Book S2

S2

CAMBRIDGE
UNIVERSITY PRESS

PUBLISHED BY THE PRESS SYNDICATE OF THE UNIVERSITY OF CAMBRIDGE
The Pitt Building, Trumpington Street, Cambridge, United Kingdom

CAMBRIDGE UNIVERSITY PRESS
The Edinburgh Building, Cambridge CB2 2RU, UK
40 West 20th Street, New York, NY 10011-4211, USA
477 Williamstown Road, Port Melbourne, VIC 3207, Australia
Ruiz de Alarcón 13, 28014 Madrid, Spain
Dock House, The Waterfront, Cape Town 8001, South Africa

http://www.cambridge.org

Printed in Italy by G. Canale & C. S.p.A., Borgaro T.se, (Turin)
Typeface Minion   *System* QuarkXPress®

A catalogue record for this book is available from the British Library.

ISBN 0 521 78545 6 paperback

Typesetting and technical illustrations by The School Mathematics Project
Other illustrations by Robert Calow, Steve Lach and Neil Stanton at Eikon Illustration
Cover image © Image Bank/Antonio Rosario
Cover design by Angela Ashton

The publishers thank the following for supplying photographs:
Pages 23, 35, 53 (B, C, D, E, K), 83 Paul Scruton
Page 29, David Cassell
Page 57 © Rufus F. Folkks/CORBIS
All other photographs by Graham Portlock

We have been unable to trace the copyright holders of the photograph on page 59 (from Robin
Fabish, *New Zealand Maori: Culture and Craft* (Auckland: Hodder Moa Beckett, 1995), p.40) and
the images on the playing cards on page 131 (created by Star Illustration Works Ltd, London)
and would be grateful for any information that would enable us to do so.

Data on page 30 from the Environment Agency; page 32, BPI Surveys; page 39, Schools Youth
Team, Christian Aid, 1997 (Factfile 98); pages 40-41, Digest of Environmental Statistics No. 20,
1998 (Department of the Environment, Transport and the Regions); page 138, Guinness World
Book of Records, 1994.

Contents

Into the bath

This is about graphs that show things changing as time passes.
The work will help you

♦ get information from graphs

♦ sketch graphs describing real situations

Peter is taking a bath.
This graph shows the level of the water in his bath.

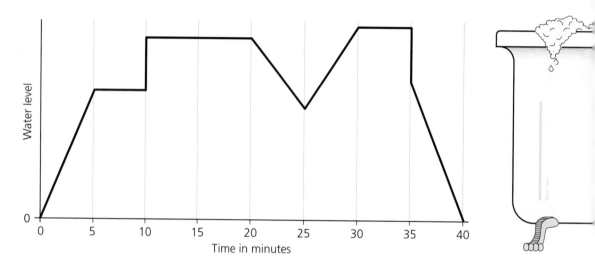

1 At 10 minutes, Peter gets into the bath.
   So the water level rises very quickly.

   (a) What is happening between 30 and 35 minutes?

   (b) What do you think happens at 35 minutes?

   (c) What is happening between 35 and 40 minutes?

2 Here are three more bath graphs.
Write down what each one tells you.
You can write it as a story if you want.
(Remember to say exactly when the taps go on and off,
and when the plug is put in or taken out.)

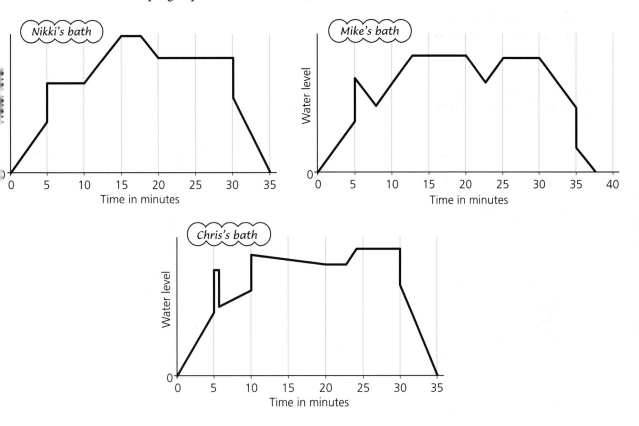

3 Sketch a graph for this bath story.

> I decided to have a long bath.
>
> First I ran the cold tap for 5 minutes,
> and then I turned on the hot tap as well.
> After 10 minutes there was enough water,
> so I turned both taps off and got in.
>
> After I had been soaking for 10 minutes, the phone rang.
> I got out and talked to Jane for 5 minutes.
>
> I got back in, but the water was cold, so after another 5 minutes
> I got out and let all the water out.

4 Sketch a bath graph of your own.
Give it to someone else and ask them to write a bath story for it.

② Ratio

This is about using ratios to describe mixtures and to compare quantities.
The work will help you

- ◆ use the notation for ratio
- ◆ understand equal ratios
- ◆ share a quantity in a given ratio
- ◆ compare ratios

A Recipes

Here is a recipe for light orange paint.

Light orange
Mix 1 tin of red with 2 tins of yellow.

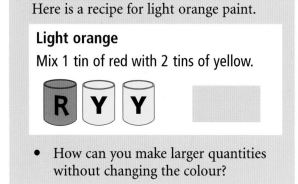

- How can you make larger quantities without changing the colour?

Here are some more shades of orange.

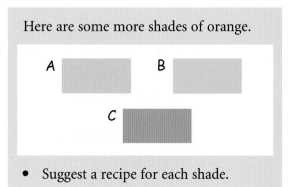

- Suggest a recipe for each shade.

A1 This is a recipe for light grey.

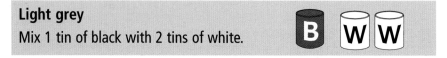

Light grey
Mix 1 tin of black with 2 tins of white.

(a) You want to make 3 times the amount in the recipe.
How many tins of white do you mix with 3 tins of black?

(b) How many tins of white do you mix with 6 tins of black?

A2 Here is a recipe for dark green.

Dark green
Mix 3 tins of blue with 2 tins of yellow.

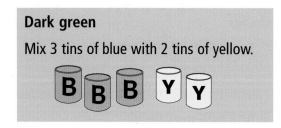

Copy and complete this mixing table.

	Blue	Yellow
2 times the recipe	6 tins	
3 times the recipe		
5 times the recipe		
10 times the recipe		

A3 This is the recipe for light pink.

Light pink
Mix 4 tins of white with 1 tin of red.

   (a) How many litres of white do you mix with 3 litres of red?

   (b) (i) How many litres of white do you mix with 2 litres of red?

        (ii) How much light pink paint would this give you altogether?

   (c) How many litres of **red** do you mix with 20 litres of white?

A4

Lemonade
Mix 1 part lemon juice with 4 parts fizzy water.

   (a) You have 2 litres of lemon juice.
      How much fizzy water do you mix with it?

   (b) (i) How much fizzy water do you mix with 5 litres of lemon juice?

        (ii) How much lemonade would this give you?

A5

Blackcurrant cordial
1 part syrup with 6 parts water

   (a) How much water do you mix with 3 cups of blackcurrant syrup?

   (b) How much blackcurrant cordial can you make with 4 litres of syrup?

A6 Here is a recipe for making light green paint.

Light green

2 parts blue to 5 parts yellow

Copy the table on the right and fill it in.

Litres of blue	Litres of yellow	Litres of light green
4		
6		
8		
10		

A7 This is how to make light purple paint.

Light purple

3 parts red to 2 parts blue

Copy the table on the right and fill it in.

Litres of red	Litres of blue	Litres of light purple
3		
6		
	6	
	8	
	12	

B Ratios

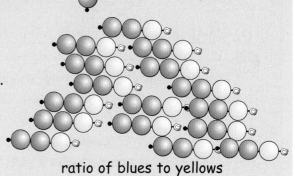

This earring is made with 2 blue beads and 1 yellow bead.

This is a pile of designs like the one above.

Whatever the size of the pile, there will always be **2 blue beads to every 1 yellow bead**.

We say the **ratio** of blues to yellows is **2 to 1**.

We can also say that the ratio of yellows to blues is 1 to 2.

ratio of blues to yellows
2 to 1

B1 What is the ratio of blue beads to yellow beads in each of these?

(a)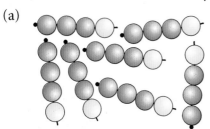

(b)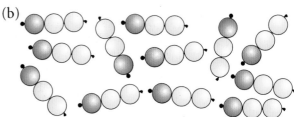

(c)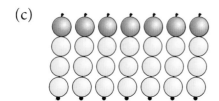

(d)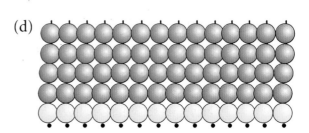

B2 You have 6 red beads and 12 yellow beads.

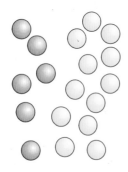

(a) Can you make the beads into designs like this with none left over?

(b) Can you make the beads into designs like this with none left over?

(c) What is the ratio of **reds** to **yellows**?

(d) What is the ratio of **yellows** to **reds**?

8

B3 Here are six sets of beads.

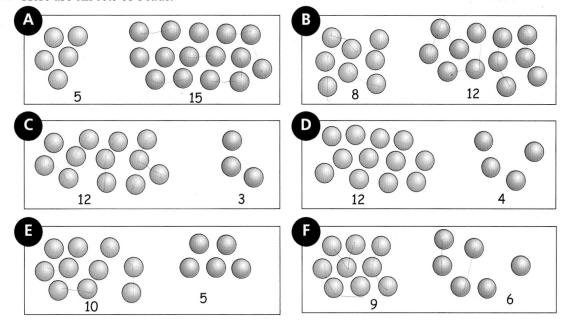

(a) Which set can be made into earrings like this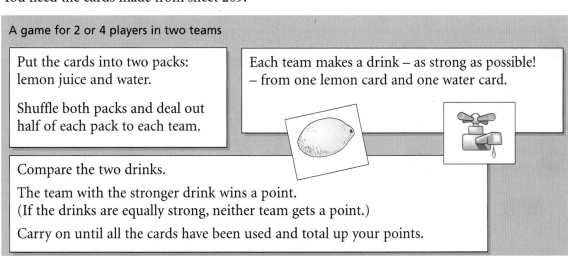
with no beads left over?
Write down the ratio of reds to blues for this set.

(b) Now match each of these designs to a set and write down the ratio of reds to blues.

(i) •◦◦◦◦•   (ii) •◦◦◦◦◦•   (iii) •◦◦●◦◦•

(iv) •◦◦◦◦◦•   (v) •◦◦◦◦•

C Strong, stronger, **strongest**

You need the cards made from sheet 209.

A game for 2 or 4 players in two teams

Put the cards into two packs: lemon juice and water.

Shuffle both packs and deal out half of each pack to each team.

Each team makes a drink – as strong as possible! – from one lemon card and one water card.

Compare the two drinks.

The team with the stronger drink wins a point.
(If the drinks are equally strong, neither team gets a point.)

Carry on until all the cards have been used and total up your points.

D Darker, lighter

For pairs or small groups

If you mix red paint and yellow paint, you get orange.

If you mix a lot of red with a little of yellow, you get a dark orange.

If you mix a little of red with a lot of yellow, you get a light orange.

There are some recipes for orange colours below.

1 Sort the recipes according to how dark the orange will be.
(If there are any you can't decide on, put them in a separate list.)

2 How many different colours are there?

3 For each different colour, make up a new recipe which will give the same colour.

4 Make up a recipe for an orange colour which is somewhere between
two of the colours that can already be made.

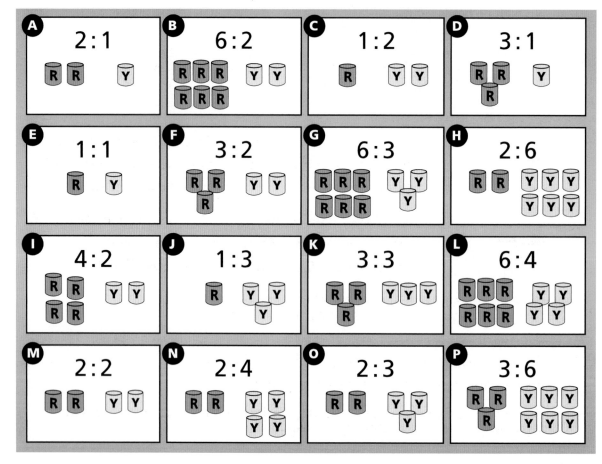

A 2 : 1   R R   Y

B 6 : 2   R R R   Y Y   R R R

C 1 : 2   R   Y Y

D 3 : 1   R R   Y   R

E 1 : 1   R   Y

F 3 : 2   R R   Y Y   R

G 6 : 3   R R R   Y Y   R R R   Y

H 2 : 6   R R   Y Y Y   Y Y Y

I 4 : 2   R R   Y Y   R R

J 1 : 3   R   Y Y   Y

K 3 : 3   R R   Y Y Y   R

L 6 : 4   R R R   Y Y   R R R   Y Y

M 2 : 2   R R   Y Y

N 2 : 4   R R   Y Y   Y Y

O 2 : 3   R R   Y Y   Y

P 3 : 6   R R   Y Y Y   R   Y Y Y

E Working with ratios

If we make orange by mixing 6 litres of red with 4 litres of yellow, the ratio of red to yellow is 6:4.

If we multiply both numbers by 3, we get the ratio 18:12.

The orange colour is the same.

We say that **6:4 is equal to 18:12.**

If we divide both numbers by 2, we get the ratio 3:2.

The orange colour is the same.

We say that **6:4 is equal to 3:2.**

6:4

multiply both by 3 × 3   × 3

18:12

6:4

÷ 2   ÷ 2 divide both by 2

3:2

3:2
is the **simplest form**
of the ratio.

E1 A recipe for grass green says 'Mix blue and yellow in the ratio 3 : 1'.
(a) How many litres of blue are mixed with 5 litres of yellow?
(b) How many litres of yellow go with 30 litres of blue?

E2 A recipe for deep purple says 'Mix blue and red in the ratio 5:2'.
(a) How many litres of blue go with 6 litres of red?
(b) How many litres of red go with 10 litres of blue?

E3 When making concrete, you have to mix sand and gravel.
For every spadeful of sand you need 2 spadefuls of gravel.
(a) Is the ratio of sand to gravel 2:1 or 1:2?
(b) How many spadefuls of gravel go with 6 spadefuls of sand?
(c) How many spadefuls of sand go with 40 spadefuls of gravel?

E4 Craig made a light green colour by mixing 20 litres of yellow with 5 litres of blue.
Write the ratio of yellow to blue in its simplest form.

E5 Dina made a pink colour by mixing 8 litres of red with 6 litres of white.
Write the ratio of red to white in its simplest form.

E6 Sergei made green by mixing 12 litres of blue with 9 litres of yellow.
   (a) Write the ratio of blue to yellow in its simplest form.
   (b) Write the ratio of yellow to blue in its simplest form.

E7 Write each of these ratios in its simplest form.
   (a) 9 : 3   (b) 15 : 10   (c) 20 : 30   (d) 8 : 14

E8 Sort these ratios into groups, so that the ratios in each group are equal.
In each group underline the simplest form.

1 : 5	4 : 6	3 : 1		4 : 20
	3 : 2	20 : 100	12 : 8	9 : 3
12 : 4	2 : 3	10 : 15	2 : 10	

E9 A recipe for pale green says 'Mix blue and yellow in the ratio 1 : 2'.
So 1 litre of blue and 2 litres of yellow will make 3 litres of pale green.

Sharmila wants to make 30 litres of pale green.
How much blue and how much yellow should she use?

makes

3 pale green

E10 Soft pink is made by mixing red and white in the ratio 1 : 3.
Kevin needs 20 litres of soft pink.
How much red and how much white should he use?

E11 Grey paint is made by mixing black and white.
Here are the recipes for three kinds of grey.

Light grey	Medium grey	Dark grey
Mix black and white in the ratio 1 : 5	Mix black and white in the ratio 2 : 5	Mix black and white in the ratio 3 : 5

   (a) Colin wants to make light grey.
        He has 3 litres of black.
        How much white does he need?
   (b) Sandra needs 30 litres of light grey.
        How much black and how much white does she need?
   (c) How much black and how much white are needed to make 14 litres of medium grey?
   (d) You want to make medium grey. You already have 12 litres of black.
        How much white do you need?
   (e) How much black and how much white do you need to make 40 litres of dark grey?

F Sharing in a given ratio

Paul and Karen have earned £20 between them.
Paul did more work, so they agree to share the money in the ratio **3 : 2**.

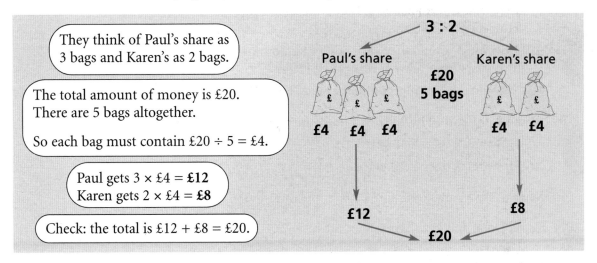

They think of Paul's share as 3 bags and Karen's as 2 bags.

The total amount of money is £20.
There are 5 bags altogether.

So each bag must contain £20 ÷ 5 = £4.

Paul gets 3 × £4 = **£12**
Karen gets 2 × £4 = **£8**

Check: the total is £12 + £8 = £20.

F1 Stuart and Shula share £12 in the ratio 2 : 1. How much does each get?

F2 Dawn and Eve share £20 in the ratio 3 : 1. How much does each get?

F3 Jake and Poppy share £15 in the ratio 1 : 2.
    (a) How much does each get?
    (b) What fraction of the money does Jake get?

F4 Martin and Priya share £20 in the ratio 1 : 3.
    (a) How much does each get?
    (b) What fraction of the money does Martin get?
    (c) What fraction of the money does Priya get?

F5 Eric and Betty share £21 in the ratio 3 : 4. How much does each get?

F6 Share each of these.
    (a) £20 in the ratio 4 : 1   (b) £60 in the ratio 2 : 3
    (c) £24 in the ratio 5 : 3   (d) £45 in the ratio 5 : 4
    (e) £12.50 in the ratio 3 : 2   (f) £6 in the ratio 3 : 1
    (g) £17.50 in the ratio 4 : 3   (h) £1.80 in the ratio 4 : 5

F7 Joy and Fran win some money.
They agree to share the money in the ratio 1 : 2.
Joy gets £40.

How much does Fran get?

F8 James and Sarah's grandmother makes a will.
When she dies, James and Sarah will have £2000 to share between them.
They are to share it in the same ratios as their ages.

 (a) James is 3 and Sarah is 5. So if their grandmother dies now,
 they would share £2000 in the ratio 3:5.
 How much would each get?

 (b) How much would they each get if grandmother dies one year from now?
 Two years from now? Investigate further.

 (c) Who does better if grandmother lives longer?

F9 Alan, Bertha and Cyril share £12 in the ratio 1:2:3.

 (a) How much does Alan get?

 (b) How much does Cyril get?

F10 Xavier, Yasmin and Zak share £200 in the ratio 1:3:6. How much does each get?

F11 Carol, Doug and Eva share £32 in the ratio 2:3:3. How much does each get?

F12 (a) Share £18 in the ratio 2:3:4.

 (b) Share £66 in the ratio 2:3:7.

G Comparing ratios

Festive pink

Mix red and white
in the ratio 4:5

Flamingo pink

Mix red and white
in the ratio 7:10

Which is the darker pink?

Grass green

Mix blue and yellow
in the ratio 5:3

Leaf green

Mix blue and yellow
in the ratio 3:2

Which is the darker green?

Bright orange

Mix red and yellow
in the ratio 4:7

Electric orange

Mix red and yellow
in the ratio 5:9

Which is the darker orange?

G1 Find the missing numbers.

 (a) 3:5 = ■:10   (b) 3:2 = 9:■   (c) 7:10 = ■:30   (d) 4:9 = 20:■

G2 Which of these two blue colours is darker? Show your method clearly.

 Pale blue   Mix blue and white in the ratio 3:4.
 Light blue   Mix blue and white in the ratio 5:8.

G3 Which of these two purple colours is darker? Show your method clearly.

Psychedelic purple   Mix blue and red in the ratio 3:4.
Passionate purple   Mix blue and red in the ratio 2:3.

G4 Find out which of these two grey colours is darker. Show your method clearly.

Squirrel grey   Mix black and white in the ratio 8:5.
Thundercloud grey   Mix black and white in the ratio 5:3.

G5 Steve made a lime drink by mixing 2 litres of juice with 3 litres of water.
Simon also made a lime drink but used 7 litres of juice and 9 litres of water.

Whose drink was stronger?

G6 Jasmine made an orange drink by mixing juice and water in the ratio 3:4.
Nita also made an orange drink by mixing juice and water in the ratio 5:7.

Whose drink was stronger?

G7 Find the missing numbers.

(a) $10:5 = ■:1$ (b) $7:4 = ■:1$ (c) $5:12 = 1:■$ (d) $0.5:3 = 1:■$

G8 Jeremy made a lemon drink by mixing juice and water in the ratio 2:7.
Ken also made a lemon drink by mixing juice and water in the ratio 5:17.

Jeremy worked out which drink was stronger by writing each ratio in the form $1:■$.

Here is part of his working.

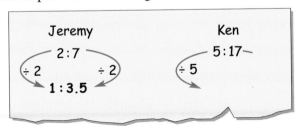

(a) Write the ratio 5:17 in the form $1:■$.

(b) Whose drink is stronger, Jeremy or Ken's?
Explain your answer.

G9 A recipe for calypso punch mixes pineapple and lime juice in the ratio 11:4.
A recipe for tangy punch mixes pineapple and lime juice in the ratio 7:3.

(a) Write each ratio in the form $■:1$.

(b) Which recipe uses the greater proportion of pineapple juice?

G10 The paint colour sugar lilac mixes purple and white paint in the ratio 10:21.
The paint colour dream lilac mixes purple and white paint in the ratio 6:13.

(a) Write each ratio in the form $1:■$.

(b) Which colour uses the greater proportion of purple paint?

What progress have you made?

Statement	Evidence

I can work out quantities from a recipe for a mixture.

1 Orange fizz is made by mixing 1 part of orange juice with 5 parts of lemonade.

   (a) How much lemonade do you mix with 3 litres of orange juice?

   (b) How much orange juice do you need to mix with 25 litres of lemonade?

I can understand the way in which ratios are written.

2 Pale pink is made by mixing red and white in the ratio 2:5.

   (a) How much white do you mix with 8 litres of red?

   (b) How much red do you mix with 15 litres of white?

3 Light grey paint is made by mixing black and white in the ratio 1:3.

   Connie needs 12 litres of light grey paint.

   How much black paint and how much white paint should she use?

I can change a ratio into its simplest form.

4 Change each of these ratios to its simplest form.

   (a) 8:6   (b) 4:16

   (c) 10:25   (d) 16:24

I can share a quantity in a given ratio.

5 (a) Harry and Will share £12 in the ratio 2:1. How much does each get?

   (b) What fraction of the money is Will's?

6 (a) Gavin and Susan share £36 in the ratio 4:5. How much does each get?

   (b) Lee, Jo and Vi share £80 in the ratio 1:3:4. How much does each get?

I can compare ratios.

7 Which of these recipes will give a darker shade of grey? Explain your answer.

   A Mix black and white in the ratio 5:8.

   B Mix black and white in the ratio 3:5.

③ Starting equations

This work will help you
- ◆ solve balance puzzles
- ◆ form and solve equations with the unknown on both sides

A Review

Picture 1

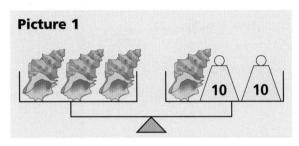

Picture 2

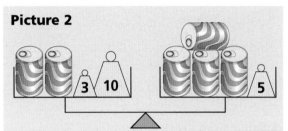

A1 The weights in the puzzles below are grams.

Write an equation for each puzzle and find the weight of each object.
Check each solution works.

(a)

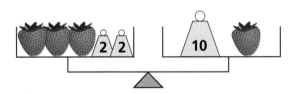

(b)

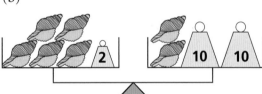

(c)

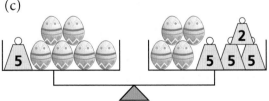

(d)

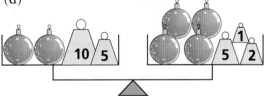

(e)

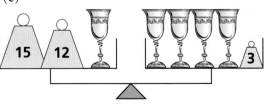

(f)

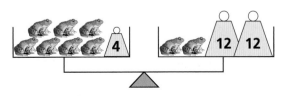

17

B Shorthand

Suppose each frog weighs *w* grams.

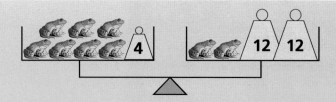

We can write the puzzle as $w + w + w + w + w + w + w + 4 = w + w + 24$

A shorter way to write the puzzle is

First we can take 2*w* off each side.

Now we can take 4 off each side.

Lastly we can divide both sides by 5.

Now we can check the solution.

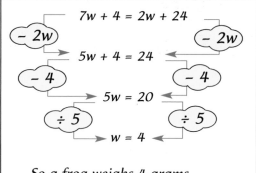

$7w + 4 = 2w + 24$

− 2w   − 2w

$5w + 4 = 24$

− 4   − 4

$5w = 20$

÷ 5   ÷ 5

$w = 4$

So a frog weighs 4 grams

Check

left side: (7 × 4) + 4 = 32

right side: (2 × 4) + 24 = 32

so both sides agree.

The weights in the puzzles below are kilograms.

B1

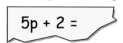

(a) Copy and complete the equation below for the balance puzzle.

$5p + 2 =$

(b) Solve the equation.

(c) Check your solution works for the puzzle.

B2 Write an equation for this balance puzzle.
Solve it and check your solution.

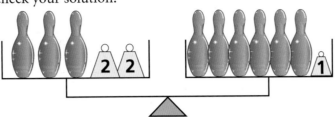

B3 Write and solve an equation for this balance puzzle.

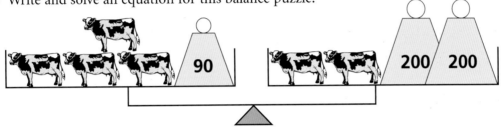

B4 Solve these equations.
Show all your working and check each solution.

(a) $4c + 1 = 3c + 8$ (b) $3d + 28 = 5d + 8$

(c) $37 + 2n = 17 + 4n$ (d) $5t + 7 = 27$

(e) $5y = 4y + 5$ (f) $4x + 20 = 8x$

(g) $5q + 11 = 3q + 21$ (h) $6m + 2 = 14 + 2m$

B5 Solve these equations.

(a) $7 + 2n = 22$ (b) $21 + 3m = 40 + m$

(c) $2f + 37 = 1 + 12f$ (d) $3h + 10 = 8h + 1$

(e) $5p + 4 = p + 41$ (f) $3r + 31 = 5 + 8r$

B6 Make up an equation and give it to a partner to solve.
Make sure you can solve it yourself first!

Equation bingo   a game for the whole class

You need a copy of this bingo card.

Choose five different numbers from 1, 2, 3, 5, 6, 7, 10, 13, 15, 20,
and write them in your white squares.

Your teacher will write an equation on the board.
Solve the equation, and cross the solution off your card if it's there.
The winner is the first to cross off all the numbers on their card and shout 'BINGO!'

C Making equations

C1 Sal has these four cards.

(a) She uses the blue and yellow cards to make this equation.

$$5x + 3 = 3x + 25$$

Solve the equation to find the value of x which makes it true.

(b) She uses the yellow and pink cards to make another equation.

$$3x + 25 = 19 + 4x$$

Solve this equation.

(c) Choose another pair of these cards and make a different equation. Solve your equation.

(d) Make two more equations from the cards and solve them.

C2 Find some different equations using these cards.

Solve each equation.

D Thinking of a number

Adie and Jaspaal are doing 'think of a number' puzzles.
They both start with the **same** number.

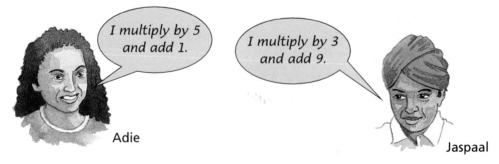

They are surprised to find their final result is the same.

- What number were they thinking of?

D1 Here is another 'think of a number' puzzle.
Ruth and Darren both start with the same number.

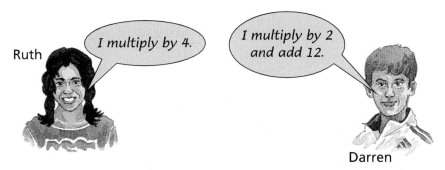

They find that their final result is the same.

(a) Copy and complete the equation below for this puzzle.

4n =

(b) Solve your equation to find the number they were thinking of.
Check your solution.

D2 Zahir and Babs start with the same number.

Zahir multiplies it by 10.
Babs multiplies it by 5 and adds 35.
Their results are the same.

(a) Which of the equations below fits this puzzle?

5n + 10 = 35

10n + 35 = 5n

10n = 5n + 35

5n + 35 = 10

(b) Solve the equation to find the number they both started with.

D3 Nikky and Dan start with the same number.

Nikky multiplies it by 4 and adds 9.
Dan multiplies it by 6.
Their results are the same.

(a) Write an equation for this puzzle.

(b) What number did they both start with?

D4 Chris and Eve start with the same number.

Chris multiplies the number by 6 and adds 8.
Eve multiplies it by 2 and adds 40.
Their results are the same.

What number did they both start with?

*D5 Jas and Yasser start with the same number.

Jas adds 3 then multiplies the result by 6.
Yasser adds 8 then multiplies the result by 4.
Their answers are the same.

(a) Copy and complete the equation below for this puzzle.

$$6(n + 3) =$$

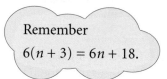

Remember
$6(n + 3) = 6n + 18$.

(b) Solve your equation to find the number
they were thinking of.

*D6 Amy and Thady start with the same number.

Amy adds 3 then multiplies the result by 4.
Thady multiplies the result by 5 and adds 3.
Their answers are the same.

What did they start with?

*D7 Kerry and Kenny start with the same number.

Kerry multiplies it by 7 and adds 0.6.
Kenny adds 1.8 then multiplies the result by 5.
Their answers are the same.

What did they start with?

*D8 Make up two problems like this and give them to someone else to solve.

What progress have you made?

Statement

I can solve equations.

Evidence

1 Solve these equations.

(a) $4t + 12 = 56$

(b) $3g + 70 = 8g + 10$

(c) $22 + 6r = 4r + 38$

I can turn number puzzles into equations
and solve them.

2 Rick and Sophie start with the same number.
Rick multiplies it by 7.
Sophie multiplies it by 5 and adds 18.
Their results are the same.

Write an equation that fits this, and solve it.
Check your answer.

4 Cuboids

This work will help you understand the idea of volume and find the volumes of cuboids.

A How many cubes?

- You have 24 cubes.
  You have to make a cuboid using all of them.
  How many different cuboids can you make?

- This is a 3 by 5 by 2 cuboid.
  How many cubes are there in it?

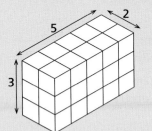

You can think of it like this   or like this   or like this.

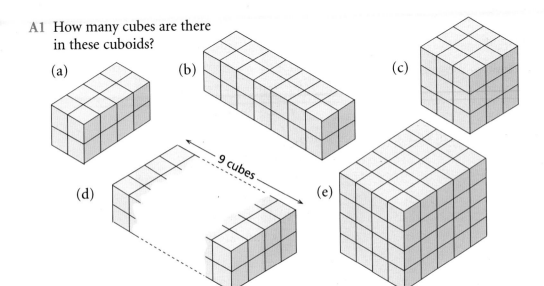

A1 How many cubes are there in these cuboids?

(a)

(b)

(c)

(d)   9 cubes

(e)

A2 How many cubes are there in these cuboids?

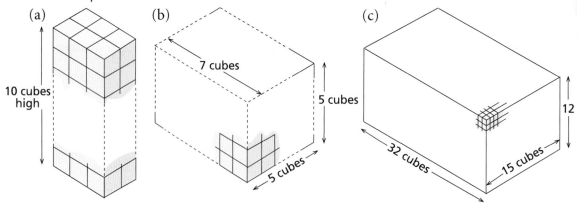

(a) 10 cubes high

(b) 7 cubes, 5 cubes, 5 cubes

(c) 32 cubes, 15 cubes, 12

A3 This cuboid is made from 12 cubes.
It is a '6 by 2 by 1' cuboid.

What other cuboids can be made from 12 cubes?
List them or draw them on triangular dotty paper.

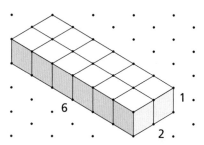

A4 List all the different cuboids that can be made from

(a) 8 cubes   (b) 20 cubes

A5 How many cuboids can be made from 23 cubes?
Why do some numbers of cubes give more cuboids than others?

B Volume of a cuboid

The volume of a three-dimensional object is the amount of space it takes up.
A cube 1 cm by 1 cm by 1 cm has a volume of 1 cm³ (one cubic centimetre).
Volumes are often measured in cm³.

1 cm   1 cm   1 cm

B1 Find the volume of each of these cuboids.

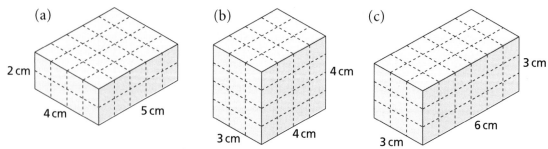

(a) 2 cm, 4 cm, 5 cm

(b) 4 cm, 3 cm, 4 cm

(c) 3 cm, 3 cm, 6 cm

B2 Find the volumes of these cuboids.

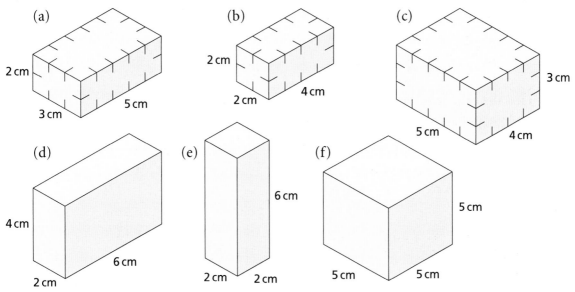

(a) 2 cm 3 cm 5 cm

(b) 2 cm 2 cm 4 cm

(c) 3 cm 5 cm 4 cm

(d) 4 cm 2 cm 6 cm

(e) 6 cm 2 cm 2 cm

(f) 5 cm 5 cm 5 cm

B3 Find the volume of each of these cuboids.

    (a) 6 cm by 2 cm by 5 cm   (b) 2 cm by 3 cm by 6 cm

    (c) 1 cm by 7 cm by 4 cm   (d) 3 cm by 3 cm by 4 cm

B4 (a) Write down a rule to calculate the
        volume of a cuboid if you know
        its length, width and height.

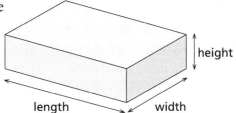

length   width   height

    (b) Use your rule to calculate the volume of this cuboid.
        Explain how you can see by counting cubes that
        the result is correct.

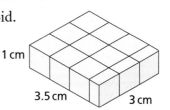

1 cm   3.5 cm   3 cm

B5 Calculate the volume of each of these cuboids.

    (a)

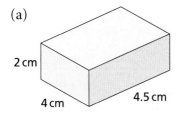

2 cm   4 cm   4.5 cm

    (b)

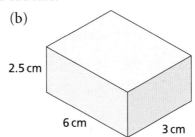

2.5 cm   6 cm   3 cm

B6 Use the rule to calculate the volume of this cuboid.
Check by counting cubes.

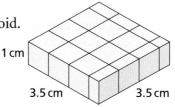

1 cm

3.5 cm   3.5 cm

B7 Find the volume of each of these cuboids.

(a) 2.5 cm by 3.5 cm by 8 cm   (b) 4.5 cm by 3 cm by 1.5 cm

B8 All these cuboids have the same volume.
Find the missing measurements.
(The diagrams are not drawn to scale.)

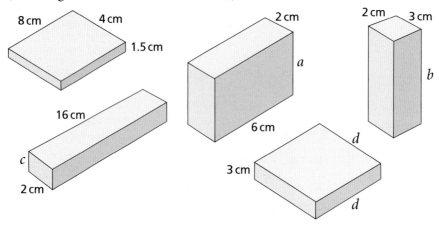

B9 A block of pastry has a volume of 250 cm³.
It is rolled out to make a rectangle 25 cm by 20 cm.
How thick is the pastry?

C Shapes made from cuboids

C1 This solid shape has been made by
putting together two cuboids, P and Q.

Find the volume of

(a) cuboid P

(b) cuboid Q

(c) the whole solid shape

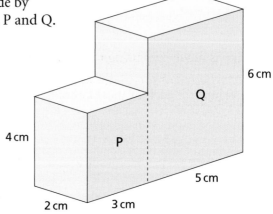

C2 Here is the solid shape from question C1 again.
The dotted lines show the hidden edges.

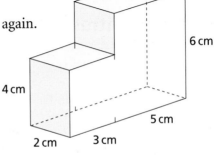

6 cm

4 cm

5 cm

2 cm   3 cm

(a) Work out the area of each of these faces.

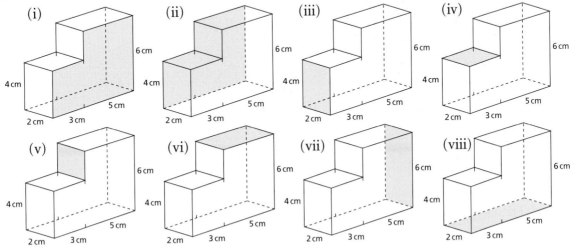

(i)   6 cm   4 cm   5 cm   2 cm   3 cm

(ii)   6 cm   4 cm   5 cm   2 cm   3 cm

(iii)   6 cm   4 cm   5 cm   2 cm   3 cm

(iv)   6 cm   4 cm   5 cm   2 cm   3 cm

(v)   6 cm   4 cm   5 cm   2 cm   3 cm

(vi)   6 cm   4 cm   5 cm   2 cm   3 cm

(vii)   6 cm   4 cm   5 cm   2 cm   3 cm

(viii)   6 cm   4 cm   5 cm   2 cm   3 cm

(b) What is the total surface area of the shape?

C3 Calculate
(a) the volume of this shape
(b) the surface area of this shape

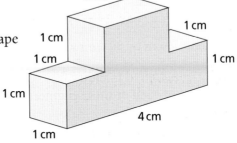

2 cm   1 cm   1 cm   1 cm   1 cm   1 cm   4 cm   1 cm

C4 This solid shape is made by putting two different sized cubes together.
(a) What is the volume of the whole shape?
(b) What is its surface area?

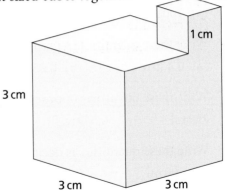

1 cm   1 cm   1 cm   3 cm   3 cm   3 cm

27

D Litres and millilitres

The **capacity** of a container is the volume it holds.
Each of these contains 1 litre.

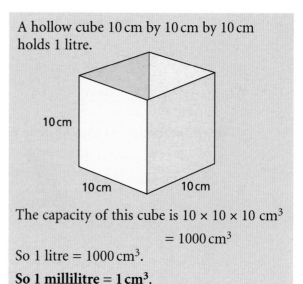

A hollow cube 10 cm by 10 cm by 10 cm holds 1 litre.

10 cm

10 cm   10 cm

The capacity of this cube is $10 \times 10 \times 10$ cm^3

$$= 1000 \text{ cm}^3$$

So 1 litre = 1000 cm^3.

So 1 millilitre = 1 cm^3.

a thousandth of a litre

D1 How many 250 ml cartons can be filled from a litre of orange juice?

D2 How many 100 ml cans can be filled from a litre of oil?

D3 How many litres of liquid would it take to fill each of these?
   (a) Ten 200 ml bottles of shampoo   (b) Six 500 ml tins of paint
   (c) Twelve 750 ml bottles of wine   (d) A carton 20 cm by 20 cm by 50 cm
   (e) A fuel storage tank 70 cm by 80 cm by 120 cm

D4 An engine's capacity is measured in either litres or c.c. (cubic centimetres, cm^3).
   What is the size in litres of each of these engines?
   (a) 2000 c.c.   (b) 3500 c.c.   (c) 500 c.c.   (d) 850 c.c.

D5 Liquid medicine is usually given in 5 ml spoonfuls.
   How many 5 ml spoonfuls are there in these?
   (a) 100 ml   (b) 750 ml   (c) 1 litre   (d) 0.5 litre

D6 Write these quantities in millilitres.
   (a) 0.4 litre   (b) 0.65 litre   (c) 0.273 litre   (d) 0.05 litre

D7 Write these quantities in order, smallest first.
   750 ml   0.5 litre   1.2 litres   60 ml   1100 cm^3

D8 Write these quantities as decimals of a litre.
   (a) 300 ml   (b) 450 ml   (c) 50 ml   (d) 1 cm^3

E Cubic metres

Large volumes are measured in cubic metres (m³).

A cube with edges 1 m has a volume of 1 m³.

- How many pupils could get into this cubic metre?
- What is the volume of each of these, roughly, in m³?

  your classroom

  a container on a lorry

  a home freezer

Believe it or not ...

In 1987 a giant iceberg, called B-9, broke away from the mainland of Antarctica.
It was roughly a cuboid 154 km long, 35 km wide and 250 m deep.

Estimate its volume.

What progress have you made?

Statement

I can find the volume of cuboids.

Evidence

1 Find the volume of these cuboids.

(a)

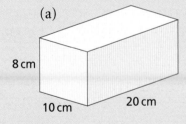

8 cm   10 cm   20 cm

(b)

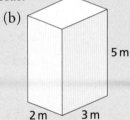

5 m   2 m   3 m

I can work with shapes made from cuboids.

2 Find
  (a) the volume and
  (b) the surface area of this shape.

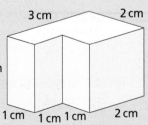

3 cm   2 cm   2 cm   1 cm   1 cm 1 cm   2 cm

I can work with cm³, litres and millilitres.

3 Write these quantities in order, smallest first.

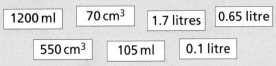

1200 ml   70 cm³   1.7 litres   0.65 litre

550 cm³   105 ml   0.1 litre

⑤ Graphs, charts and tables

This is about displaying information.

The work will help you read and produce graphs, charts and tables.

A **Regional differences**

This picture shows the regions of Great Britain and the results of a survey of children's income.

What information is given for each region?

How does your region compare with other regions?

A1 (a) What is the largest income shown?

(b) Where did children get most income?

(c) Where did children get least income?

(d) What is the difference between the greatest and smallest amounts?

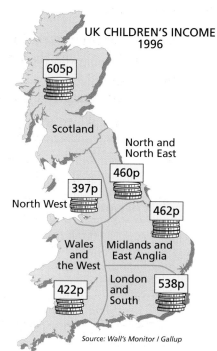

UK CHILDREN'S INCOME 1996

605p
Scotland
North and North East
460p
397p
North West
462p
Wales and the West
Midlands and East Anglia
London and South
422p
538p

Source: Wall's Monitor / Gallup

A2 From 1992 to 1994, hundreds of water samples from rivers and canals were tested. These are the results for eight water regions.

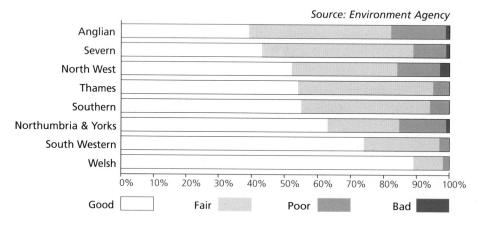

Source: Environment Agency

Anglian
Severn
North West
Thames
Southern
Northumbria & Yorks
South Western
Welsh

0% 10% 20% 30% 40% 50% 60% 70% 80% 90% 100%

Good ☐   Fair ▨   Poor ▨   Bad ▨

(a) Which region had the highest percentage of 'good' samples?

(b) Which regions had no 'bad' samples?

(c) Which had more than 60% of their samples 'good'?

(d) Which region had the greatest percentage of 'fair' samples?

(e) Which had the greatest percentage of 'poor' samples?

(f) Which do you think had the worst water quality? Give your reasons.

B Changes over time

This graph is about the number of complaints made about noise.

B1 (a) In what year was the highest number of complaints made?

(b) (i) In which two years were there the same number of complaints?

(ii) About how many complaints were made in each of these years?

(c) Between which two years did the number of complaints drop?

(d) Between which two years did the number of complaints rise the most?

B2 Complaints went up between 1986 and 1987. By how many roughly?

B3 Copy and complete this story

Between 1983 and 1985 complaints rose steadily. Then ...

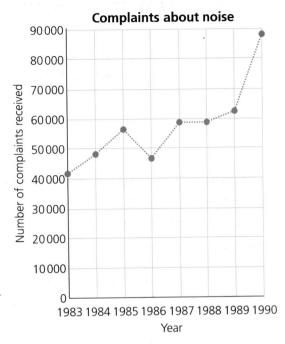

Complaints about noise

Complaints about noise are investigated. Often the complaints are found to be untrue.

This graph shows the number of complaints found to be true.

B4 Look closely at the numbering on the vertical scale.

Why is there a jagged line at the bottom of the scale, between 0 and 12 000?

B5 Between which two years was there the biggest drop in complaints found to be true?

B6 In what year was there the lowest number of complaints found to be true?

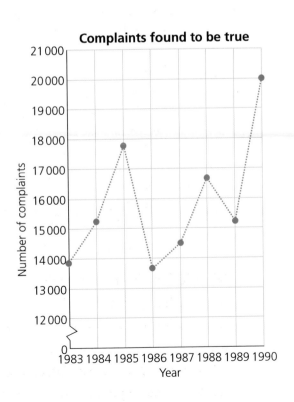

Complaints found to be true

31

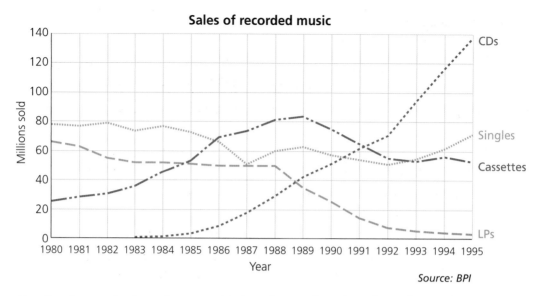

Sales of recorded music

Millions sold (vertical axis: 0 to 140)

Year (horizontal axis: 1980 1981 1982 1983 1984 1985 1986 1987 1988 1989 1990 1991 1992 1993 1994 1995)

CDs, Singles, Cassettes, LPs

Source: BPI

B7 On the graph above, between 1980 and 1995 the sales of LPs dropped, stayed steady and then went down again.

(a) What happened to the sales of CDs?

(b) What happened to the sales of cassettes?

(c) When did CD sales overtake LP sales?

(d) When did cassette sales reach 70 million?

(e) Roughly how many singles were sold in 1982?

B8 What was the most popular way of buying recorded music in

(a) 1980　　　　　　　(b) 1989　　　　　　　(c) 1995

B9 If CD sales kept growing the same way, what do you estimate the 1996 sales were?

B10 When do you think CD sales reached 200 million?

B11 This table shows the temperature of an oven in °C at 1 minute intervals from switching on.

Time in minutes	0	1	2	3	4	5	6	7	8
Temperature in °C	20	78	129	157	173	184	192	196	198

(a) On graph paper, draw and label a time axis going across and and a temperature axis going upwards.

Plot a point for each of the temperature readings.

Join the points with dotted lines.

(b) Describe how the temperature changes over time. Is it easier to do this by looking at the table or by looking at the graph?

B12 This table shows the average daily maximum temperature in °C in London and Auckland (New Zealand).

	Jan	Feb	Mar	Apr	May	Jun	Jul	Aug	Sep	Oct	Nov	Dec
London	7	7	10	13	16	20	22	21	19	15	10	8
Auckland	24	23	22	21	17	15	14	16	16	18	19	21

(a) On graph paper, draw a time axis going across, labelled with the months.
Draw a temperature axis going upwards.

Plot the points for London and join them with dotted lines.
Do the same for Auckland.

(b) Describe two ways in which the graphs for the two cities are different.

(c) If you were choosing between these two cities for a holiday in September and warm weather was the main attraction for you, which would you choose?

(d) Which would you choose in April?

B13 Draw a graph to show the number of new cases of flu recorded each day in a certain area over a fortnight.

Day	1	2	3	4	5	6	7	8	9	10	11	12	13	14
Number of cases	3	7	8	11	16	24	22	26	19	15	15	7	3	1

B14 Draw a graph to show these temperatures one night in a certain place.

Time	18:00	19:00	20:00	21:00	22:00	23:00	00:00	01:00	02:00
Temperature in °C	14	12	9	4	1	⁻1	⁻4	⁻6	⁻3

Reading between plotted points

B15 This is the beginning of a graph of the **midday** temperatures each day in Tolero.

The time that is halfway between midday on day 1 and midday on day 2 is midnight.

Is it sensible to read off midnight temperatures halfway between the plotted points?
If not, why not?

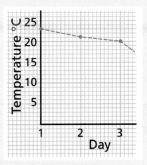

B16 Is it sensible to read off temperatures halfway between the plotted points on the graph you drew for B11?

B17 Is it sensible to read off temperatures halfway between the plotted points on your graph for B14?

C Frequency charts and tables

Pupils' test scores

37	41	28	60	56	39	17	39	73	64
58	25	44	66	34	32	78	35	46	76
18	39	56	38	75	53	49	55	38	47
53	86	34	64	26	36	22	18	73	91
64	86	15	27	53	72	76	52	57	28
74	24	46	39	74	53	33	70	28	30

Times taken (in seconds) to run 100 metres

21.31	19.64	17.56	17.84	20.48	16.91	22.51	23.03
19.23	18.17	17.36	26.15	19.35	24.08	21.37	18.63
17.52	22.23	25.11	18.85	21.47	24.68	18.99	23.90
27.01	19.30	17.73	20.05	25.16	20.43	17.39	16.50
17.73	23.23	18.01	24.57	26.18	19.93	18.44	23.74

Drawing a frequency bar chart

- *Find the smallest and largest values.*
- *Decide on class intervals.*
- *Make a table of frequencies.*
- *Find the highest frequency.*
- *Decide on a scale for each axis.*
- *Draw and label the axes.*
- *Draw the bars.*
- *Write the title of the chart.*

C1 Draw a frequency bar chart for this set of ages of people living in a village.

41	25	75	64	14	9	23	64
88	34	45	2	69	33	53	51
27	38	70	22	4	19	16	72
66	40	38	41	77	80	38	44
11	46	61	50	13	3	22	59
52	71	60	72	18	37	44	56

C2 Draw a frequency bar chart for this set of weights in kg of newborn babies.

3.27	3.11	2.45	2.90	4.39	2.06	2.59	3.71	2.88	1.65
2.05	3.77	4.08	2.96	2.71	3.50	2.55	3.19	3.47	1.95
3.47	1.64	1.81	3.70	2.69	2.27	3.37	2.40	1.94	2.56

C3 (a) Copy this table. ➡

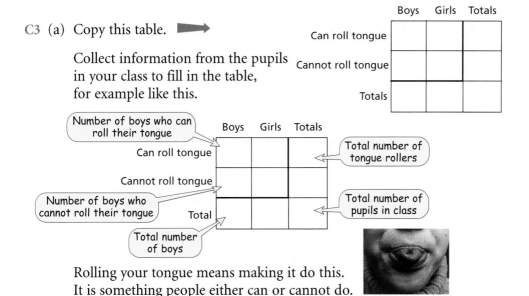

	Boys	Girls	Totals
Can roll tongue			
Cannot roll tongue			
Totals			

Collect information from the pupils in your class to fill in the table, for example like this.

Number of boys who can roll their tongue

Can roll tongue

Total number of tongue rollers

Cannot roll tongue

Number of boys who cannot roll their tongue

Total

Total number of pupils in class

Total number of boys

	Boys	Girls	Totals
Can roll tongue			
Cannot roll tongue			
Total			

Rolling your tongue means making it do this.
It is something people either can or cannot do.

(b) In your class, can a greater proportion of boys than girls roll their tongue? How did you calculate this?

Two-way tables like the one in in C3 are useful for displaying frequency data and making comparisons.

You could collect other frequency data from your class and present it as a two-way table. The top or side headings of the table could be these, or ideas of your own:

Left-handed/Right-handed   Has school dinner/Does not have school dinner

Walks to school/Does not walk to school   Wears glasses/Does not wear glasses

C4 974 year 7 pupils and 8602 year 10 pupils were asked how long they spent watching TV after school the previous day. These are the results.

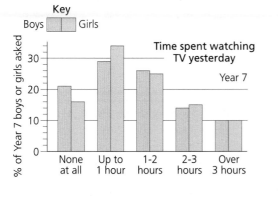

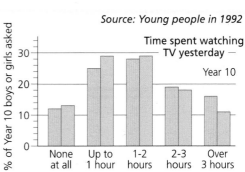

Source: Young people in 1992

(a) In year 7, did more boys than girls watch no TV?

(b) In year 10, did more girls than boys watch over 3 hours of TV?

(c) Roughly what percentage of year 7 girls watched 2–3 hours?

(d) For year 7 boys which class interval shows the greatest frequency?

(e) On the whole, who watched more TV, year 7 or year 10? How did you decide?

What progress have you made?

Statement

I can draw and interpret a graph showing how a quantity changes over time.

Evidence

1 Draw a graph to illustrate this data, which shows how a plant grew.

Number of days after planting	0	10	20	30	40	50
Height in cm	3.4	5.0	8.5	12.7	15.6	17.2

(a) How tall do you think the plant was halfway between day 20 and day 30?

(b) How tall would you expect the plant to be on day 60?

2 This shows rainfall over a year in Bangkok.

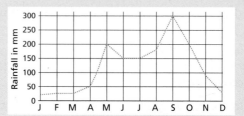

(a) Which is the wettest month?

(b) Between which two months did the amount of rainfall change the most?

I can draw and interpret a frequency bar chart.

3 Draw a grouped frequency bar chart for these pupils' test marks.

34	17	23	22	20	18	42
16	11	28	41	35	44	23
19	15	40	17	26	29	13
46	25	36	33	27	36	32
36	38	24	30	36	33	28
31	17	14	23	24		

4 This shows the heights of pupils at a camp. Who are generally taller, boys or girls? How did you decide?

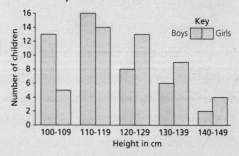

6 Fractions, decimals and percentages

This work will help you

◆ revise fractions, decimals and percentages

A Review

Fractions

A chimpanzee's weight is $\frac{2}{3}$ of the weight of an orang-utan.

An orang-utan weighs 75 kg.

$\frac{1}{3}$ of $75 = 75 \div 3 = 25$

so $\frac{2}{3}$ of 75 is $25 \times 2 = 50$

So a chimpanzee weighs 50 kg.

A chimpanzee weighs 50 kg.
An African elephant weighs 5000 kg.

$$\frac{50}{5000} \overset{\div 10}{\underset{\div 10}{=}} \frac{5}{500} \overset{\div 5}{\underset{\div 5}{=}} \frac{1}{100}$$

So a chimpanzee's weight is $\frac{1}{100}$ of the weight of an African elephant.

A1 Evaluate these.

(a) $\frac{1}{8}$ of 24   (b) $\frac{1}{3}$ of 90   (c) $\frac{1}{7}$ of 147   (d) $\frac{3}{4}$ of 60

(e) $\frac{2}{3}$ of 36   (f) $\frac{7}{10}$ of 120   (g) $\frac{4}{5}$ of 25   (h) $\frac{5}{6}$ of 12

A2 The weights of some animals are shown in the table.

Animal	Weight (kg)
African elephant	5000
Giant panda	160
Giraffe	1200
Lion	250
Tiger	300
Hippopotamus	

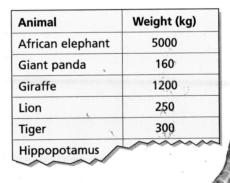

(a) The weight of a hippopotamus is $\frac{2}{5}$ of the weight of an African elephant.

What is the weight of a hippopotamus?

(b) What fraction of the weight of a giraffe is a tiger?

(c) Say whether each of these is true or false.

(i) The weight of a lion is $\frac{1}{20}$ of an African elephant.

(ii) The weight of a giant panda is $\frac{2}{15}$ of a giraffe.

(iii) The weight of a giraffe is $\frac{5}{12}$ of an African elephant.

(iv) The weight of a lion is $\frac{5}{6}$ of a tiger.

(d) What fraction of the weight of a tiger is a giant panda?

37

Fractions and decimals

$\frac{4}{5} = 4 \div 5 = 0.8$ $\qquad\qquad$ $\frac{2}{3} = 2 \div 3 = 0.67$ (to two decimal places)

A3 Write these fractions as decimals, rounding to two decimal places where necessary.

(a) $\frac{3}{4}$ $\qquad$ (b) $\frac{3}{5}$ $\qquad$ (c) $\frac{1}{50}$ $\qquad$ (d) $\frac{6}{11}$ $\qquad$ (e) $\frac{4}{7}$

A4 Write these decimals as fractions in their simplest form.

(a) 0.5 $\qquad$ (b) 0.25 $\qquad$ (c) 0.1 $\qquad$ (d) 0.4 $\qquad$ (e) 0.05

Percentages and decimals

$48\% = \frac{48}{100} = 48 \div 100 = 0.48$

A5 Write these percentages as decimals.

(a) 75% $\qquad$ (b) 94% $\qquad$ (c) 30% $\qquad$ (d) 3% $\qquad$ (e) 84%

A6 Write these decimals as percentages.

(a) 0.21 $\qquad$ (b) 0.34 $\qquad$ (c) 0.9 $\qquad$ (d) 0.08 $\qquad$ (e) 0.2

Fractions and percentages

$\frac{13}{20} = 13 \div 20 = 0.65 = 65\%$ $\qquad\qquad$ $\frac{2}{7} = 2 \div 7 = 0.29$ (to 2 d.p.) $= 29\%$

A7 Write these fractions as percentages, to the nearest 1%.

(a) $\frac{7}{20}$ $\qquad$ (b) $\frac{6}{8}$ $\qquad$ (c) $\frac{1}{25}$ $\qquad$ (d) $\frac{4}{10}$ $\qquad$ (e) $\frac{5}{12}$

(f) $\frac{12}{13}$ $\qquad$ (g) $\frac{14}{24}$ $\qquad$ (h) $\frac{1}{32}$ $\qquad$ (i) $\frac{4}{9}$ $\qquad$ (j) $\frac{8}{11}$

Finding a percentage of a quantity

23% of 73.5 $= 0.23 \times 73.5 = 16.905 = 16.9$ (to one decimal place)

A8 Calculate these (to one decimal place).

(a) 32% of 24 kg $\qquad$ (b) 95% of 5 tonnes $\qquad$ (c) 43% of 650 g

(d) 2% of 6.9 kg $\qquad$ (e) 10% of 78 kg $\qquad$ (f) 45% of 12 kg

A9 The weight of a house mouse is about 27% of the weight of a golf ball.
A golf ball weighs about 45 g.

Find the weight of a house mouse to the nearest gram.

A10 John is a man who weighs about 73.5 kg.
About 17% of the weight of an adult person is bones.

Estimate the weight of John's bones in kg, to one decimal place.

Writing one number as a percentage of another

A birdwatcher sees 42 birds in her garden one afternoon.
6 of these birds are starlings.

$\frac{6}{42} = 6 \div 42 = 0.14$ (to two decimal places)

So about 14% of the birds she sees are starlings.

A11 The table shows all the birds the birdwatcher sees.

Copy and complete the table.

Bird	Number	Percentage
Sparrow	9	
Blue tit	7	
Starling	6	14%
Blackbird	5	
Chaffinch	8	
Greenfinch	7	

The birdwatcher saw 42 birds altogether.

B Mixed percentage problems

B1 In 1997, 28% of the money spent on the National Lottery went to good causes.
Helen spent £60 on lottery tickets in 1997.
How much of this money went to good causes?

B2 Out of 23 million UK households, about 6 million have a pet dog.
What percentage of households have a pet dog?

B3 The chart shows where the money spent on a UK packet of tea goes.

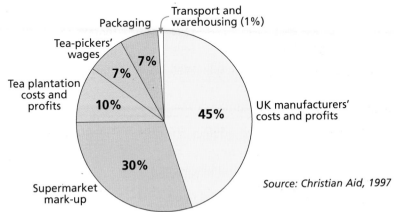

Source: Christian Aid, 1997

I buy a packet of tea for £2.69 in a supermarket.

How much of this money goes on

(a) supermarket mark-up

(b) tea-pickers' wages

(c) packaging

(d) UK manufacturers' costs and profits

B4 China produces about 187 200 000 tonnes of rice each year.
The world's rice production each year is about 534 700 000 tonnes.

What percentage is produced by China?

B5 In 1997, a total of 1785 people in England and Wales were asked which environmental issues made them 'very worried'.

They were allowed to choose as many issues as they wished.
The table shows the results for some issues.

Source: DETR

Number in sample	Global warming	Ozone depletion	Over-fishing of the seas	Not enough recycling	Vacant/ derelict land
1785	633	821	530	326	315

© Crown copyright

(a) Which of these issues did most people worry about?

(b) What percentage were worried about global warming?

(c) Find the percentage worried about over-fishing.

C A load of rubbish

This table shows some information about aluminium can recycling in the UK.

Aluminium cans		*Source: DETR*
Year	Consumption (tonnes)	Weight of cans recycled (tonnes)
1989	48 400	1200
1990	72 900	4000
1991	74 200	8200
1992	73 450	11 700
1993	92 700	19 600
1994	106 000	25 440
1995	109 000	30 260
1996	78 000	23 900

© Crown copyright

C1 Decide if each statement about aluminium cans is true or false.

(a) In 1994, nearly $\frac{1}{4}$ of cans were recycled.

(b) In 1990, about 55% of cans were recycled.

(c) In 1989, nearly $\frac{1}{4}$ of cans were recycled.

(d) In 1996, about 3% of cans were recycled.

C2 (a) What percentage of aluminium cans in 1989 were recycled?

(b) Work out the percentages for the other years and show your results in a table.

This table shows some information about steel can recycling in the UK.

Steel cans		Source: DETR
Year	Consumption (tonnes)	Weight of cans recycled (tonnes)
1989	700 000	57 156
1990	700 000	65 103
1991	700 000	69 640
1992	700 000	83 000
1993	675 000	89 973
1994	650 000	91 550
1995	600 000	82 000
1996	650 000	79 000

© Crown copyright

C3 (a) In 1989, what percentage of steel cans were recycled?

(b) Work out the percentages for the other years and show your results in a table.

C4 Comment on the trends in the percentages of aluminium and steel cans recycled in the UK between 1989 and 1996.

C5 In 1997, the average UK household produced 635 kg of rubbish.

(a) Use the diagram to copy and complete this table for 1997.

Household waste in the UK

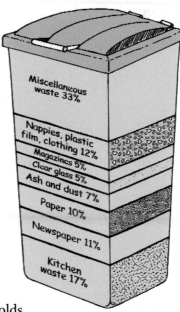

Waste	Average weight (kg)
Kitchen waste	108
Newspaper	
Paper	
Ash and dust	
Clear glass	
Magazines	
Nappies, plastic film, clothing	
Miscellaneous waste	

(b) In 1997, Manchester had about 150 000 households. Estimate the amount of clear glass waste produced by these households that year.

*(c) In 1997, there were about 23 million households in the UK. A tree provides about 600 kg of paper.

About how many trees would be needed to make newspapers for these households for one day?

41

C6 This table shows what the USA and Japan do with their waste each day.

Country	Incinerate	Landfill	Recycle	Compost	Total (tonnes)
USA	81 000	317 000	104 000	18 000	520 000
Japan	44 000	20 000	44 000	1000	109 000

(a) What percentage of the USA's waste is recycled?

(b) For each country, draw a pie chart to show what it does with its waste.
Label each category with its percentage.

(c) Write a short report to compare what these countries do with their waste each day.

What progress have you made?

Statement

I can work with fractions.

I can work with percentages.

Evidence

1 (a) A walrus weighs 1200 kg.
The weight of a giant panda is $\frac{2}{15}$ of the weight of a walrus.
What is the weight of a giant panda?

(b) A polar bear weighs 700 kg.
A spectacled bear weighs 140 kg.
What fraction of the weight of a polar bear is the weight of a spectacled bear?

2 The weight of a humpback whale is about 20% of the weight of a blue whale.
A blue whale weighs 130 tonnes.
About how heavy is a humpback whale?

3 This table shows land use in France.

Cultivated	Grazing	Forest	Other
35%	20%	27%	18%

The area of France is 545 630 km^2.
What area of land is in each category
(to the nearest 1000 km^2)?

4 These figures show land use in Rwanda.

Cultivated	Grazing	Forest	Other	Total (km^2)
11 980	4490	5490	2990	24 950

What percentage of land is in each category?

7 Using rules

This work will help you

◆ use rules written in words or using letters

A Katy's Catering

Katy's Catering provide everything you need for a children's party.

Katy uses rules to work out how much food and how many plates, cups and so on are needed for a party.

Here are some of the rules she uses.

> The number of chicken legs needed is 6 more than the number of people.

> You need 3 sausage rolls for each person plus 10 spare.

> Number of paper cups = number of people × 2

> You need half as many bottles of lemonade as there are people.

> You need 6 party poppers for each person plus 20 extra.

> Number of rubbish bags = $\dfrac{\text{number of people}}{2}$

A1 Here is the rule for sausage rolls.

> You need 3 sausage rolls for each person plus 10 spare.

(a) How many sausage rolls would Katy's Catering take for

    (i) 6 people   (ii) 20 people   (iii) 50 people

(b) To one party, they take 100 sausage rolls.
How many people did they expect?

A2 This is the rule for chicken legs.

> *The number of chicken legs needed is 6 more than the number of people.*

(a) How many chicken legs would Katy's Catering take for

    (i) 10 people   (ii) 40 people   (iii) 25 people

(b) To one party, they take 60 chicken legs.
How many people did they expect?

A3 Here is the rule for party poppers.

> *You need 6 party poppers for each person plus 20 extra.*

(a) How many party poppers would they take to a party of 50 people?

(b) They take 800 party poppers to one party!
How many people are expected?

A4 This is the rule for lemonade.

> *You need half as many bottles of lemonade as there are people.*

(a) How many bottles of lemonade are needed for

    (i) 10 people   (ii) 20 people

(b) The caterers take 30 bottles of lemonade to a party.
How many people are they catering for?

A5 Here is the rule for paper cups.

> *Number of paper cups = number of people × 2*

(a) How many cups are needed for

    (i) 7 people   (ii) 12 people

(b) They take 36 cups to one party.
How many people do they expect?

A6 This is the rule for rubbish bags.

> *Number of rubbish bags = $\dfrac{\text{number of people}}{2}$*

How many rubbish bags will they take for

(a) 20 people   (b) 16 people   (c) 100 people

B Shorthand

Katy's Catering decide to write their rules using a shorthand.

Hats

Here is the rule for the number of hats they need.

> Number of hats = number of people + 2

They write   *n* to stand for the *number of people*
                 h to stand for the *number of hats*

So the hat rule becomes $h = n + 2$

> Any letters can be used as long as it is clear what they stand for.

Paper cups

Here is the rule for the number of paper cups they need.

> Number of paper cups = number of people × 2

They write   *n* to stand for the *number of people*
                 p to stand for the *number of paper cups*

You can write the cup rule as $p = n \times 2$ or, even shorter, as $p = 2n$

B1 This is the rule Katy's Catering use for mince pies.

$m = n + 6$

   n stands for the *number of people*
   m stands for the *number of mince pies* they take

   (a) If there are 12 people, how many mince pies will they take?
   (b) If $n = 20$, work out what *m* is.
   (c) If $n = 32$, what is *m*?

B2 This is the rule Katy's Catering use for straws.

$s = 3n$

   n stands for the *number of people*
   s stands for the *number of straws* they take

   (a) If there are 8 people, how many straws will they take?
   (b) If $n = 10$, work out what *s* is.
   (c) If $n = 20$, what is *s*?

B3 Here are three other rules Katy's Catering use.

$$p = 4n \qquad k = n + 5 \qquad j = \frac{n}{5}$$

n stands for the *number of people*
p stands for the *number of paper plates*
k stands for the *number of plastic knives*
j stands for the *number of bowls of jelly*

40 people go to a party.

(a) How many paper plates do they need?

(b) How many plastic knives are needed?

(c) How many bowls of jelly should Katy's Catering take?

B4 Here is the sausage roll rule as a sentence.

> You need 3 sausage rolls for each person plus 10 spare.

Here it is in shorthand. $\quad r = 3n + 10$

n stands for the *number of people*
r stands for the *number of sausage rolls*

(a) If n is 20, what is r?

(b) If n is 15, what is r?

(c) 50 people come to a party. How many sausage rolls are needed?

B5 Here is a rule for iced buns. $\quad b = 5n + 15$

n stands for the *number of people*
b stands for the *number of iced buns*

(a) Work out b when n = 8.

(b) What is b when n = 20?

(c) Copy and complete this sentence for the iced buns.

You need ... iced buns for each person, and another ... extra.

B6 Sometimes Katy's Catering take crackers to parties.
Here is the rule as a sentence.

Take one cracker for each person, with 6 extra.

Which of these rules is correct for crackers?

$$c = 6n \qquad c = n + 6$$

$$c = 6n + 1 \qquad c = n + 1 + 6$$

n stands for the *number of people*
c stands for the *number of crackers*

B7 This is the rule for serviettes. | *Take three serviettes for each person.*

(a) Which of these is correct?

    A *Number of people = number of serviettes × 3*

    B *Number of serviettes = number of people + 3*

    C *Number of serviettes = number of people × 3*

    D *Number of people = number of serviettes + 3*

(b) Which of these shorthand rules is the right one?

$n = 3s$ $s = 3n$ $3s = n$ *n* stands for the *number of people*
                                   s stands for the *number of serviettes*

$s = n + 3$ $n = s + 3$

B8 This is the rule for loaves of bread. | You need half a loaf of bread for each person.

(a) Copy and complete this rule.

    Number of loaves of bread needed = number of people ....

(b) Which of these shorthand rules is correct?

$b = \frac{1}{2} + n$ $\frac{b}{2} = n$ *n* stands for the *number of people*
                                  b stands for the *number of loaves of bread*

$b = 2n$ $b = \frac{n}{2}$

B9 Write each of these rules in shorthand.
Choose your own letters in your rules, but say what each letter stands for.

(a) *Number of lucky bags = number of people + 2*

(b) *Number of jam doughnuts = (number of people × 3) – 6*

(c) *Number of peanut butter sandwiches = (4 × number of people) + 8*

(d) *Number of plastic forks = (number of people × 2) + 10*

B10 Write shorthand rules for each of these sentences.
Choose your own letters in your rules, but say what each letter stands for.

(a) You need six marshmallows for each person.

(b) You need twice as many bread rolls as people, plus 6 more.

(c) Take one bag of crisps for each person, and 10 extra.

(d) You need one bowl of trifle for every six people.

(e) Take two cheese sandwiches for each person, with 6 extra.

C Working out formulas

Expocamp supply equipment to expeditions.

They use rules to decide how many of each thing to take.
In each rule, n stands for the number of people on the expedition.

$$t = \frac{n + 8}{4}$$

t is the number of tents

$$s = 4(n - 1)$$

s is the number of cans of sardines

$$r = 2(n + 2)$$

r is the number of climbing ropes

$$p = 12n + 2$$

p is the number of packets of porridge

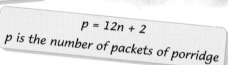

C1 Expocamp plan an expedition for 40 people.
  (a) How many tents will they take?
  (b) Work out how many of each of the other items they will take.

C2 (a) How many of each item would Expocamp take on an expedition of 12 people?
  (b) Work out how many of each item would be needed for 100 people.

C3 Ms Price orders stock for the maths department.
Naturally she uses rules to decide what to buy.

Here are some of the rules she uses.
(c stands for the number of children in that year.)

$$t = \frac{c}{4}$$

t is the number of textbooks

$$m = 2(c - 20)$$

m is the number of mirrors

$$k = 4(c + 50)$$

k is the number of multilink cubes

$$w = \frac{c}{10} - 10$$

w is the number of wallcharts

Work out how many of each item she has to buy for
  (a) 200 children   (b) 100 children   (c) 1000 children

C4 Ms Price buys two pencils for each child, plus an extra 50.
Write this as a shorthand rule.

C5 Use the rule $n = 3(m + 5)$ to work out n when
    (a) $m = 5$ (b) $m = 10$ (c) $m = 1$ (d) $m = 0$

C6 Use the rule $y = 2x - 6$ to work out y when
    (a) $x = 20$ (b) $x = 5$ (c) $x = 3$ (d) $x = 100$

C7 Use the rule $f = \frac{x}{4} - 6$ to work out f when
    (a) $x = 40$ (b) $x = 100$ (c) $x = 50$ (d) $x = 1000$

C8 Use the rule $j = \frac{d + 2}{10}$ to work out j when
    (a) $d = 18$ (b) $d = 98$ (c) $d = 8$

C9 In the rule $a = b^2$, b^2 means $b \times b$.
    (a) Work out what a is when $b = 6$.
    (b) Work out what a is when $b = 5$.
    (c) Can you say what b would have to be to make $a = 100$?

C10 If $y = x^2 + 10$, what is y when
    (a) $x = 3$ (b) $x = 5$ (c) $x = 1$

C11 If $s = t^2 - 1$, what is s when
    (a) $t = 6$ (b) $t = 8$ (c) $t = 1$

C12 Work these out.
    (a) $h^2 - 5$ when $h = 6$ (b) $d^2 + 8$ when $d = 1$

C13 Work these out.
    (a) $5(e - 4)$ when $e = 10$ (b) $5e - 4$ when $e = 10$
    (c) $2(f + 12)$ when $f = 6$ (d) $4(12 - g)$ when $g = 2$
    (e) $12 + \frac{b}{4}$ when $b = 20$ (f) $\frac{h + 2}{3}$ when $h = 19$
    (g) $5(t - 1)$ when $t = 12$ (h) $2(k + 2)$ when $k = 0$

C14 Here is a rule. $r = 5(g + h)$
    Work out r when
    (a) $g = 13$ and $h = 5$ (b) $g = 6$ and $h = 1$ (c) $g = 0$ and $h = 10$

C15 Here is a rule. $z = \frac{(y - x)}{2}$
    Work out z when
    (a) $y = 5$ and $x = 1$ (b) $y = 4$ and $x = 0$ (c) $y = 100$ and $x = 10$

What progress have you made?

Statement	Evidence

I can use a rule in words.

1 When I take my class on a picnic, I take 4 sandwiches for each child, plus 6 extra. How many sandwiches will I take for 12 children?

2 I always take tablecloths on picnics. I work out how many to take using the rule

$$Number\ of\ tablecloths = \frac{number\ of\ children}{3}$$

How many tablecloths will I take for 24 children?

I can use simple rules written with letters.

3 This is the rule I use for working out how many paper hankies to take on picnics.

$$h = 2c + 10$$

h is the *number of hankies*
c is the *number of children*

How many hankies will I take for 10 children?

4 This is the rule I use for sticking plasters.

$$p = \frac{c}{2} + 5$$

p is the *number of plasters*
c is the *number of children*

How many plasters do I take for 12 children?

I can use more complicated rules using letters and brackets.

5 Here is a rule. $h = 4(c - 3)$

Work out h when

(a) $c = 10$ (b) $c = 3$ (c) $c = 100$

6 Use the rule $y = \frac{x + 1}{4}$ to work out y when

(a) $x = 3$ (b) $x = 11$ (c) $x = 99$

Review 1

1 John and Adrian share £60 in the ratio $1:2$.

   (a) How much does each get?

   (b) What fraction of the money is John's?

2 Solve these equations.

   (a) $5c + 9 = 44$ (b) $8d = 5d + 18$ (c) $25 + 4e = 6e + 9$

3 Darren uses this rule to work out how many films for his camera he should take on holiday.

$$f = \frac{d}{2} + 3$$

   d is the number of days. f is the number of films.

   How many films will Darren take for a 14-day holiday?

4 (a) These containers are in the shape of cuboids.
       Find the volume of water each could hold in cm³.

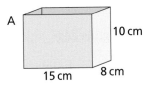 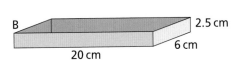

   (b) A bottle holds 2.5 litres of water. How many millilitres is this?

   (c) Would the contents of the bottle fit into container B? Explain your answer.

5 Change each of these ratios to its simplest form.

   (a) $3:12$ (b) $20:8$ (c) $18:16$ (d) $100:125$

6 The graph shows the number of people on a platform at a station.

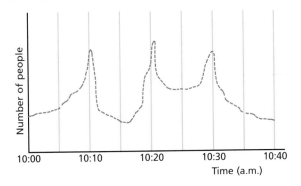

   (a) At what time did the first train arrive after 10:00 a.m.?

   (b) At approximately what time were there most people on the platform?

   (c) At 10:15 a.m. were more people arriving on the platform or leaving it?

7 Some biscuits contain 19% fat. What is the weight of the fat in a 15 g biscuit?

8 An artist wants 200 ml of olive-green paint made by mixing yellow, blue and black paint in the ratio 2:5:1. How much of each colour does she need?

9 Use the formula $y = 3x - 4$ to find y when $x = 20$.

10 The table shows the populations, in millions, of Africa and Europe over 200 years.

Date	1800	1850	1900	1950	2000
Africa	107	111	133	224	784
Europe	203	276	408	547	729

© Crown copyright 2001   Source: National Statistics

 (a) On graph paper, draw and label a horizontal date axis and a vertical population axis.

 (b) On these axes, draw two graphs to show the information in the table.

 (c) When, approximately, did the population of Africa become greater than the population of Europe?

 (d) Describe one way in which the graphs for the two continents are different.

11 A concrete mix uses cement and sand in the ratio 2:5.

 (a) If 10 kg of cement is used, how much sand is needed?

 (b) If 350 kg of concrete is required, how much cement will be needed?

12 Of the 54 million visits abroad by UK residents, 46 million were for holidays.
What percentage of visits abroad were for holidays?
Give your answer to the nearest 1%.

13 In 100 g of sterling silver, there is 92 g of silver and the rest is copper.

 (a) Write the ratio of silver:copper in its simplest form.

 (b) How much copper is contained in 75 g of sterling silver?

14 Polly and Jane start with the same number.
Polly multiplies the number by 5 then adds 3.
Jane multiplies the number by 3 then adds 21.
Their results are the same.

 Form an equation and solve it to find their starting number.

15 (a) If $p = 5(r + 6)$ find the value of p when $r = 4$.

 (b) If $m = \frac{30 - x}{4}$ find the value of m when $x = 6$.

16 Calculate

 (a) the volume of this solid

 (b) the surface area of this solid

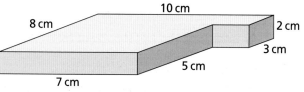

Decimals and area

This work will help you

◆ deal with decimals when calculating areas of rectangles and right-angled triangles

◆ calculate the areas of shapes made up from simpler shapes

A Area of a rectangle

• The charge for displaying a poster on a poster site for a week is £1 per square metre.
How much does each of these posters cost for a week?
Explain why.

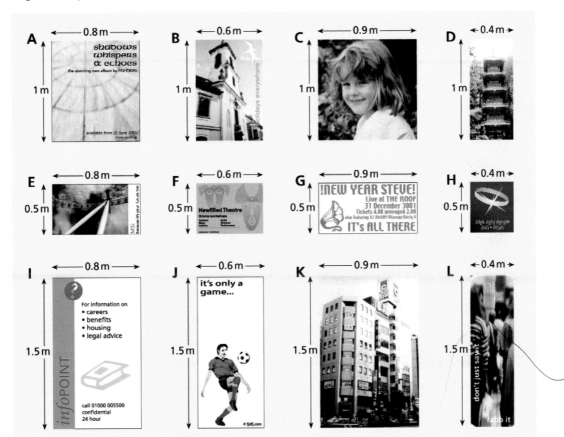

A1 Work out the cost for a poster 0.5 m by 0.7 m.

A2 Do the same for posters with these sizes.

(a) 1.5 m by 2 m   (b) 0.5 m by 1.5 m   (c) 2 m by 0.7 m   (d) 0.3 m by 0.5 m

If you divide a square metre into ten equal parts, each part is 0.1 m².

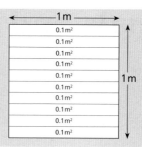

A3 Write each green area as a decimal of a square metre.

(a)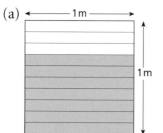

(b)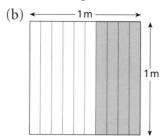

(c)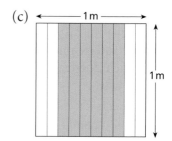

If you divide a square metre into squares 0.1 m by 0.1 m, you get 100 of them.
So each small square is $\frac{1}{100}$ of a square metre, or 0.01 m².

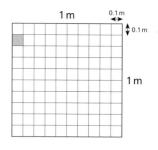

A4 (a) What would $\frac{7}{100}$ m² look like on a square metre divided up like this?

(b) What would 0.03 m² look like?

A5 Which two values go with which each blue area?

0.4 m² $\frac{16}{100}$ m²

0.16 m² $\frac{4}{100}$ m²

$\frac{40}{100}$ m²   0.04 m²

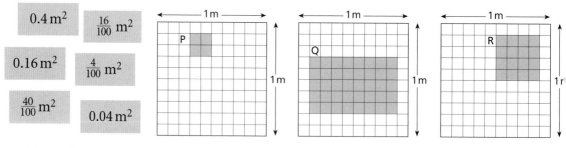

A6 Write each orange area

(i) in hundredths of a square metre   (ii) as a decimal of a square metre

(a)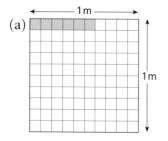

(b)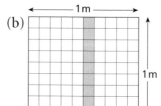

(c)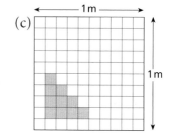

3 tenths of a square metre and 7 hundredths
have been coloured here.

So 0.37 m² is coloured.

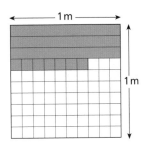

A7 What is 0.37 m² in hundredths of a square metre?

A8 Write each of these shaded areas

    (i) as a decimal of a square metre   (ii) in hundredths of a square metre

(a) 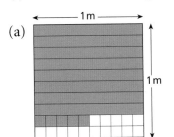 (b) 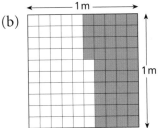 (c)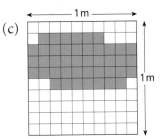

A9 This poster has been placed on a metre square.

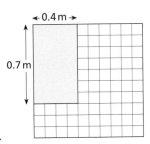

    (a) How many hundredths of a square metre
         does the poster cover?

    (b) What is that as a decimal?

    (c) Work out the area of the poster by doing
         0.4 × 0.7 on your calculator.
         Compare the result with your answer to (b).

A10 For each of these posters,

    (i) write how many hundredths of a square metre it covers

    (ii) give this as a decimal

    (iii) check with a calculator

(a) 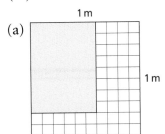 (b) 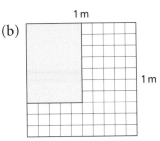 (c)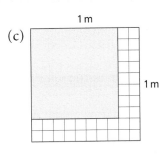

A11 Work out the areas of posters with these sizes.

    (a) 0.4 m by 0.9 m   (b) 0.3 m by 0.6 m   (c) 0.7 m by 0.9 m

A12 (a) A poster has area 0.45 m² and is 0.5 m wide. How long is it?

    (b) Another has area 0.18 m² and is 0.3 m wide. How long is it?

    (c) Another has area 0.72 m² and is 0.9 m long. How wide is it?

A13 Justin says:

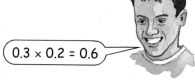

0.3 × 0.2 = 0.6

Is he right?
Use a diagram like those on the previous page to explain.

A14 Work out the areas of posters with these sizes.

(a) 0.2 m by 0.4 m   (b) 0.3 m by 0.4 m   (c) 0.3 m by 0.3 m

A15 This large poster has been placed on
four metre squares.

(a) Work out each of the areas A, B, C and D.

(b) Work out the total of these areas.

(c) Multiply the length and width of
the whole poster on a calculator.
Compare the result with the answer to (b).

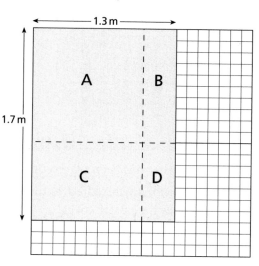

A16 Work out the area of this poster.

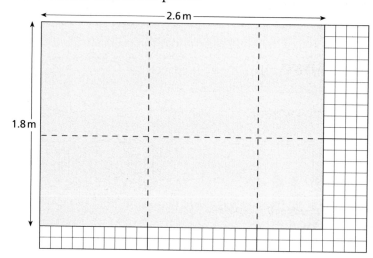

A17 Work out the areas of these posters.

(a) 1.7 m by 1.9 m   (b) 2.4 m by 2.4 m   (c) 1.6 m by 2.9 m
(d) 1.8 m by 3.0 m   (e) 2.1 m by 3.5 m   (f) 2.8 m by 3.5 m

*A18 (a) A poster has area 4.5 m² and is 1.8 m wide. How long is it?

(b) Another has area 2.4 m² and is 3.2 m long. How wide is it?

(c) Another has area 0.1 m² and is 0.2 m wide. How long is it?

A19 Measure each gift tag and work out its area in cm² to 1 d.p.

(a)

(b)

(c)

B Areas of other shapes

B1 These are the dimensions of one letter on the famous Hollywood sign.

(a) Make a sketch showing how it can be split into two rectangles.
Mark the dimensions of the rectangles.

(b) Find the total area of the letter in square metres, to the nearest whole square metre.

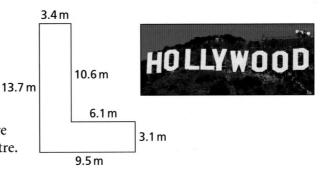

3.4 m

13.7 m

10.6 m

6.1 m

3.1 m

9.5 m

B2 (a) What is the area of this rectangle?

(b) What fraction of the rectangle is coloured green?

(c) What is the area of the green triangle?

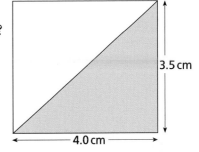

3.5 cm

4.0 cm

B3 Calculate the areas of these right-angled triangles.
Give your answers in cm² to 1 d.p.

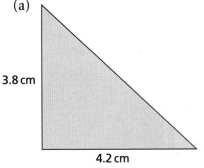

(a)

3.8 cm

4.2 cm

(b)

2.8 cm

4.0 cm

(c)

4.6 cm

3.4 cm

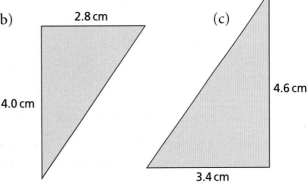

57

B4 The price for putting tarmac on a house drive depends on its area in square metres.

Find the area of each of these drives to the nearest whole square metre.

(a)

6.2 m 2.8 m 3.1 m 1.8 m

(b)

2.7 m 7.3 m 2.8 m 1.4 m

(c)

4.3 m 2.4 m 1.8 m 6.8 m 4.4 m 2.5 m 2.0 m

What progress have you made?

Statement

I can work with areas of rectangles where measurements are decimals.

Evidence

1 Work out the area of this rectangle.

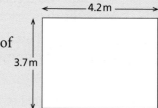

4.2 m
3.7 m

2 Work out the missing length.

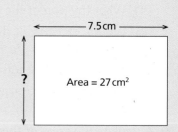

7.5 cm
?
Area = 27 cm²

I can calculate areas of shapes made up from simpler shapes.

3 Find the area of this Hollywood letter, to the nearest whole square metre.

3.4 m   3.4 m
5.3 m
3.4 m
13.7 m   3.1 m
5.3 m

⑨ Finding rules

This work will help you
◆ find and use expressions and formulas from geometric patterns

A Maori patterns

Some of the geometric patterns in this work are based on the weaving and stitching patterns used by Maori people in New Zealand.

The Maori women in this photograph are weaving flax strips through wooden slats.

These *tukutuku* panels are then used to decorate the walls of the Maori great houses.

An example of Maori patterns	Pattern 1	Pattern 2	Pattern 3
	XXX X	XXXXX X X	XXXXXXX X X X

A1 Look at the patterns on the right.

(a) Sketch pattern 4 and pattern 5.

(b) Explain what pattern 10 would look like.

Pattern 1   Pattern 2   Pattern 3

(c) Copy and complete this table.

Pattern number	1	2	3	4	5
Number of crosses	5				

(d) How many crosses will there be in
   (i) pattern 10   (ii) pattern 50   (iii) pattern 100

(e) Write an expression for the number of crosses in pattern n.

A2 Here is another weaving design.

(a) Sketch pattern 4 and pattern 5.

(b) Explain what pattern 10 would look like.

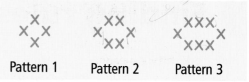

Pattern 1   Pattern 2   Pattern 3

(c) Copy and complete this table.

Pattern number	1	2	3	4	5
Number of crosses	4	6	8		

(d) Work out how many crosses there would be in pattern 100.

(e) Find an expression for the number of crosses in the nth pattern.

(f) One of these patterns has 56 crosses. Which one is it?

A3 This Maori design is called *tapatoru*.

(a) Sketch pattern 3 and pattern 5.

(b) How many crosses are there in each of these four patterns? Show your results in a table.

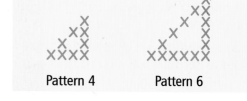

Pattern 4   Pattern 6

(c) How many crosses would there be in pattern 10? Explain how you worked it out.

(d) How many crosses would there be in the 100th pattern?

(e) How many crosses would there be in the nth pattern?

A4 (a) Sketch pattern 4 and pattern 6 for this design.

(b) Explain what pattern 10 would look like.

(c) How many crosses are there in each of these patterns?

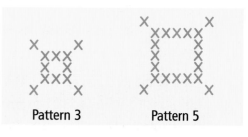

Pattern 3   Pattern 5

(d) Work out how many crosses are in the 100th pattern.

(e) Find a formula for the number of crosses in the nth pattern.

(f) One pattern has 84 crosses. Which one is it?

A5 On squared paper, invent a weaving design of your own. Draw some of the patterns.

Explain in words how to find the number of crosses in the 10th and 100th patterns.

Find a formula for the nth pattern of your design.

B Matchstick patterns

B1 Here is a sequence of matchstick designs.

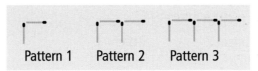

Pattern 1   Pattern 2   Pattern 3

(a) Sketch pattern 4.

(b) Copy and complete this table.

Pattern number	1	2	3	4	5
Number of matches	2				

(c) How many matches are added to each pattern to make the next?

(d) Find how many matches you would need to make

    (i) pattern 10   (ii) pattern 100

(e) Choose the formula for the number of matches in pattern n.

$m = n + 1$ $m = 2n$ $m = n + 2$ $m = 2n + 1$

B2 Here is another sequence.

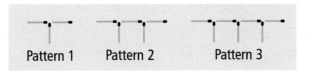

Pattern 1   Pattern 2   Pattern 3

(a) Sketch pattern 4.

(b) How many matches are added to each pattern to make the next?

(c) Find how many matches you would need to make

    (i) pattern 10   (ii) pattern 100

(d) Choose the formula for the number of matches in pattern n.

$m = n + 1$ $m = 2n$ $m = n + 2$ $m = 2n + 1$

B3 (a) Sketch pattern 4 for this sequence.

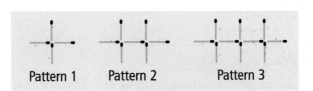

Pattern 1   Pattern 2   Pattern 3

(b) How many matches are added to each pattern to make the next?

(c) How many matches you would need to make pattern 20.

(d) Find a formula for the number of matches in pattern n.

B4

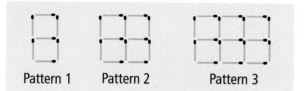

Pattern 1   Pattern 2   Pattern 3

(a) Sketch pattern 4 for this sequence.

(b) How many matches are added to each pattern to make the next?

(c) Find how many matches you would need to make pattern 100.

(d) Find a formula for the number of matches in pattern n.

C Finding formulas

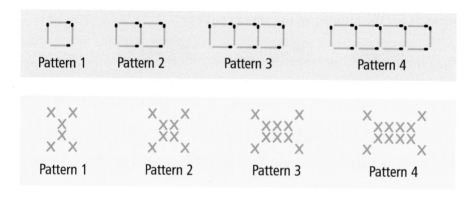

Pattern 1   Pattern 2   Pattern 3   Pattern 4

Pattern 1   Pattern 2   Pattern 3   Pattern 4

- What do you add to each pattern to make the next?
- What is a formula for pattern n in each design?
- Is there a link?
- Can you explain it?

C1

Pattern 1   Pattern 2   Pattern 3

(a) Count the crosses in pattern 3.

(b) How many crosses will be in pattern 4?

(c) How many crosses are added to each pattern to make the next?

(d) Find a formula for the number of crosses in the nth pattern.

(e) Use your formula to work out the number of crosses in the 20th pattern.

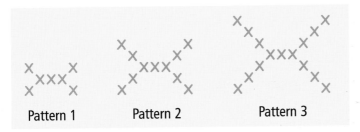

Pattern 1   Pattern 2   Pattern 3

(a) How many crosses are added to each pattern to make the next?

(b) Find a formula for the number of crosses in the nth pattern.

(c) Use your formula to work out the number of crosses in the 10th pattern.

(d) Which pattern uses 83 crosses?

C3

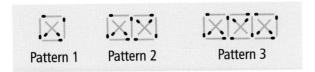

Pattern 1   Pattern 2   Pattern 3

(a) Find a formula for the number of matches in the nth pattern.

(b) Use your formula to work out the number of matches in the 50th pattern.

(c) What is the number of the largest pattern you can make with 100 matches?

C4 Jamie is investigating some matchstick patterns.

Here are his tables for two designs.
Work out a formula for each table.

(a)

Pattern number (n)	1	2	3	4	5
Number of matches (m)	5	7	9	11	13

(b)

Pattern number (n)	1	2	3	4	5
Number of matches (m)	8	11	14	17	20

C5

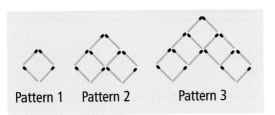

Pattern 1   Pattern 2   Pattern 3

(a) Find a formula for the number of matches in the nth pattern.

(b) Use your formula to work out the number of matches in the 20th pattern.

(c) What is the number of the largest pattern you can make with 150 matches?

D Pattern problems

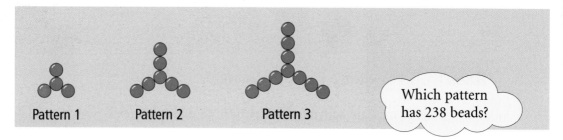

Pattern 1 Pattern 2 Pattern 3

Which pattern has 238 beads?

D1 This is a cross design made with beads.

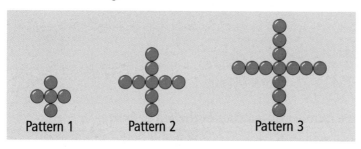

Pattern 1 Pattern 2 Pattern 3

(a) How many beads will be in pattern 4?

(b) How many beads will there be in the 100th pattern?

(c) Write down an expression for the number of beads in pattern n.

(d) Work out the number of beads in pattern 45.

(e) One of these patterns has 349 beads in it.
Form an equation and solve it to find n.

D2 This is a hexagon design made with beads.

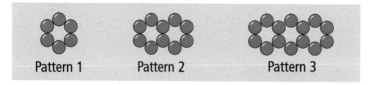

Pattern 1 Pattern 2 Pattern 3

(a) Make a table to show the number of beads in
each of the first five hexagon designs.

(b) Find an expression for the number of beads in pattern n.

(c) One of these patterns has 470 beads in it.
Form an equation and solve it to find n.

(d) Is it possible to make a hexagon design with exactly 100 beads?
Explain how you decided on your answer.

D3 Look at this H design.

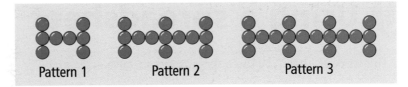

Pattern 1   Pattern 2   Pattern 3

(a) Find an expression for the number of beads in pattern n.

(b) One of these patterns has 148 beads in it.
Form an equation and solve it to find n.

(c) What is the largest design you can make with 500 beads?
Explain how you decided on your answer.

What progress have you made?

Statement	Evidence

I can work out a rule from a design.

1

Pattern 2   Pattern 4

(a) For the design above, sketch pattern 3 and pattern 5.

(b) Copy and complete this table.

Pattern number	2	3	4	5
Number of crosses				

(c) How many crosses would be in pattern 10?

(d) Find an expression for the number of crosses in the nth pattern.

I can use a rule.

(e) Work out the number of crosses in the 100th pattern.

(f) One of these patterns has 163 beads in it.
Form an equation and solve it to find n.

(g) Is it possible to make one of these designs with exactly 100 beads?
Explain how you decided on your answer.

Using a spreadsheet

This work will help you use a spreadsheet to solve problems.

Notation   * stands for ×   / stands for ÷   ^ stands for a power (3^2 means 3^2)

Formulas in spreadsheets start with **=**.

The formula **= 2*A1** works out 2 × the number in A1.

Spot the formula   for pairs of pupils

The first person puts a number into cell **A1**.
Then they put a formula into another cell.

	A	B
1	10	
2		
3	= 3*A1 + 12	
4		
5		

Now they just click in another cell.

	A	B
1	10	
2		
3	42	
4		
5		

The second person has to try to find out the formula by trying different numbers in **A1**.

When they think they know the formula, they type it into the spreadsheet.

	A	B
1	10	
2		
3	42	
4		= 4*A1 + 2
5		

They check they are right by trying some more numbers in **A1**.

	A	B
1	5	*Oh blow!*
2		
3	27	
4		22
5		

Challenge

The second person has to find a formula that undoes the first person's.

So in the example above, the undoing formula would start with 42 and produce 10.

Making a sequence

Type 1, 2, 3, 4, … into the first column.

	A	B
1	1	
2	2	
3	3	
4	4	
5	5	
	6	

Find a formula you can **fill down** to get this sequence.

	A	B
1	1	1
2	2	3
3	3	5
4	4	7
5	5	9
	6	11

Now see if you can find a formula you can fill down to get each of these.

1

1	2
2	4
3	6
4	8
5	10
6	12
7	14

2

1	2
2	5
3	8
4	11
5	14
6	17
7	20

3

1	6
2	11
3	16
4	21
5	26
6	31
7	36

4

1	1
2	4
3	9
4	16
5	25
6	36
7	49

5

1	0
2	3
3	8
4	15
5	24
6	35
7	48

6

1	1
2	3
3	6
4	10
5	15
6	21
7	28

Big, bigger, biggest

Set up your spreadsheet like this.

	A	B
1		2
2		3
3		5
4		4
5		
6	Sum	?
7		
8	Product	?
9		

You can type any four numbers into these four cells.

Put a formula in this cell that adds up your four numbers.

Put a formula here that multiplies your four numbers together.

1 (a) Can you find four numbers whose sum is 14 and whose product is 84?

(b) Find four numbers with a sum of 14 and a product of 108.

(c) What is the largest product you can find with four numbers whose sum is 14?

2 (a) Can you find four numbers whose sum is 15 and whose product is 180?

(b) Find four numbers with a sum of 15 and a product of 137.5.

(c) Find the largest product you can get with four numbers that add up to 15.

Ways and means

Put two numbers into your spreadsheet, one above the other.

	A	B
1		
2		
3		2
4		8
5		
6		
7		
8		

Put a formula to find the mean of the two numbers into the next cell.

	A	B
1		
2		
3		2
4		8
5		5
6		
7		
8		

Drag and drop the formula down the column.

	A	B
1		
2		
3		2
4		8
5		5
6		6.5
7		5.75
8		6.125

- What do you notice?
- Investigate how the numbers you start with affect the result.
- Investigate what happens when you start with three numbers and find their mean. What about four numbers?

Parcel volume

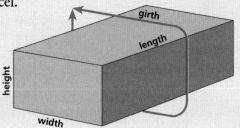

PARCEL DELIVERY
Individual parcels can weight up to 30 kg, with a maximum length of 1.5 m and a total of 3 m when length and girth are combined.

Parcel Force have a rule about the biggest sized parcel you can send.

It depends on the length and the girth of the parcel. (The girth is the distance all the way round it.)

What is the largest volume of parcel you can send?
Set up a spreadsheet to investigate this.
One way to organise it might be like this.

	A	B	C	D	E	F
1	Height	Width	Length	Girth	Length+Girth	Volume
2						

Furry festivals

Furry sell souvenirs at festivals.
They sell T-shirts, badges and pens.

At one festival they sold 60 items altogether.
(They sold at least one of everything.)
They took £200 for the items.

Use a spreadsheet to help you work out how many of each item they sold.
Is there only one answer?

Furry festivals

T-shirts	£22
Badges	£2
Pens	£1

Put here the number of T-shirts you think they sold.

Put a formula here for the cost of the T-shirts.

	A	B	C	D	E	
1						
2		Cost each (£)	Number		Total cost (£)	
3	T-shirts	22				
4	Badges	2				
5	Pens	1				
6						
7		Total number		Grand total		
8						

Put formulas here for the cost of badges and pens.

Put here the number of items they sold.

Put a formula here for the cost of all the items they sold.

Breakfast time

Foods contain different proportions of protein, carbohydrate and fat, as shown, for example, in the table below.

Food	% protein	% carbohydrate	%fat	Amount (g)
Cornflakes	8	25	0.7	
Milk	3	5	4	
White bread	8	4	2	
Butter	0.5	0	82	
Jam	0.6	69	0	

Put the table into a spreadsheet and enter these amounts.

Cornflakes	30 g
Milk	150 g
White bread	120 g
Butter	5 g
Jam	10 g

Add three extra columns 'Amount of protein', 'Amount of carbohydrate', 'Amount of fat'. Use suitable formulas to find the total amounts of protein, fat and carbohydrate in the breakfast above.

# Estimation

This work will help you

◆ estimate distances

◆ convert between metric and imperial measures

A Good judgement

How long is one centimetre?

The nail of your index finger is about 1 cm across.
Check this with a ruler.

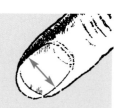

- Use your fingernail to estimate the length of your pencil.
  Check your estimate by measuring with a ruler.

- Use your fingernail to estimate the lengths of some other things on your desk.

How long is one metre?

- Mark a line on the ground (or use a wall).
  Ask everyone to place a counter exactly 1 m away from the line (or wall).
  Check who was closest with a metre rule.
  Then try estimating 2 m, 3 m, ... Check the estimates with a tape measure.

- Estimate, without measuring, the dimensions (length, width and height) of your classroom and the length of the corridor.

How long is 100 metres?

- Mark a line (or use one marked already) on a field or playground.
  Everyone walks to a place they estimate is 100 m from the line.
  Measure to see who is closest.

- About how big are the sports pitches at your school?
  Estimate some other distances around the school.
  Using a trundle wheel or long tape measure, check how good your estimates were.

How far is one kilometre?

- Make a list of places you think are exactly one kilometre from your school.
  Check your guesses with a map.

- Estimate how far you and your friends have to travel to school.
  Make a list of local places and estimate how far they are from your school.

Do not measure for these problems.

A1 Decide which of these metric units completes each sentence.

millimetres   metres   centimetres   kilometres

(a) The height of my living room is 3 ___ .

(b) The length of my hand is 15 ___ .

(c) Each day I walk 2 ___ to school.

(d) My thumbnail is 12 ___ wide.

(e) My garden is 8 ___ long.

(f) The length of my index finger is 70 ___ .

A2 Roughly how far will you have to walk to your next lesson?
Estimate the distances for all your walks between lessons today.

Roughly how far do you walk in a school day?

A3 If tables were put around the walls of your classroom,
how many chairs could you fit along the edge?

A4 How wide does a car parking space need to be?
Estimate the length of a suitable wall in your school.
How many car parking spaces could fit along this wall?

A5 The Skylon Tower in Toronto has 154 floors.
Estimate the height of your classroom.
Use this to estimate the height of the Skylon Tower.

*A6 Estimate the length of a small car.
Imagine a single line of cars, nose to tail, stretching along the 1270 km
of road between Penzance and Wick.
About how many cars would be in the line?

B Converting lengths

Here are some approximate rules for converting some metric and imperial lengths.

To change kilometres to miles, divide by 8 then multiply by 5

To change inches to centimetres, divide by 2 then multiply by 5

To change feet to metres, multiply by 3 then divide by 10

Try to find rules for changing
- miles to kilometres
- centimetres to inches
- metres to feet

B1 Change the distances given in km in these road signs to miles.

Calais	16
Boulogne	24

Firenze	64
Siena	32

Limerick	52
Ennis	20

B2 Convert these clothing measures in inches into centimetres.

(a) 32 inch waist   (b) 40 inch hips   (c) 16 inch collar

B3 A classroom is 30 feet long.
About how long is this in metres?

B4 Decide if each statement is true or false.

(a) Suneet is $3\frac{1}{2}$ feet tall which is under one metre.

(b) The distance from Liverpool to Leeds is 121 km which is just over 75 miles.

(c) Jane needs 21 inches of ribbon to go round a cake.
This is over 50 cm of ribbon.

B5 Greg is 6 feet tall.
About how tall is he in metres?

B6 Stranraer is 500 miles from Plymouth.
About how far is this in kilometres?

B7 Convert these speed limits in miles per hour to kilometres per hour (km/h).

(a) 30 miles per hour   (b) 50 miles per hour   (c) 70 miles per hour

B8 (a) About how many inches are equivalent to 5 cm?

(b) (i) Sam's handspan is 15 cm. What is this length in inches?

(ii) Helen's one-year-old baby is 70 cm tall. About how tall is the baby in inches?

B9 Fiona is 1.5 metres tall. About how tall is she in feet?

B10 The width of my palm is $7\frac{1}{2}$ cm. About how wide is this in inches?

B11 Decide if each statement is true or false.

(a) It is 303 miles from Shrewsbury to Land's End. This is over 500 kilometres.

(b) Sarah's pencil is 16 cm long which is just under 6 inches.

(c) The doors in my house are 2 metres high which is just under 7 feet.

B12 The height of a horse is measured from the ground to the shoulders.
This is usually measured in 'hands'.
A 'hand' is the width of a hand and is 4 inches in length.

Estimate the heights in cm of these horse breeds.

(a) Arab (15 hands)   (b) Shire (17 hands)   (c) Suffolk Punch (16 hands)

C Liquid measures

There are about $4\frac{1}{2}$ litres in a gallon.
To roughly **convert gallons into litres** multiply by 4 and add another half.

So 10 gallons = $(4 \times 10) + (\frac{1}{2}$ of 10$)$
= 40 + 5
= 45 litres

C1 About how many litres are there in

(a) 8 gallons (b) 20 gallons (c) 50 gallons (d) 200 gallons

C2 There are exactly 8 pints in a gallon.
A group of friends are regular blood donors.

The table show how many pints
of blood they have each given so far.

Change these into gallons and work out roughly
how many litres of blood each person has given.

Wayne	16 pints
Zak	48 pints
Irvine	40 pints
Stephen	240 pints

To convert litres into gallons

- Divide by 4 to give a rough estimate.

- To get a better estimate take away one tenth of the answer.

- So 32 litres gives 32 ÷ 4 = 8 gallons as a rough estimate.
  But 8 − 0.8 = 7.2 gallons is a better estimate.

C3 A saleswoman notes how many litres of petrol she puts in her car in a week.

(a) Copy this list but estimate
the amounts in gallons.

Monday	32 litres
Tuesday	24 litres
Wednesday	28 litres
Thursday	20 litres
Friday	40 litres
Saturday	36 litres

(b) About how many gallons
did she use in total?

(c) She has driven 1200 miles that week.
Roughly how many miles per gallon does her car travel?

C4 A few years ago it was suggested that pubs stopped
selling pints of beer and used $\frac{1}{2}$ litres.

Which is the larger amount? Explain why.

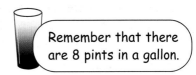

Remember that there
are 8 pints in a gallon.

C5 About how many pints are in a litre?

D Weights

There are about 2.2 pounds in a kilogram.

To roughly **convert kilograms into pounds**
- multiply by 2
- find $\frac{1}{10}$ of your result
- add your two answers together

So 20 kilograms gives
$$20 \times 2 = 40$$
$$\frac{1}{10} \text{ of } 40 = 4$$
$$40 + 4 = 44 \text{ pounds}$$

D1 About how many pounds are there in

(a) 30 kilograms   (b) 5 kilograms   (c) 35 kilograms   (d) 8 kilograms

D2 There are 14 pounds in one stone.
Which of these people weigh over 10 stones?

Janet 60 kg   Tony 70 kg   Jo 65 kg   Rob 63 kg

D3 Jim is baking some bread and needs $6\frac{1}{2}$ pounds of flour.
He has 3 kg of flour.
Does he have enough flour for his baking? Explain your answer.

D4 Which is heavier, one pound of sugar or 500 grams of sugar?
Explain your answer.

What progress have you made?

Statement	Evidence
I can estimate lengths.	1 Estimate the width of your desk in cm.
I can use metric and imperial units.	2 Which is further, 80 km or 60 miles? Explain your answer.
	3 Kay's waist measures 28 inches. About how much is this in centimetres?
	4 Jen's car holds 12 gallons of petrol. About how many litres of petrol is this?
	5 Gill's new baby weighs 3.5 kg. About how heavy is this in pounds?
	6 Could you fit 2 pints of orange juice into a 1 litre jug? Explain your answer.

② Quadrilaterals

This work will help you

◆ recognise special quadrilaterals (shapes with four straight sides)
◆ draw them
◆ learn about their properties
◆ see that some quadrilaterals are special types of other quadrilaterals

A Special quadrilaterals

These are some special quadrilaterals.
What is special about each one?

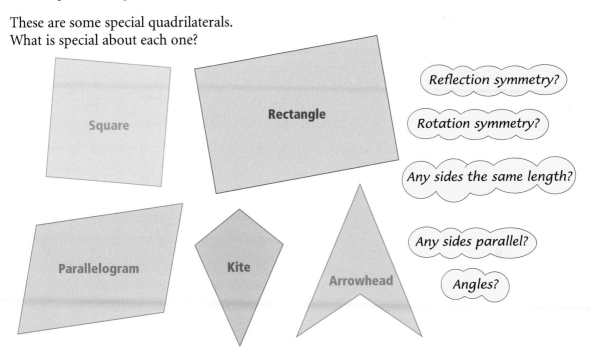

A1 In each of these, two sides of a square have been drawn.
Copy the two sides on dotty paper, then finish the square.

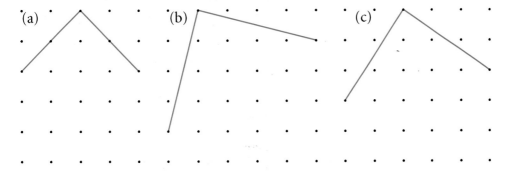

A2 In each of these, two sides of a rectangle have been drawn.
Copy the two sides on dotty paper, then finish the rectangle.

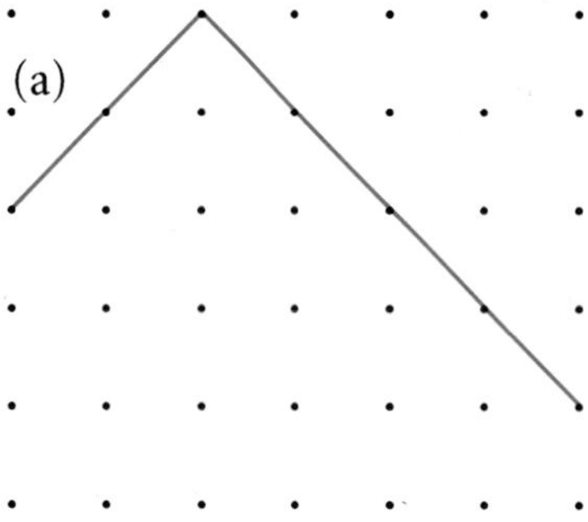

(a)

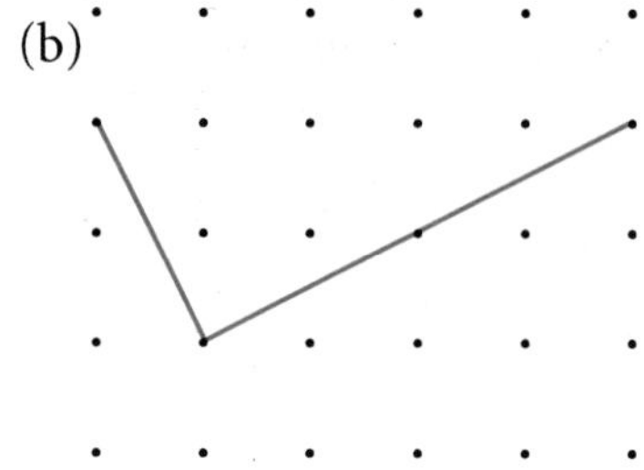

(b)

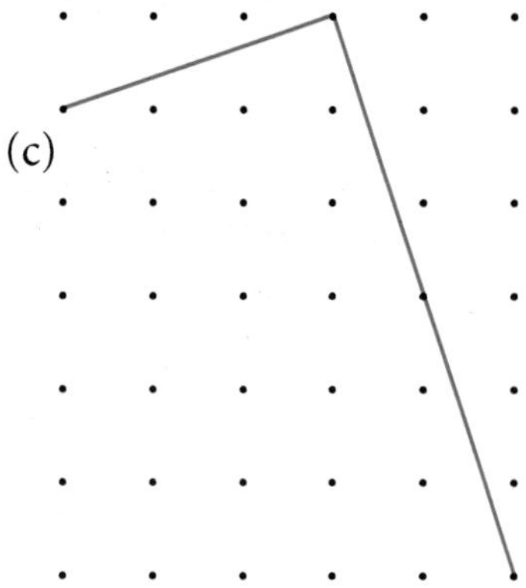

(c)

A3 In each of these, two sides of a parallelogram have been drawn.
Copy the two sides, then finish the parallelogram.

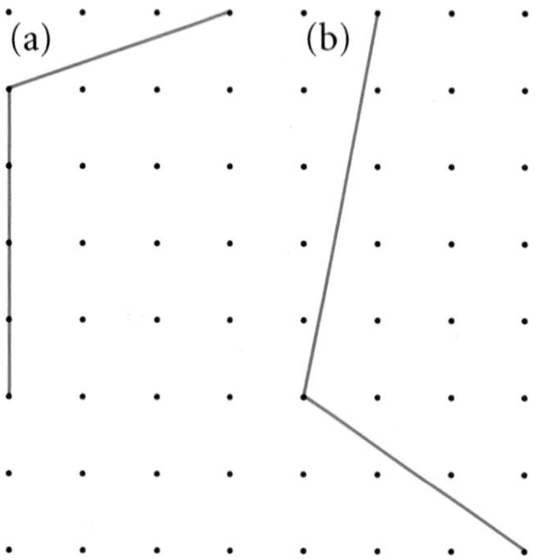

(a)

(b)

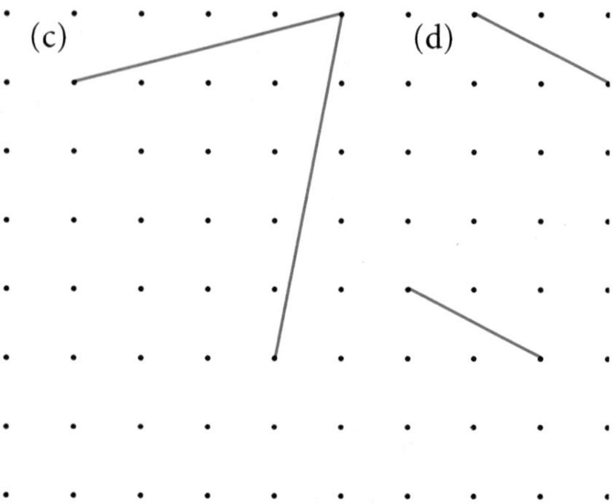

(c)

(d)

A4 Copy and complete these two sides to make
(a) a kite
(b) a parallelogram

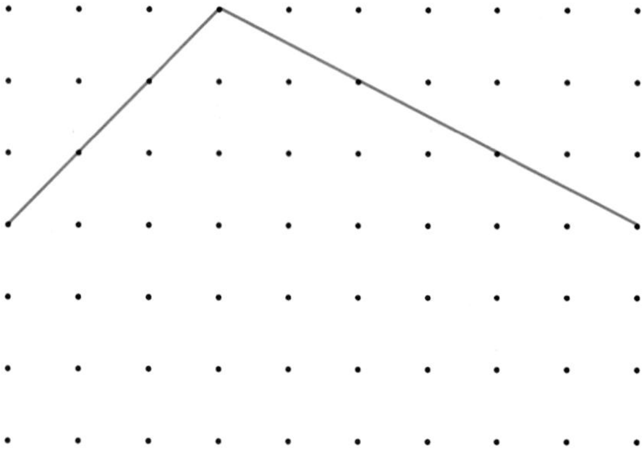

A **rhombus** is a parallelogram that has all four sides the same length.

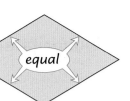

A5 In each of these, two sides of a rhombus have been drawn.
Copy the two sides, then finish the rhombus.

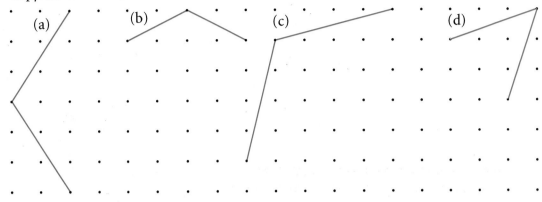

(a) (b) (c) (d)

On each rhombus, mark any lines of reflection symmetry.
If there is a centre of rotation symmetry, mark it with a cross and
write the order of rotation symmetry under your drawing.

A **trapezium** has a pair of opposite parallel sides,
but the parallel sides do not have to be the same length.

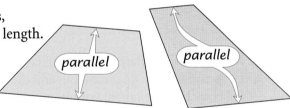

A6 (a) Which of these quadrilaterals are trapeziums?

(b) Describe any symmetry that the trapeziums have.

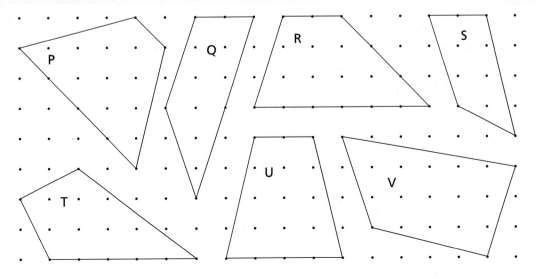

B Quadrilaterals from triangles

Use the triangles on sheet 164.

B1 Cut out the two scalene triangles
   with no right angle.

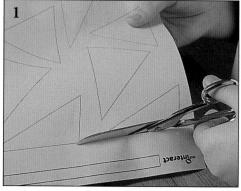

   Fit them together on your exercise
   book to make a quadrilateral.

   Draw round it carefully.

   Draw in a diagonal to show how it was
   made from the triangles.

   Label your quadrilateral to show
   what kind it is.

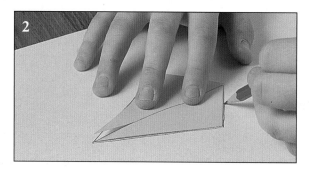

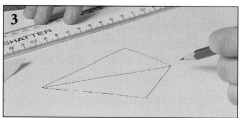

Make as many different quadrilaterals as you can with these two scalene triangles.
Draw round each quadrilateral, and draw a diagonal to show how it was made.
Label each quadrilateral with its name.

B2 If your scalene triangles had been shaped like this,
   which of the quadrilaterals could you not make?

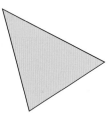

B3 Cut out the two isosceles triangles.
   Use the same method to draw as many quadrilaterals as you can.
   Show how each one was made and write its name.

B4 If your isosceles triangle had been like this,
   what difference would it have made?

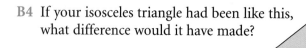

B5 Cut out the two equilateral triangles.
Show what quadrilaterals you can make with them.

B6 (a) Show what quadrilaterals you can make from the two right-angled triangles.

(b) Show what triangles you can make from the two right-angled triangles.

B7 If your right-angled triangles had been like this, what difference would it have made?

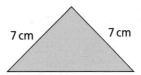

7 cm   7 cm

B8 What fraction of each quadrilateral is blue?

(a) 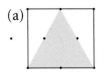   (b) 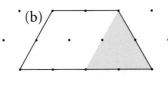   (c) 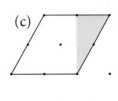   (d)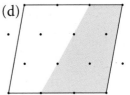

C Angles of a quadrilateral

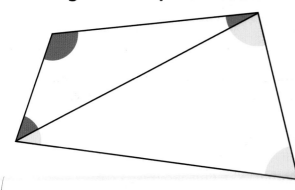

- What do the three red angles add up to?
- What do the three yellow angles add up to?
- What do the four angles of the quadrilateral add up to?

C1 Draw a quadrilateral. It can be any shape or size.
Measure its angles. What do they add up to?

C2 Work out the size of the angles marked with letters.
The drawings are not accurate, so don't try to measure.

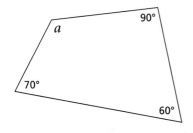

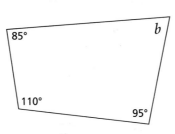

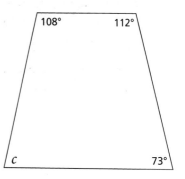

These are some other angle relationships that you should know.

Angles round a point add up to 360°.

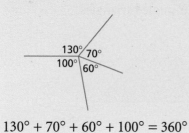

$130° + 70° + 60° + 100° = 360°$

Angles on a straight line add up to 180°.

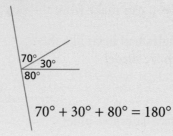

$70° + 30° + 80° = 180°$

Vertically opposite angles are equal.

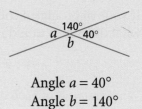

Angle $a = 40°$
Angle $b = 140°$

C3 Calculate the angles marked with letters.

 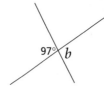 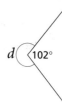

C4 Calculate the angles marked with letters.

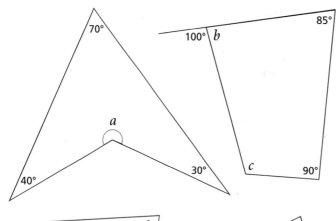 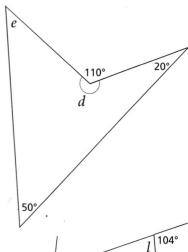

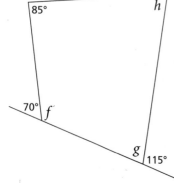 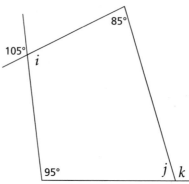 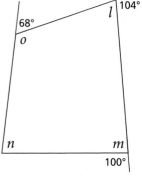

80

C5 These quadrilaterals are symmetrical. Work out the angles marked with letters.

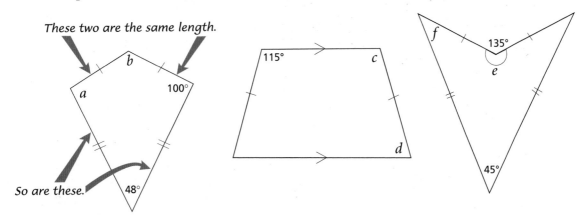

These two are the same length.

So are these.

C6 These are instructions to draw a quadrilateral on a computer.

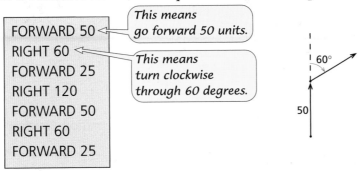

```
FORWARD 50
RIGHT 60
FORWARD 25
RIGHT 120
FORWARD 50
RIGHT 60
FORWARD 25
```

This means go forward 50 units.

This means turn clockwise through 60 degrees.

(a) What kind of quadrilateral is it?

(b) Write a version of the instructions that will draw a rhombus.

(c) Write a version that will draw a square.

(d) Write a version to draw a rectangle that is not a square.

*C7 Work out the values represented by the letters.

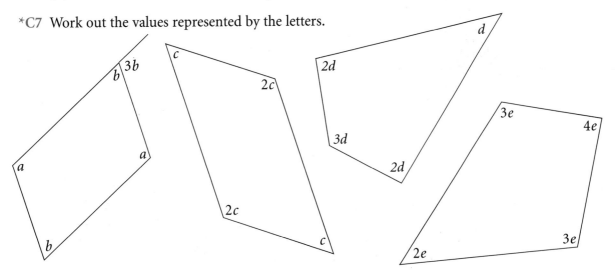

Parallelograms and angles

- Here two set of parallel lines make some parallelograms.
  What are the missing angles?

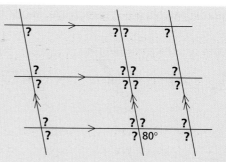

- What are the missing angles here?

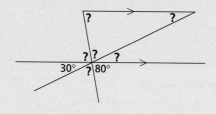

- What are the missing angles here?
  What do you your answers tell you about the angles of the coloured triangle?

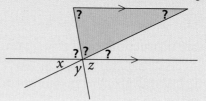

D Drawing and describing

Labelling points with capital letters helps when describing a mathematical drawing.

'AB' means the line from A to B (or its length).

'Angle DAB' means the angle with A at its vertex and D and B along its arms.
You can also write ∠DAB or D̂AB.

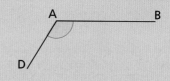

D1 Do accurate drawings of these quadrilaterals.
    For each one, first decide carefully what order you will draw the lines.

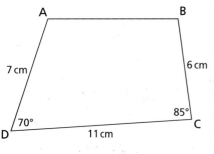

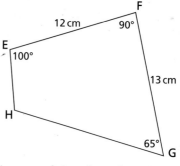

D2 Check the accuracy of your drawings by measuring these lengths and comparing your measurements with someone else's.

(a) AB   (b) HG   (c) IL

D3 Now use these angles to check the same way.

(a) Angle DAB   (b) Angle ABC   (c) Angle ILK

D4 This shows a quadrilateral and its diagonals.

   (a) Draw the diagonals accurately.
      Now join the points ABCD to make the quadrilateral.

   (b) What type of quadrilateral have you drawn?

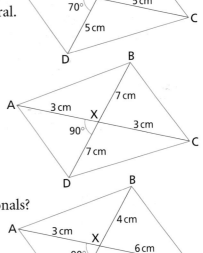

D5 Do the same as in D4 with this quadrilateral.
What type of quadrilateral do you get?

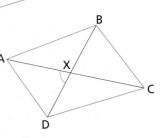

*D6 What kind of quadrilateral do you get with these diagonals?
(Try to decide without drawing, then draw to
see if you were right.)

*D7 What kind of quadrilateral do you get with these diagonals?

   (a) AX = 4 cm, XC = 4 cm, BX = 4 cm, XD = 4 cm, angle AXD = 90°

   (b) AX = 4 cm, XC = 4 cm, BX = 6 cm, XD = 6 cm, angle AXD = 80°

   (c) AX = 5 cm, XC = 7 cm, BX = 5 cm, XD = 7 cm, angle AXD = 85°

E Stand up if your drawing …

What did the teacher ask for?

What progress have you made?

Statement

I know the names of special quadrilaterals and their properties.

Evidence

1 Draw

  (a) a trapezium   (b) a rhombus

2 What special quadrilaterals have just one line of reflection symmetry?

3 What quadrilateral has four lines of reflection symmetry?

I can work out angles in quadrilaterals.

4 Work out the angles marked with letters.

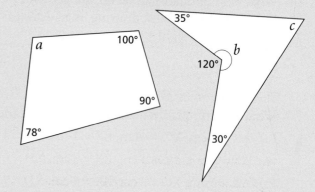

I can draw quadrilaterals accurately.

5 Draw quadrilaterals from these sketches.

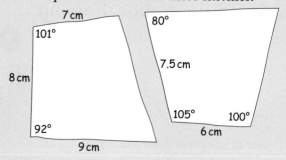

I know that some quadrilaterals are special types of other quadrilaterals.

6 Which of these are always parallelograms?

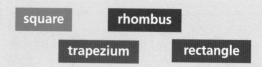

square   rhombus   trapezium   rectangle

⑬ Negative numbers

This work will help you

◆ use all four operations, +, −, × and ÷, with negative numbers

A Adding

$$^-5 + {}^-2 =$$ $$8 + {}^-2 =$$ $$4 + {}^-7 =$$ $$15 + {}^-9 =$$

$$^-13 + {}^-8 =$$ $$1 + {}^-20 =$$ $$9 + {}^-17 =$$ $$^-24 + 6 =$$

A1 Here is a set of five numbers.

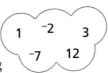

1 ⁻2 3
⁻7 12

The number 8 can be made by adding some of them together

$$3 + 12 + {}^-7 = 8$$

(a) How can you make   (i) 2   (ii) ⁻5

(b) What other numbers can you make?
(You can only use each number once, and you can only add them.)

A2 Copy and complete these addition squares.

(a)
+	⁻3	5
2		
⁻1		

(b)
+	6	⁻1
⁻4		
6		

(c)
+	12	⁻8
⁻7		
10		

(d)
+	35	
13		
⁻3	32	⁻22

A3 Copy and complete this addition wall.
The number on each brick is found by
adding the number on the two bricks below.

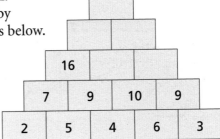

85

A4 Copy and complete these addition walls.

(a)
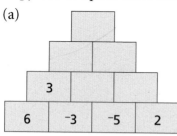

(b)
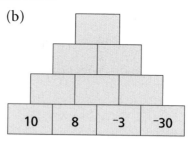

(c)
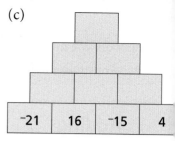

(d)
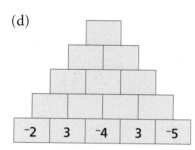

(e)
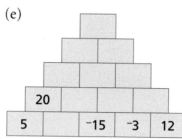

(f)
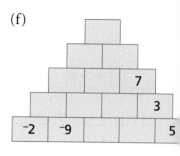

A5 In the puzzles below the number in a square is the sum of the numbers in the circles on each side of it.

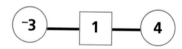

Copy and solve these.

(a)
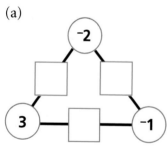

(b)
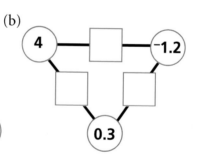

(c)
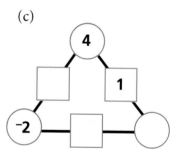

(d)
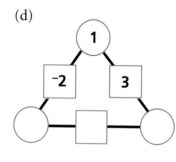

(e)
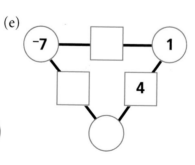

(f)
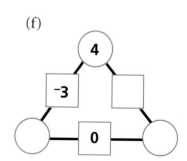

B Subtracting

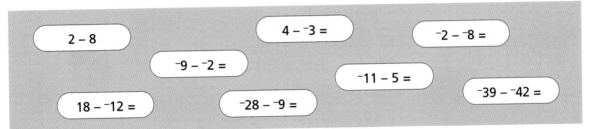

2 − 8

4 − ⁻3 =

⁻2 − ⁻8 =

⁻9 − ⁻2 =

⁻11 − 5 =

18 − ⁻12 =

⁻28 − ⁻9 =

⁻39 − ⁻42 =

This is a subtraction strip. How does it work?

| 2 | 4 | | | → | 2 | 4 | ⁻2 | | → | 2 | 4 | ⁻2 | 6 | → | 2 | 4 | ⁻2 | 6 | ⁻8 |

* Can you complete these subtraction strips?

| 20 | 14 | | |

| 10 | 1 | | |

| 1 | 2 | | |

| ⁻3 | ⁻1 | | |

| 9 | | 5 | | |

| 1 | | 2 | | |

| ⁻3 | | 7 | | |

B1 Copy and complete these subtraction strips.

(a)

| 16 | 14 | | |

(b)

| 13 | 2 | | |

(c)

| 8 | 9 | | |

(d)

| 10 | ⁻5 | | |

(e)

| ⁻6 | 3 | | |

(f)

| ⁻2 | ⁻5 | | |

B2 Copy and complete these subtraction strips.

(a)

| 11 | | 2 | | |

(b)

| | 4 | 2 | | |

(c)

| | 5 | ⁻2 | | |

(d)

| | 3 | | ⁻1 |

(e)

| | 2 | | ⁻1 |

(f)

| | ⁻2 | | 1 |

B3 (a) For each calculation, fit these three numbers
into the squares to make it true.

⁻3   ⁻1   2

(i) ☐ − ☐ − ☐ = 0

(ii) ☐ − ☐ − ☐ = ⁻4

(b) What is the largest answer you can get for ☐ − ☐ − ☐ =
using the three numbers in the cloud above?

C Multiplying

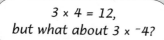

> $3 \times 4 = 12$,
> but what about $3 \times {}^-4$?

> It's 3 lots of negative four.

> So it's the same as
> ${}^-4 + {}^-4 + {}^-4$

> What is $4 \times {}^-5$?

> What is $5 \times {}^-4$?

$1 \times {}^-3 = {}^-3$
$2 \times {}^-3 = {}^-6$
$3 \times {}^-3 = {}^-9$
$4 \times {}^-3 =$
.....

> How do the patterns continue?

$4 \times {}^-3 = {}^-12$
$3 \times {}^-3 = {}^-9$
$2 \times {}^-3 = {}^-6$
$1 \times {}^-3 =$
.....

×	4	3	2	1	0	⁻1	⁻2	⁻3	⁻4
4				4	0	⁻4			
3				3	0	⁻3	⁻6		
2			4	2	0	⁻2	⁻4	⁻6	
1		3	2	1	0	⁻1	⁻2	⁻3	⁻4
0	0	0	0	0	0	0	0	0	
⁻1					0	1	2		
⁻2					0	2			
⁻3									
⁻4									

C1 Use any patterns you noticed to help you do these.

(a) $5 \times {}^-5$ (b) $^-6 \times 5$ (c) $^-5 \times {}^-6$ (d) $10 \times {}^-2$

(e) $^-6 \times 3$ (f) $3 \times {}^-6$ (g) $^-3 \times 6$ (h) $^-6 \times {}^-3$

C2 Work these out.

(a) $^-2 \times {}^-2$ (b) $^-4 \times {}^-4$ (c) $5 \times {}^-3 \times {}^-2$ (d) $^-2 \times {}^-2 \times {}^-3$

(e) $3 \times {}^-3 \times 4$ (f) $^-4 \times {}^-3 \times {}^-3$ (g) $6 \times 10 \times {}^-3$ (h) $^-2 \times {}^-2 \times {}^-2$

C3 Copy and complete these multiplication squares.

(a)
×	2	4
3		
⁻2		

(b)
×	5	⁻3
2		
⁻1		

(c)
×	⁻1	
⁻3		
⁻4	4	32

(d)
×	⁻6	
3		⁻21
	42	

C4 (a) Fit numbers from this set into the squares to make each calculation true.

(i) ☐ × ☐ = ⁻4

(ii) ☐ × ☐ = 12

(iii) ☐ × ☐ × ☐ = 24

(iv) ☐ × ☐ × ☐ = ⁻8

(b) What is the smallest answer you can get to ☐ × ☐ × ☐ = using three different numbers from the set?

C5 Copy and complete this multiplication wall. The number on each brick is found by multiplying the number on the two bricks below.

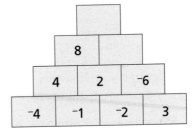

C6 Copy and complete these multiplication walls.

(a)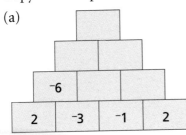

(b)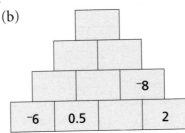

(c)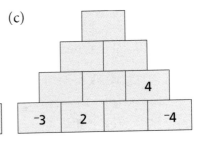

C7 In multiplication strips you find each new number by multiplying the two numbers before it. For example,

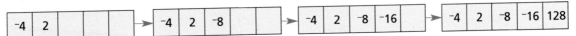

Copy and complete these multiplication strips.

(a)

(b) 2 | ⁻2

(c) ⁻3 | 1

(d) ⁻1 | | ⁻3

(e) ⁻2 | | 4

(f)  ⁻20 | 200

*C8 Copy and complete these multiplication strips.

(a) 2 | | | | ⁻4

(b) ⁻1 | | | | 8

(c) 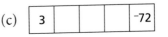 3 | | | | ⁻72

89

D Dividing

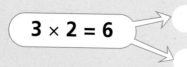

$3 \times 2 = 6$

$6 \div 3 = 2$ $\frac{6}{3} = 2$

$6 \div 2 = 3$ $\frac{6}{2} = 3$

What two divisions do we get from $4 \times {}^-5 = {}^-20$?

What two divisions do we get from ${}^-6 \times {}^-3 = 18$?

D1 Write the two divisions you get from each of these.

(a) $^-5 \times 3 = {}^-15$ (b) $^-7 \times {}^-3 = 21$ (c) $4 \times {}^-3 = {}^-12$ (d) $^-2 \times 8 = {}^-16$

(e) $^-4 \times {}^-5 = 20$ (f) $^-2 \times 7 = {}^-14$ (g) $2 \times {}^-7 = {}^-14$ (h) $^-2 \times {}^-7 = 14$

D2 Look through your answers to question D1.
Copy and complete these rules for dividing positive and negative numbers.

- positive ÷ positive = positive

- negative ÷ positive = _____

- positive ÷ negative = _____

- negative ÷ negative = _____

D3 Work these out.

(a) $^-16 \div {}^-4$ (b) $^-20 \div {}^-2$ (c) $^-36 \div {}^-9$ (d) $25 \div {}^-5$

(e) $^-32 \div {}^-4$ (f) $^-40 \div {}^-10$ (g) $56 \div {}^-8$ (h) $^-45 \div 9$

(i) $49 \div {}^-7$ (j) $100 \div {}^-10$ (k) $^-120 \div {}^-4$ (l) $^-144 \div 8$

D4 Work these out.

(a) $\dfrac{30}{^-6}$ (b) $\dfrac{^-48}{8}$ (c) $\dfrac{^-49}{^-7}$ (d) $\dfrac{42}{^-6}$

(e) $\dfrac{^-60}{15}$ (f) $\dfrac{^-24}{^-6}$ (g) $\dfrac{81}{^-9}$ (h) $\dfrac{144}{^-12}$

(i) $\dfrac{^-39}{13}$ (j) $\dfrac{40}{^-10}$ (k) $\dfrac{15}{^-10}$ (l) $\dfrac{^-5}{^-10}$

D5 These rules are used to make number chains.

- If the number is even, divide by $^-2$
- If the number is odd,   multiply by $^-3$, then add 1

Copy and continue this chain.      6 ⟶ $^-3$ ⟶ 10 ⟶ ...

Investigate chains for other starting numbers.

E Mixed problems

E1 Work these out.

(a) $^-3 + {}^-2$ (b) $^-2 - 9$ (c) $2 - {}^-5$ (d) $2 \times {}^-5$

(e) $^-3 \times {}^-4$ (f) $^-3 - {}^-7$ (g) $^-12 \div 2$ (h) $^-16 \div {}^-8$

E2 Work these out.

(a) $\dfrac{^-3 + {}^-5}{^-2}$ (b) $\dfrac{12}{^-3} - 1$ (c) $^-2(3 + {}^-7)$ (d) $3 \times {}^-5 - 8$

(e) $^-3(5 - {}^-4)$ (f) $\dfrac{24}{^-2 - 1}$ (g) $(^-4)^2 - 3$ (h) $\dfrac{^-4 - {}^-10}{^-3}$

E3 Work these out when $a = {}^-3$.

(a) $a - 2$ (b) $2a + 1$ (c) $3(1 - a)$ (d) $a^2 + 5$

E4 Work these out when $a = {}^-6$ and $b = {}^-2$.

(a) $a + b$ (b) $a \times b$ (c) $b - a$ (d) $a - b$

(e) $\dfrac{a}{b}$ (f) $b(a + 9)$ (g) $\dfrac{a + b}{4}$ (h) $a^2 + b^2$

E5 Copy and complete these addition squares.

(a)
+	3
	6
5	3

(b)
+	1	
$^-3$	2
	8

(c)
+		4
	$^-15$	$^-1$
	$^-13$

(d)
+		
9	$^-3$
$^-9$	$^-3$

E6 In these strips each number is the sum of the two numbers before it.
Copy and complete the strips.

(a) [ ] [ ] [12] [ ] [15] [ ]   (b) [ ] [ ] [ ] [$^-7$] [10]   (c) [ ] [$^-5$] [ ] [2] [ ]

E7 Copy and complete these multiplication squares.

(a)
×	$^-2$
	$^-6$
$^-4$	20

(b)
×			
3	6	$^-9$
$^-12$

(c)
×		$^-5$
	$^-20$	10
	15

(d)
×			
$^-1$	$^-1$	0.2
	$^-0.5$

E8 The numbers 16 and 17 can be made using four negative fours ($^-4, {}^-4, {}^-4, {}^-4$) and mathematical symbols.

$$^-4(^-4 - {}^-4 + {}^-4) = 16$$

$$(^-4 \times {}^-4) + \frac{^-4}{^-4} = 17$$

What other numbers can you make with four $^-4$s?

Get to 1 or ⁻1

- Choose a number from this set. You cannot use this number again.

- Your aim is to reach 1 or ⁻1 in as few stages as possible.

  You can use ×, ÷ or − any number of times each.
  You cannot use +.
  You can use any of the other numbers in the set **once**.

- For example, Kim and Jo both chose ⁻2.
  They both did it in three stages.

  Kim:

  Jo:

  Can you do better than Kim or Jo?

- Find the shortest way of reaching 1 or ⁻1 starting from other numbers in the set.

What progress have you made?

Statement

I can use all four operations with negative numbers.

Evidence

1 Work these out.

  (a) $6 + {}^-3$ (b) $8 - {}^-4$ (c) ${}^-10 - {}^-7$

2 Work these out.

  (a) ${}^-4 \times 6$ (b) ${}^-3 \times {}^-9$ (c) $5 \times {}^-10$

  (d) ${}^-60 \div 12$ (e) ${}^-80 \div {}^-20$ (f) $30 \div {}^-5$

  (g) $\dfrac{12}{{}^-4}$ (h) $\dfrac{{}^-20}{5}$ (i) $\dfrac{{}^-15}{{}^-3}$

3 Work these out.

  (a) ${}^-3(1 - 5)$ (b) ${}^-5(2 - {}^-1)$

  (c) ${}^-2(7 + {}^-12)$ (d) $({}^-3)^2 - ({}^-2)^2$

  (e) $\dfrac{{}^-8 + 2}{{}^-2}$ (f) $\dfrac{48}{{}^-10 - {}^-2}$

4 Work these out when $a = {}^-8$ and $b = {}^-4$.

  (a) $2b + 10$ (b) $a + b$

  (c) $3(b - a)$ (d) $a^2 - 60$

Percentage change

The work will help you

◆ calculate the result of a percentage increase or decrease

A Increasing and decreasing

Percentage cards

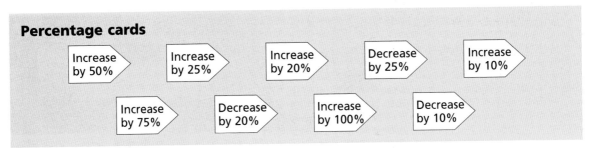

● Find the output for this flow diagram. £20 → Increase by 50% → ?

● Find the output for each of the other percentage cards.

● Which percentage card goes with each of these?

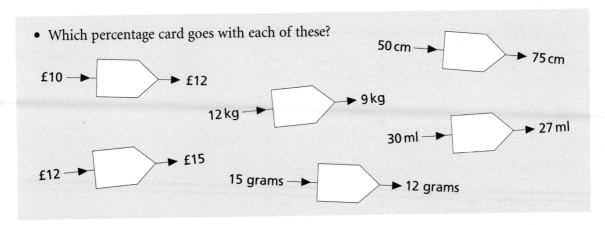

Do not use a calculator for these questions.

A1 What is the output for each flow diagram?

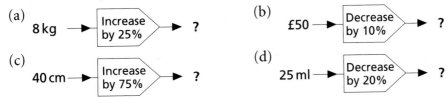

(a) 8 kg → Increase by 25% → ?

(b) £50 → Decrease by 10% → ?

(c) 40 cm → Increase by 75% → ?

(d) 25 ml → Decrease by 20% → ?

93

A2 What is the percentage increase in each flow diagram?

(a) £16 → | Increase by ?% | → £20

(b) 30 kg → | Increase by ?% | → 36 kg

A3 What is the percentage decrease in each flow diagram?

(a) £18 → | Decrease by ?% | → £9

(b) £40 → | Decrease by ?% | → £36

More than one percentage change

The diagram shows the result of two percentage changes on £20.

£20 → | Increase by 50% | £30 | Increase by 10% | → £33   The final result is £33.

A4 What is the final result for each flow diagram?

(a) 50 kg → | Increase by 20% | → | Increase by 10% | → ?

(b) £24 → | Decrease by 25% | → | Decrease by 50% | → ?

A5 What is the final result for each flow diagram?

(a) 50 → | Increase by 10% | → | Decrease by 20% | → ?

(b) 80 → | Increase by 25% | → | Decrease by 10% | → ?

A6 What is the final result for this flow diagram?

£250 → | Increase by 20% | → | Decrease by 20% | → ?

A7 Solve the puzzles on sheet 212.

*A8 What is the missing amount in each flow diagram?

(a) ? → | Increase by 25% | → £40

(b) ? → | Decrease by 20% | → £40

B Percentage increases and their multipliers

If an amount goes up by 25%, this means 25% of the
old amount is added on to make the new amount.

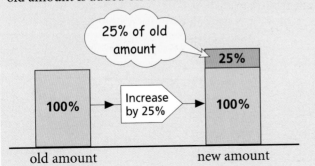

• Which of these multipliers will
increase an amount by 25%?

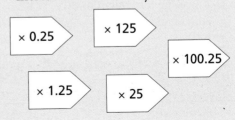

B1 A bus company increases all its fares by 25%.
Calculate the new fare after a 25% increase when the old fare is

(a) £28   (b) £4.80   (c) £57   (d) £21   (e) £6.60

B2 (a) Which of these multipliers will increase an amount by 12%?

 × 0.12   × 112   × 1.12   × 12   × 100.12

(b) A railway company increases its fares by 12%.
Calculate the new fare when the old fare is £30.

B3 (a) What multiplier will increase an amount by 23%?

(b) A book is priced at £8.00.
The bookshop then increases its prices by 23%.
What is the price of the book after the increase?

B4 A hairdressing salon increases its prices by 15%.

(a) A haircut previously cost £16.00.
What is the cost of a haircut after the increase?

(b) Highlights previously cost £25.00.
Work out the cost of highlights after the increase.

B5 (a) Increase £65 by 38%.   (b) Increase 50 kg by 46%.

(c) Increase 25 cm by 14%.   (d) Increase £12 by 73%.

B6 (a) Which of these multipliers will increase an amount by 5%?

 × 1.5   × 0.5   × 1.05   × 0.05   × 105

(b) A bakery increases its prices by 5%.
Calculate the new cost of a cake that used to cost £1.60.

C Percentage decreases and their multipliers

If an amount goes down by 38%, this means 38% of the old amount is taken away to leave the new amount.

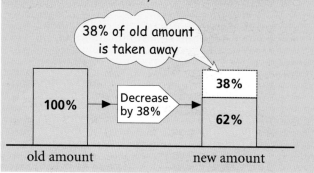

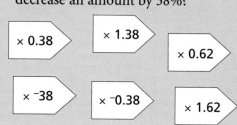

• Which of these multipliers will decrease an amount by 38%?

C1 Reduce each of these prices by 38%.

(a) £20 (b) £38 (c) £72 (d) £68.50 (e) £49.50

C2 Match each percentage decrease to its multiplier.

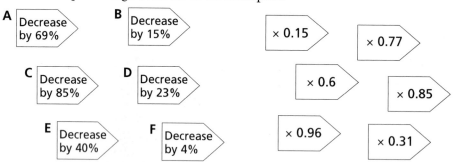

C3 In a sale a shop reduces all its prices by 15%.
Reduce each of these prices by 15%.

(a) £30 (b) £76 (c) £5.40
(d) £98.60 (e) £27.20 (f) £235

C4 (a) What number do you multiply by to reduce prices by 28%?

(b) In a sale, a clothes shop reduces its prices by 28%.
A dress was priced at £24.50.
What is its sale price?

C5 (a) Decrease £4 by 45%. (b) Decrease £6.50 by 14%.

(c) Decrease 700 kg by 63%. (d) Decrease 75 kg by 29%.

C6 (a) What number do you multiply by to decrease by 8%?

(b) Decrease 90 kg by 8%.

D Mixed questions

D1 Between the ages of eleven and twelve Jake's weight increased by 10%.
If he weighed 37.0 kg at age eleven years, what did he weigh at age twelve years?

D2 A shop reduces its prices by 25% in a January sale.
What is the sale price of a jumper that used to cost £40?

D3 Every percentage increase or decrease corresponds to a multiplier.
Match these percentage changes to their multipliers.

D4 The value of a car decreased by 19% over the last year.
The car was worth £5600 a year ago.

How much is the car worth now?

D5 The population of a new town is planned to increase by 11% during this year.
The population at the start of the year was 20 000.

What is the planned population at the end of the year?

D6 (a) Increase £80 by 42%. (b) Decrease 25 kg by 35%.
(c) Decrease 4200 by 6%. (d) Increase 45 kg by 18%.

What progress have you made?

Statement	Evidence
I can increase or decrease an amount by a given percentage.	1 Do not use a calculator. (a) Increase £10 by 50%. (b) Decrease £50 by 20%. 2 A shop increases its prices by 14%. What is the new price of a top that was marked at £15.00? 3 A shop reduces its prices by 8% for a spring sale. A TV costs £260 before the sale. What is its sale price?

Review 2

1 Here is a pattern made with counters.

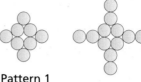

Pattern 1

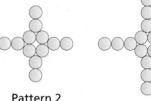

Pattern 2

Pattern 3

(a) Sketch pattern 4 and pattern 5.

(b) How many counters are added to each pattern to make the next?

(c) How many counters would be needed for the 10th pattern?

(d) Find a formula for the number of counters in the nth pattern.

(e) One pattern needs 64 counters. Which one is it?

(f) What is the number of the largest pattern you can make with 150 counters?

2 A rectangular room has length 3.2 m and width 2.7 m. What is its area?

3 (a) Name a quadrilateral that has exactly two lines of reflection symmetry.

(b) Is this the only possible answer? If not, name another quadrilateral with exactly two lines of reflection symmetry.

4 Work these out.

(a) $5 \times {}^-2$ (b) $8 + {}^-9$ (c) $7 - {}^-3$ (d) ${}^-6 \times {}^-4$

(e) ${}^-15 \div 3$ (f) ${}^-5 - 4$ (g) $18 \div {}^-6$ (h) ${}^-9 - {}^-2$

5 (a) Increase £40 by 20%.   (b) Decrease £16 by 25%.

6 What is the area of a poster that measures 0.5 m by 0.8 m?

7 (a) Estimate your armspan in metres.

(b) Estimate the number of people needed to make a 'human chain' all the way round a park, a distance of 3 km.

8 (a) Draw a sketch of a rhombus.

(b) Draw in one of its diagonals, splitting it into two triangles. What type of triangles are they?

9 Work out the area of the right-angled triangle. Give your answer in cm^2 to 1 d.p.

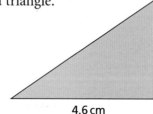

2.1 cm

4.6 cm

10 Here is a table for a design using counters.

Pattern number (n)	1	2	3	4	5
Number of counters (c)	8	13	18	23	28

    (a) Find a formula for the nth pattern.

    (b) Use your formula to find how many counters would be needed for the 100th pattern.

11 Work out the sizes of the lettered angles in these diagrams.

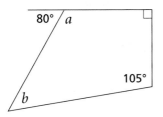 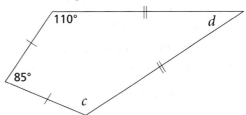

12 Work these out.

    (a) $(^-9)^2$ (b) $^-4(2 + {}^-7)$ (c) $\dfrac{^-10 + 4}{^-3}$ (d) $\dfrac{4 - {}^-6}{^-8 + 3}$

13 A shop reduces its prices by 15% in a sale.
   What is the sale price of a shirt that was £20 before the sale?

14 (a) Draw these two
       quadrilaterals accurately.

    (b) Measure

        (i) angle BCD

        (ii) angle PQR

    (c) What type of
       quadrilateral is

        (i) ABCD   (ii) PQRS

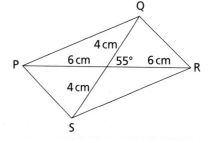

15 (a) Which is heavier, a 5 kilogram bag of potatoes or a 10 pound bag
       of potatoes? Explain your answer.

    (b) Approximately how far is 160 km in miles?   Barcelona   160 km

    (c) One of Gran's old cake recipes needs to be baked in an 8 inch tin.
       Approximately how many centimetres is this?

16 If $r = {}^-3$ and $t = {}^-5$, find the values of these.

    (a) $2r + 3t$ (b) $r - t$ (c) $r^2 + t^2$ (d) $\dfrac{12t}{r}$

17 The number of members of a club increased by 35%.
   If it previously had 80 members, how many members does it have
   after the increase?

Probability from experiments

This is about experiments involving chance.
The work will help you

◆ understand relative frequency
◆ use relative frequency as an estimate of probability

A Experiments

Dropping a spoon For pupils working in pairs

When you drop a spoon, it can land the right way up

or upside down

Which way it lands is a matter of chance.

- Which do you think is more likely?
- What do you think is the probability of landing the right way up?

  (You could mark your estimate on a probability scale from 0 to 1.)

Drop a spoon 10 times and record which way it lands.

Collect together the results for the whole class and find the **relative frequency** of 'right way up' landings.

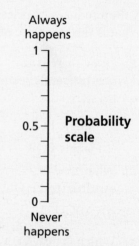

Relative frequency of 'right way up' $= \dfrac{\text{number of times spoon landed right way up}}{\text{number of times it was dropped}}$

The results of the experiment can be recorded on sheet 200, for example as shown at the top of the opposite page.

> R means 'right way up' and U means 'upside down'.
>
> A 'success' is the spoon landing right way up.

You can stop the experiment after the relative frequency settles down to a particular value.

Outcomes	Number of successes	Total number of successes so far	Total number of trials so far	Relative frequency
R R U R U U R R R	7	7	10	0.7
U R U U R R U R R U	5	12	20	0.6
R R R U R U R R U U	6	18	30	0.6
U R R U U R U R U R	5	23	40	0.58
R U R R R U R R R R	8	31	50	0.62
U R U R R R U R U R	6	37	60	0.62
U U R U R U R R R U	5	42	70	0.6
R R U R R R R U U R	7	49	80	0.61
R R R U R R U R R R	8	57	90	0.63
U R U U R R R R U R	6	63	100	0.63

You can use the relative frequency as an **estimate** of the probability that the spoon lands the right way up.

Here is a further experiment to try. There is another one on the next page.

Dropping a drawing pin

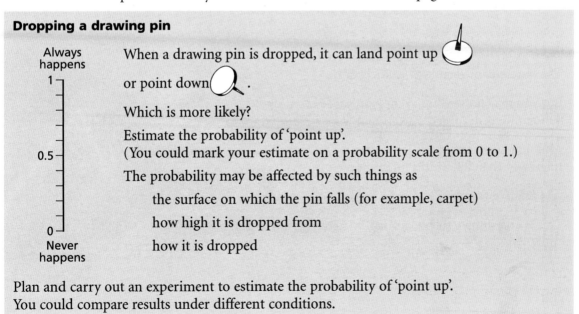

Always happens
1
0.5
0
Never happens

When a drawing pin is dropped, it can land point up

or point down .

Which is more likely?

Estimate the probability of 'point up'.
(You could mark your estimate on a probability scale from 0 to 1.)

The probability may be affected by such things as

the surface on which the pin falls (for example, carpet)

how high it is dropped from

how it is dropped

Plan and carry out an experiment to estimate the probability of 'point up'.
You could compare results under different conditions.

Dropping a multilink cube

When you drop a multilink cube, there are four ways it can land.

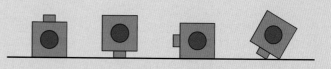

Before doing the experiment, guess the probability of each of these ways.

Now plan and carry out an experiment to estimate the probabilities.
It saves time if you drop ten cubes at a time.

You can work out some probabilities **theoretically**, using **equally likely outcomes**.
For example, when a fair dice is rolled, each face is equally likely to come up,
so the probability of each face coming up is $\frac{1}{6}$.

With a spoon there are no equally likely outcomes.
You have to use experimental data to estimate the probability.
The more data you have, the better the estimate.

B Relative frequency

Beth and Steve were doing a traffic survey.

They stood by a junction where traffic could turn either left or right.

They noted down which way each vehicle turned.

Their record started like this (R = right, L = left).

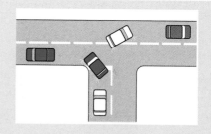

R R L R L L R R L R R R L R L R L L R R L R R L R

L L R R R L R L R R L R R R R L R R L L R R R R L

There is no pattern here. You cannot predict what the next turn will be.
The outcome of each turn is **uncertain**.

But you may notice that R happens more often than L.
50 turns were recorded. 31 of them were right turns.

Although you cannot predict which way a car will turn, it is **more likely** to turn right than left at this junction.

The **relative frequency** of right turns was $\frac{31}{50}$, or 0.62.

This is an estimate of the probability of a right turn at this junction.

B1 Here is a record made at another road junction.

Estimate the probability of a right turn at this junction.

> R L L R L L L R L L R L L R L L L L R L L R L L R
> L L L R L L R L L R L L R L R L L R L L L R L R L

B2 Gavin sells ice-cream in three flavours – vanilla, strawberry and chocolate.

He keeps a record of the flavours people ask for. It goes like this.

> S C S V V S C S V C S V S S C V V S C V
> V S S V S C S C S V C S C V S S C S V S

Estimate the probability that a person will ask for

(a) vanilla (b) strawberry (c) chocolate

Check that the three probabilities add up to 1.

B3 Nina has a coin which she suspects is unfair.

Here are the results when she throws it 50 times.

> H H T H T T H H T H H H T H T H T H H H T H T H H
> H T H H T H H T H H T T H H H H T T T H T H H T H H

What is the relative frequency of

(a) head (b) tail

Does the coin seem to be unfair?

B4 Fred stands by a newspaper stall and notes down which paper each person buys.

Here is his record after half an hour.

Paper	Tally
Mirror	ⅢⅢⅢⅢ II
Sun	ⅢⅢⅢ III
Express	ⅢⅢ II
Mail	ⅢⅢⅢ II
Star	ⅢⅢ I
Telegraph	ⅢⅢⅢ
Times	ⅢⅢ I
Guardian	ⅢⅢ
Independent	Ⅲ III

(a) Work out the relative frequency for each paper.
Write them as decimals, to two decimal places. Do they add up to 1?

(b) Estimate the probability that the next paper asked for is the *Sun*.

B5 Dervinia stood beside a road and noted how many people were in each car as it passed.

Here are her results so far.

Number of people in car	1	2	3	4	5
Number of cars	62	93	51	27	17

Estimate the probability that

(a) the next car to pass has one person in it

(b) the next car to pass has at least four people in it

B6 471 out of 9803 computers tested in a factory are found to be faulty.

(a) Estimate the probability (to 3 d.p.) that the next computer tested will be faulty.

(b) Using your answer to (a) give an estimate of the probability that the next computer will **not** be faulty.

C How often?

Relative frequency or probability can be used to estimate how often something will happen.

For example, if a coin is fair, the theoretical probability that it lands 'head' is $\frac{1}{2}$.
If the coin is thrown 50 times, we would expect about $\frac{1}{2}$ of 50 = 25 throws to be heads.

C1 (a) If a coin is fair, what is the theoretical probability of it landing 'tail'?

(b) If you throw a fair coin 260 times, about how many of those throws would you expect to be tails?

C2 (a) If an ordinary dice is fair, what is the theoretical probability of it showing a six when it is thrown?

(b) If you throw a fair dice 300 times, about how many times would you expect to get a six?

(c) If you throw it 300 times, about how many times would you expect to get

    (i) a one   (ii) an even number   (iii) a score of two or more

C3 A fair spinner is divided into five sectors the same size like this.

If the arrow is spun 150 times, roughly how many times would you expect it to stop on

(a) red   (b) yellow   (c) blue

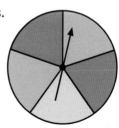

C4 Jan did an experiment with a drawing pin. In 100 throws, it landed point up 40 times.

(a) Estimate the probability that this drawing pin will land point up.

(b) If the same drawing pin is thrown 400 times, about how many times would you expect it to land point up?

C5 Karla dropped another drawing pin 100 times. It landed point up 44 times.

(a) Estimate the probability that this drawing pin will land point up.

(b) If Karla drops the pin 250 times, about how many times would you expect it to land point up?

C6 Steve made a solid shape whose faces were hexagons and pentagons. He rolled it 80 times. It stopped on a hexagonal face 56 times and on a pentagonal face 24 times.

If the same solid is rolled 500 times, about how many times would you expect it to stop on a hexagonal face?

C7 Laura cycles past a set of traffic lights on her way to work. For several days she records how often she is stopped by the lights and estimates from this that the probability of being stopped is 0.62 .

(a) What is the probability of **not** being stopped?

(b) She will cycle to work 240 times next year. Roughly how many times should she expect to get to work without being stopped by the lights?

What progress have you made?

Statement	Evidence
I can estimate a probability using relative frequency.	1 A plastic square-based pyramid is thrown 50 times. It lands on its base 12 times. Estimate the probability that the pyramid lands on its base.
	2 A study shows that 806 out of 2384 shoppers who enter a certain store make a purchase. Estimate the probability (to 2 d.p.) that the next shopper who enters will make a purchase.
I can use probability to estimate how often something will happen.	3 A fair five-sided spinner is numbered from 1 to 5. If it is spun 400 times, about how often would you expect it to land on the number 4?
	4 From an experiment it is estimated that the probability of a certain type of seed germinating is 0.62 . If 2500 seeds are sown in conditions like the experiment, about how many would be expected to germinate?

Squares, cubes and roots

This work will help you

◆ work with square and cube numbers
◆ find square roots (positive and negative) and cube roots

A Squares and cubes

Can you make a square patio that uses 40 of these tiles?

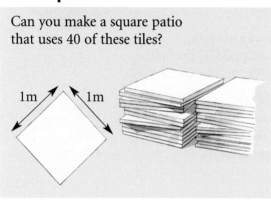

1m   1m

Can you make a large wooden cube that uses 27 of these cubes?

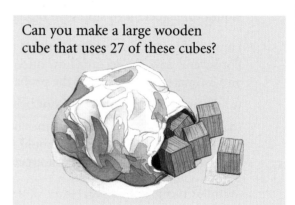

Do not use a calculator for questions A1 to A8.

A1 James has 60 square slabs.
He makes the largest square patio he can without breaking any slabs.
How many slabs does he have left over?

A2 Find two square numbers that add to give 20.

A3 Write down the value of each of these.

(a) The square of 5   (b) 6 squared
(c) 3^2 (d) 7^2

A4 Julie has 90 sugar cubes.
She makes the largest cube she can without breaking any of the sugar cubes.
How many sugar cubes does she use?

A5 Write down the value of each of these.

(a) 2 cubed   (b) The cube of 4
(c) 5^3 (d) 1^3

A6 Which two cube numbers add to give 9?

A7 Find a square number and a cube number that add to make 52.

A8 Some numbers can be written as the difference between two square numbers.

For example, $3 = 4 - 1$ $\qquad$ $20 = 36 - 16$

Write each of these as the difference between two square numbers.

(a) 5 $\qquad$ (b) 8 $\qquad$ (c) 11 $\qquad$ (d) 24 $\qquad$ (e) 13

A9 Write down all the square numbers between 90 and 150.

A10 Find a cube number between 500 and 600.

A11 Find a number that fits each statement.

(a) $\blacksquare^2 = 169$ $\qquad$ (b) $\blacksquare^3 = 216$ $\qquad$ (c) $\blacksquare^2 = 484$ $\qquad$ (d) $\blacksquare^3 = 1331$

A12 What is the smallest cube number that is larger than 1000?

A13 Work these out.

(a) 1.2^2 $\qquad$ (b) 3.5^3 $\qquad$ (c) 0.9^2 $\qquad$ (d) 0.5^3

A14 Find a number that fits each statement.

(a) $\blacksquare^2 = 2.56$ $\qquad$ (b) $\blacksquare^3 = 2.197$ $\qquad$ (c) $\blacksquare^2 = 14.44$ $\qquad$ (d) $\blacksquare^3 = 0.064$

A15 Without using a calculator, work these out.

(a) $(^-2)^2$ $\qquad$ (b) $(^-2)^3$ $\qquad$ (c) $(^-3)^2$ $\qquad$ (d) $(^-3)^3$

A16 What is the missing number in $\blacksquare^3 = {}^-64$

B Roots

6 squared is $\quad 6^2 = 6 \times 6 = 36$ $\qquad$ so the **positive square root** of 36 is 6.

$(^-6)$ squared is $\quad (^-6)^2 = {}^-6 \times {}^-6 = 36$ $\qquad$ so the **negative square root** of 36 is $^-6$.

Do not use a calculator for questions B1 to B8.

B1 Calculate $\qquad$ (a) 4^2 $\qquad$ (b) $(^-4)^2$ $\qquad$ (c) 5^2 $\qquad$ (d) $(^-5)^2$

B2 (a) Use the fact that $21^2 = 441$ to write down the value of $(^-21)^2$.

$\quad$ (b) (i) Write down the positive square root of 441.

$\qquad$ (ii) Write down the negative square root of 441.

B3 What is the positive square root of 100?

B4 Write down the negative square root of 25.

B5 Which of these numbers are the square roots of 64?

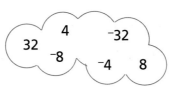

B6 The positive square root of 625 is 25.
What is the negative square root of 625?

B7 Find two numbers that fit each statement.

(a) $\blacksquare^2 = 49$ (b) $\blacksquare^2 = 4$ (c) $\blacksquare^2 = 1$ (d) $\blacksquare^2 = 81$

---

5 cubed is $5^3 = 5 \times 5 \times 5 = 125$ so the **cube root** of 125 is 5.

($^-$2) cubed is $(^-2)^3 = {}^-2 \times {}^-2 \times {}^-2 = {}^-8$ so the **cube root** of $^-8$ is $^-2$.

B8 Find the cube root of each of these.

(a) 8 (b) 27 (c) 1 (d) 64 (e) $^-27$

B9 What is the cube root of 0.125?

B10 (a) A cube has a volume of 729 cm³.
What is the length of one edge?

(b) What is the cube root of 729?

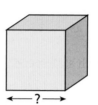

B11 Find the cube root of each of these.

(a) 512 (b) 2197 (c) 8000 (d) 3.375 (e) $^-1728$

C Using graphs

- Here is a table of squares.

Number	$^-4$	$^-3$	$^-2$	$^-1$	0	1	2	3	4
Square	16	9	4	1	0	1	4	9	16

- The values are plotted on a graph and a smooth curve is drawn through the points.

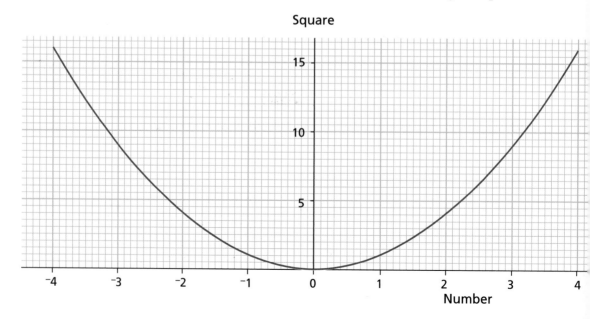

C1 Use the graph to estimate

(a) the square of 3.5   (b) the square of 1.4   (c) 2.6^2

C2 Use the graph to estimate

(a) the positive square root of 8   (b) the negative square root of 14

C3 (a) Use a calculator to find the value of 4.4^2.

(b) What is the value of 4.5^2?

(c) Why do your results show that the positive square root of 20 is between 4.4 and 4.5?

(d) Use the square root key on your calculator to find this number correct to 2 d.p.

(e) What is the negative square root of 20 correct to 2 d.p.?

C4 (a) What is the value of 4.6^3?

(b) What is the value of 4.7^3?

(c) Why do your results show that the cube root of 100 is between 4.6 and 4.7?

(d) Find the cube root of 100 correct to 2 d.p.

What progress have you made?

Statement	Evidence
I know about square and cube numbers.	1 Work out (a) 8^2 (b) 2^3
	2 What is the square of 4?
	3 Which two cube numbers add to make 28?
	4 Work out (a) $(^-5)^2$ (b) $(^-1)^3$
I can work out square and cube roots.	5 Work out
	(a) the positive square root of 49
	(b) the negative square root of 81
	(c) the cube root of 27
	(d) the cube root of $^-27$
	6 (a) Use the graph of squares opposite to estimate the square roots of 15.
	(b) Joe uses his calculator to work out that
	$3.8^2 = 14.44$ and $3.9^2 = 15.21$
	Explain how this shows that the positive square root of 15 is between 3.8 and 3.9.

17 Area

This work will help you find the area of a parallelogram, triangle and trapezium.

A Area of a parallelogram

- Cut out one copy of parallelogram P (on sheet 213).
- Cut it so you can make a rectangle from the pieces.

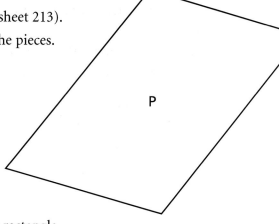

- Cut another copy of P to make a different rectangle.
- Does this give an area for P that you expected?

A1 Draw this parallelogram accurately.

By drawing or cutting, show how to make it into a rectangle.

Find the area of the parallelogram.

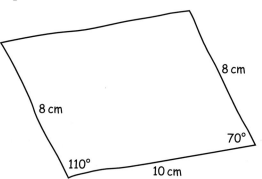

A2 Find the area of this parallelogram the same way as in A1.

Is there more than one way to make it into a rectangle?

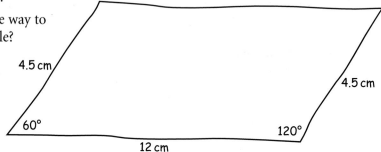

A3 This rectangle is split into two congruent right-angled triangles A and B with a parallelogram P between them.

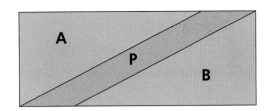

Triangle A slides along to touch triangle B. The original rectangle is now split into A, B and a rectangle R.

What can you say about the areas of P and R?

Explain the reason for your answer.

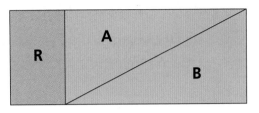

A4 Work out the area of each of these parallelograms. They are not drawn accurately.

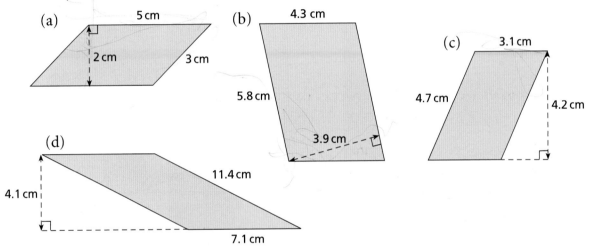

(a) 5 cm 2 cm 3 cm

(b) 4.3 cm 5.8 cm 3.9 cm

(c) 3.1 cm 4.7 cm 4.2 cm

(d) 4.1 cm 11.4 cm 7.1 cm

A5 Draw axes on squared paper. Label both axes from ⁻5 to 5.

(a) Draw a parallelogram with vertices at (3, 2), (5, 5), (1, 5) and (⁻1, 2). Calculate its area in square units.

(b) Draw a parallelogram with vertices at (4, 0), (⁻2, ⁻1), (⁻2, ⁻3) and (4, ⁻2). Calculate its area.

(c) Draw and find the area of a parallelogram with vertices at (⁻3, 0), (⁻4, 5), (⁻4, 1) and (⁻3, ⁻4).

A6 Measure this parallelogram and calculate its area.

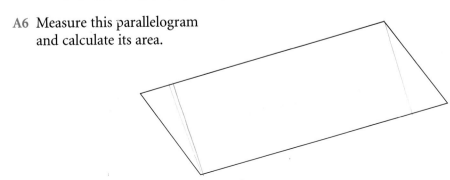

The rule for finding the area of a parallelogram can be written

area = base × height

The height must be measured at right angles to the base.

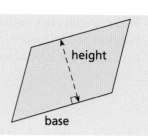

A7 Find the lengths marked with letters.
The diagrams are not drawn accurately.

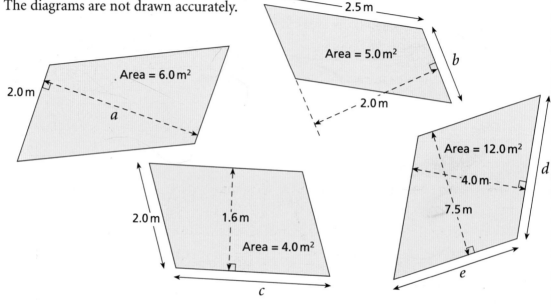

*A8 Find the lengths marked with letters.
The diagrams are not drawn accurately.

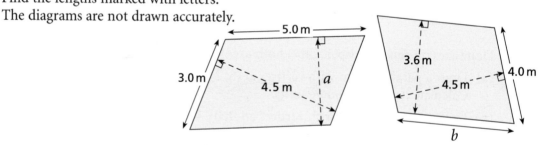

B Area of a triangle

- What fraction of the parallelogram is triangle A?
- Measure the parallelogram and work out its area.
- What is the area of triangle A?
- Could you use a different parallelogram to work out the area of triangle A?

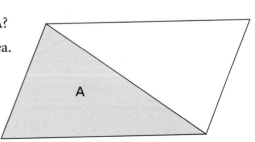

B1 For each diagram, • find the area of the parallelogram
• find the area of the pink triangle

(a)

(b)

(c)

6.0 cm

3.7 cm

3.4 cm

6.3 cm

5.8 cm

4.2 cm

4.0 cm

6.5 cm

4.1 cm

2.3 cm

(d)

2.8 cm

B2 For each triangle,

• take measurements and record them on a sketch
• work out the area
• find the area using different measurements and check that you get the same result

(a)

(b)

(c)

B3 Work out the area of each triangle.
(Be careful to use the correct lengths.)

(a)

6.0 cm

3.9 cm

5.0 cm

(b)

2.8 cm

7.6 cm

4.9 cm

(c)

4.2 cm

3.4 cm

5.9 cm

(d)

5.5 cm

5.2 cm

3.7 cm

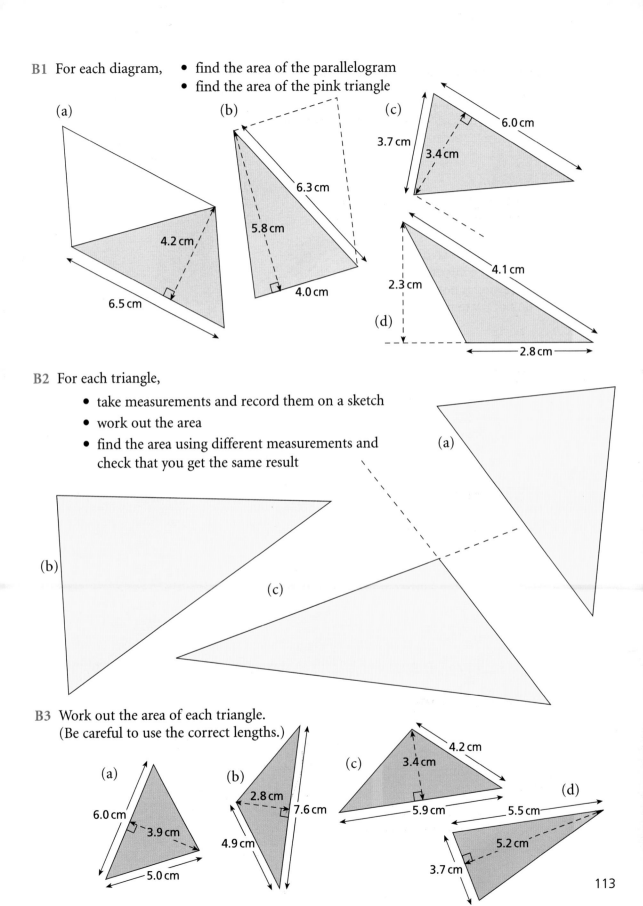

113

These formulas all say the same thing.

Area of triangle = $\dfrac{\text{base} \times \text{height}}{2}$ $\qquad A = \frac{1}{2}bh \qquad A = \dfrac{bh}{2}$

Think of them as meaning

'work out base × height and halve it'.

Remember that b can be the length of any side of the triangle, but h must be measured at right angles to b.

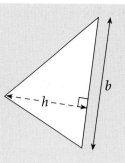

B4 This triangle has an area of 15 cm². Work out the missing length. The drawing is not accurate, so do not try to measure.

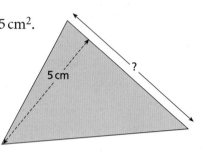

B5 All these triangles have the same area. Work out the missing lengths.

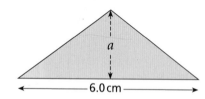
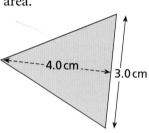
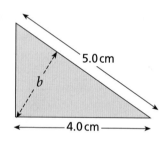

C Area of a trapezium

• These trapeziums are drawn on cm² paper. What is the area of each one?

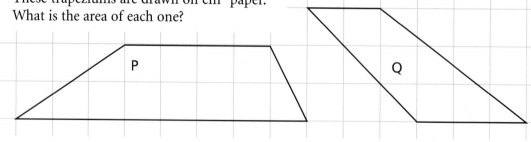

• How could you find the area of this trapezium?

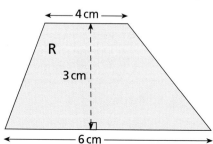

C1 Work out the areas of these trapeziums.
They are not drawn accurately.

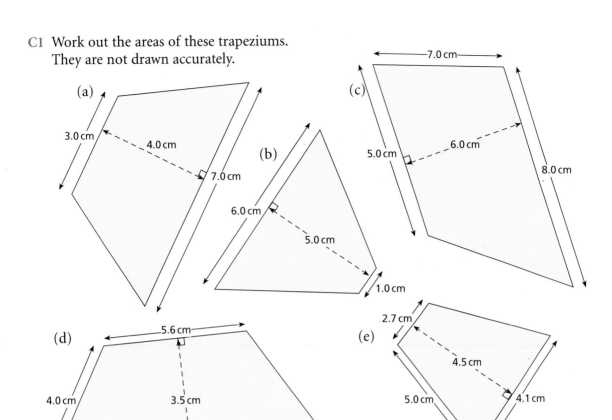

(a) 3.0 cm 4.0 cm 7.0 cm

(b) 6.0 cm 5.0 cm 1.0 cm

(c) 7.0 cm 5.0 cm 6.0 cm 8.0 cm

(d) 5.6 cm 4.0 cm 3.5 cm 6.8 cm

(e) 2.7 cm 4.5 cm 5.0 cm 4.1 cm

C2 Calculate the area of this trapezium.

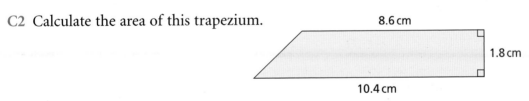

8.6 cm
1.8 cm
10.4 cm

C3 Measure each trapezium and work out its area.

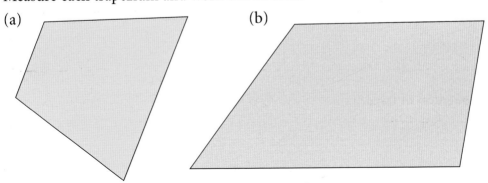

(a)

(b)

Splitting into two triangles gives this as a formula for the area of a trapezium:

$$A = \tfrac{1}{2}ah + \tfrac{1}{2}bh$$

But these are more usual ways of writing the formula:

$$A = \tfrac{1}{2}(a + b)h \qquad A = \frac{(a + b)h}{2}$$

You can think of them as saying

'add the lengths of the parallel sides,
multiply by the distance between them,
then halve'.

Remember that h must be measured at right angles to a and b.

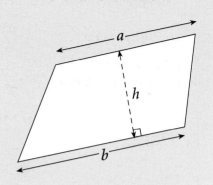

What progress have you made?

Statement

Evidence

I can work out areas of parallelograms.

1 Work out the area of this parallelogram.

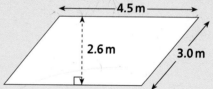

2 Work out the missing length.

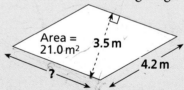

I can work out areas of triangles.

3 Measure this triangle and work out its area.

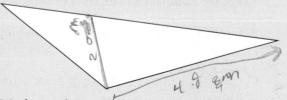

I can work out areas of trapeziums.

4 Work out the area of this trapezium.

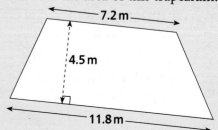

⑧ Equivalent expressions

This work will help you
◆ simplify expressions
◆ use algebra to explain things

A Walls

• Can you complete these walls?

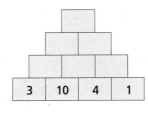

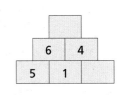

A1 Copy and complete these walls.

(a)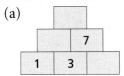

(b)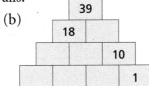

(c)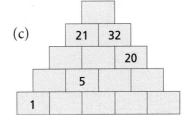

A2 This wall uses 1, 4 and 9 on the bottom row.

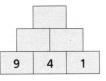

(a) What will be the total on the top brick?

(b) Draw a different wall with 1, 4 and 9 on the bottom row.

What is the total on the top brick for this wall?

(c) Using 1, 4 and 9 on the bottom row, what different totals are possible for the top brick?

A3 What is the highest total possible on the top brick for a wall with 2, 4 and 6 on the bottom row?

A4 This wall uses 1, 2, 3 and 5 on the bottom row.

(a) What is the total on the top brick for this wall?

(b) Draw a different wall with 1, 2, 3 and 5 in a different order on the bottom row.

Work out the total on the top brick.

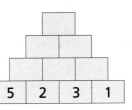

(c) Using 1, 2, 3 and 5 on the bottom row, what is the lowest possible total for the top brick?

117

A5 Copy and complete the walls below.

(a)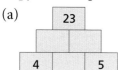

(b)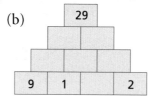

A6 (a) For this wall, find the total on the top brick when the number on the yellow brick is

(i) 1

(ii) 4

(b) Copy and complete this table for the wall.

Number on yellow brick	Number on top brick
1	
2	
3	
4	
5	
10	

(c) What rule links the number on the yellow brick with the total on the top brick?

(d) Use your rule to find the total on the top brick when the number on the yellow brick is 100.

B Building in algebra

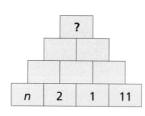

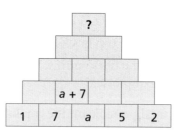

B1 (a) Copy and complete this wall.

(b) (i) What number will be on the top brick when $n = 5$?

(ii) Check your result by drawing the wall.

B2 (a) Copy and complete this wall.

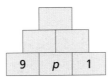

(b) (i) What value for p will give 20 on the top brick?

(ii) Check your result by drawing the wall.

B3 (a) Copy and complete this wall.

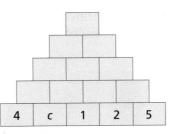

(b) What number will be on the top brick when $c = 10$?

(c) (i) What value for c will give 35 on the top brick?

(ii) Check your result by drawing the wall.

B4 Copy and complete these walls.

(a)

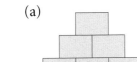

(b)

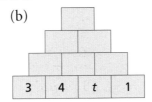

(c)

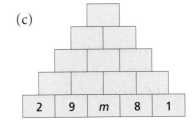

B5 Copy and complete these walls.

(a)

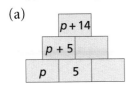

(b)

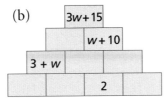

(c)

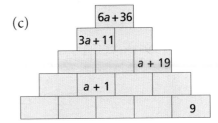

B6 (a) Choose a value for n.
Copy and complete wall A **and** wall B for your value.

What do you notice?

(b) Repeat with a different value for n.

What do you notice?

(c) Use algebra to show that the numbers on the top bricks will be the same for all possible values of n.

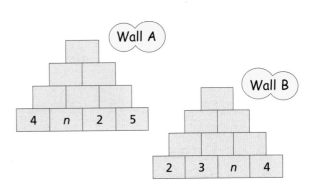

C Perimeters

The perimeter of a shape is the total length of its outside edge.

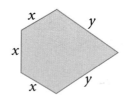
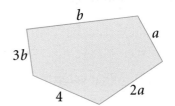

C1 Find an expression for the perimeter of each of these shapes. Write each expression in its simplest form.

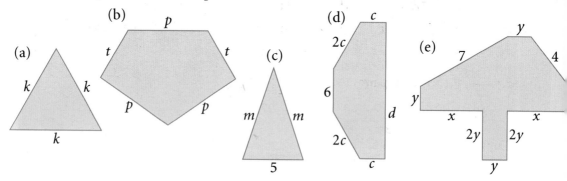

(a) (b) (c) (d) (e)

C2 Write each of these in a simpler way.

(a) $x + x + y + y + y$ (b) $3m + 2m + n$ (c) $2p + 6p + 3q + 2q$

(d) $3g + 7h + 5g + h$ (e) $4x + 5y + 3x + 6 + 1$ (f) $7 + p + 8q + 4p + 2$

C3 Sketch each shape and write expressions for the missing lengths.

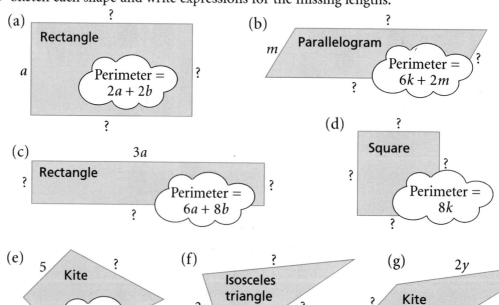

(a) Rectangle   ? a Perimeter = $2a + 2b$?

(b) Parallelogram   ? m Perimeter = $6k + 2m$?   ?

(c) Rectangle $3a$?   ?   Perimeter = $6a + 8b$?

(d) Square   ?   ?   ?   Perimeter = $8k$?

(e) Kite   5   ?   ?   Perimeter = $6p + 10$?

(f) Isosceles triangle   ? $2x$?   Perimeter = $2x + 14$

(g) Kite $2y$?   ?   Perimeter = $4y + 10z$

D Subtracting

A $a + 4a - 3a$	**B** $5a - a + 2a$	**C** $7a - 1 - 3a + 7$	**D** $9a - 2a - a$
E $9 + 2a - 6 - 3$	**F** $6 + 3a - 1 - 9a$	**G** $4 - a + 2 + 5a$	**H** $3 - 4a - 2a + 2$

T

D1 Simplify the following.

(a) $6p + 3p - 5p$ (b) $7q - 3q + q$ (c) $2r + 6 - r + 7$

(d) $3t + 5 + t - 8 + 2t$ (e) $8u - 4u - 2u$ (f) $5v - 4 - 2v + 3$

(g) $6x - 8x + 5x$ (h) $2 + 3y + 5 - y - 2y$

D2 Find three matching pairs.

A $3 - 2b + 3b$

B $3a - a + b$

C $b + 3$

D $3a + 4b - 2a - b$

E $a + 3b$

F $b + 2a$

D3 Simplify the following.

(a) $4s - 2s + 3t$ (b) $7p - 3p + q + 8q$ (c) $2n + 6m - n + 7m$

(d) $4j + 5k - 3j - 2k$ (e) $3g + 5 + h - 8 - 2g$ (f) $10e - 2f - 3f + 5e$

(g) $5c - 4d - 2c + 7d$ (h) $6b - 2a + 5b + 3a - 2b$

D4 Simplify the following.

(a) $4 + 3t - 5t + 6$ (b) $7 - 3v - 5v$ (c) $7 + 2w - 6 - 3w$

(d) $5 - 6x + 8 + 2x$ (e) $1 - 8y + y + 4$ (f) $7 + z - 4 - 9z$

D5 Simplify the following.

(a) $4m + 6n - 8n + 3m$ (b) $5r + 2s - r - 6s$ (c) $10 - 3p + q - 5p + 2q$

(d) $t + v - 3 + 2t - 5v$ (e) $w + 2 + x - 5 - 2x$ (f) $3y - 6z + 5y - z + 3z$

E Magic squares

A magic square is a square grid of numbers where the numbers in each **row**, **column** and **diagonal** add to give the **same total**.

The total for this magic square is 24.

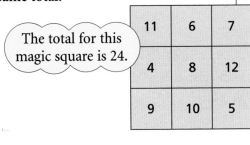

Totals

$11 + 6 + 7 = 24$

$4 + 8 + 12 = 24$

$9 + 10 + 5 = 24$

$11 + 8 + 5 = 24$

$7 + 8 + 9 = 24$

$4 + $

11	6	7
4	8	12
9	10	5

E1 Are these magic squares?

(a)

7	7	4
3	6	9
8	5	5

(b)

8	3	4
1	5	9
6	10	2

E2 (a) Make a grid of numbers by replacing each expression with its value when $v = 2$.

(b) Make a grid of numbers by replacing each expression with its value when $v = 3$.

(c) Which of these is a magic square?

$5 + 2v$	$8 - v$	$v + 4$
$3v - 2$	$5 + v$	$5v$
$10 - v$	$v + 6$	$2v + 1$

E3 (a) Make a grid of numbers by replacing each expression with its value when $w = 1$.

(b) Is your grid a magic square?

(c) Jane adds the expressions in the top row.

$w + 2 + 3w + 8 + 5 - w =$

$w + 2$	$3w + 8$	$5 - w$
$8 - w$	$5 + w$	$3w + 2$
$5 + 3w$	$2 - w$	$w + 8$

Copy and complete her working.

(d) Add the expressions in each of the other two rows.

(e) Now add the expressions in each column and diagonal.

(f) Explain why your results show you make a magic square with **any** value for w.

E4 (a) Make a grid of numbers by replacing each expression with its value when a = 2 and b = 1.

(b) Is your grid a magic square?

(c) Paul adds the expressions in the top row.

$3a - 2b + 8a + 5b + 7a =$

$3a - 2b$	$8a + 5b$	$7a$
$10a + 3b$	$6a + b$	$2a - b$
$5a + 2b$	$4a - 3b$	$9a + 4b$

Copy and complete his working.

(d) Add the expressions in each of the other two rows.

(e) Now add the expressions in each column and diagonal.

(f) Explain why your results show you make a magic square with **any** values for a and b.

E5 Which of these always gives magic squares?

(a)

$2x + 2$	$3 + x$	$6x - 2$
$7x - 3$	$3x + 1$	$5 - x$
4	$4x$	$5x - 1$

(b)

$2y + 4z$	$6y$	$y - z$
$7y - 3z$	$5z - y$	$3y + z$
$2z$	$4y - 2z$	$5y + 3z$

(c)

$8y - 3z$	$3y - 4z$	$4y + z$
$y + 2z$	$5y - 2z$	$9y - 6z$
$6y - 5z$	$7y$	$2y - z$

*E6 Copy and complete these grids to give magic squares.

(a)

$8 + 6k$		
	$5 + k$	$9 + 6k$
		$2 - 4k$

(b)

$2b$	$5a - 3b$	$4a - 2b$
	$b + a$	

F Brackets

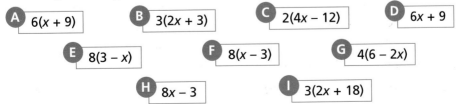

A $4(6 + a)$ B $12(2 - a)$ C $3(4a - 24)$ D $4a + 6$

E $2(2a + 3)$ F $12(a - 6)$ G $4(6 - 3a)$ H $4a + 24$

F1 Multiply out the brackets from these.

(a) $5(n + 3)$ (b) $3(m + 1)$ (c) $4(2 + p)$

(d) $2(q - 6)$ (e) $7(r - 5)$ (f) $10(6 + s)$

(g) $5(7 - t)$ (h) $8(4 - v)$ (i) $9(w - 2)$

F2 Find four pairs of equivalent expressions.

A $6(x + 9)$ B $3(2x + 3)$ C $2(4x - 12)$ D $6x + 9$

E $8(3 - x)$ F $8(x - 3)$ G $4(6 - 2x)$

H $8x - 3$ I $3(2x + 18)$

F3 Multiply out the brackets from the following.

    (a) $3(2q + 4)$ (b) $2(5r + 1)$ (c) $4(2 + 5s)$ (d) $5(3 + 4n)$

    (e) $3(2m - 5)$ (f) $4(3p - 5)$ (g) $2(7 - 2t)$ (h) $4(3 - 8v)$

    (i) $9(2w - 5)$ (j) $3(1 - 2x)$ (k) $5(4 - 6y)$ (l) $10(4z - 9)$

F4 Copy and complete each statement.

    (a) $2(w + 5) = 2w + \blacksquare$ (b) $4(\blacksquare - 3) = 8x - 12$

    (c) $6(\blacksquare - y) = 6 - 6y$ (d) $2(5 - \blacksquare) = 10 - 6z$

F5 Which two expressions give
the perimeter of this shape?

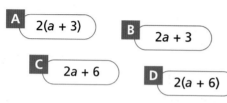
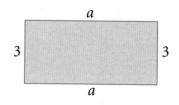

F6 List the shapes that have a perimeter of $3(2x + 1)$.

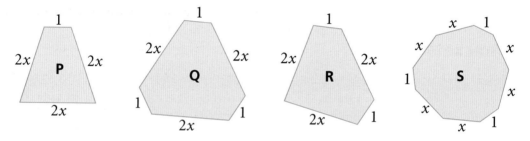

F7 Find four pairs of equivalent expressions.

F8 Which two expressions give
the perimeter of this shape?

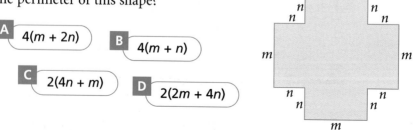

124

F9 Find two expressions for the perimeter of each shape.

(a)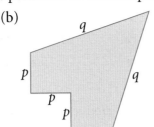

(b)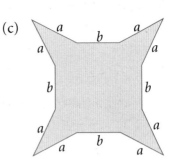

(c)

What progress have you made?

Statement

I can use algebra to solve problems.

Evidence

1 (a) Copy and complete this wall.

| 5 | 3 | a | 1 |

(b) (i) What number will be on the top brick when $a = 2$?

(ii) Check by drawing the wall.

(c) What value for a gives 18 on the top brick?

2 Simplify $2h + 6 + 3h + 5$.

I can simplify expressions like $2m + 3n + 5m + 4$.

3 Find an expression, in its simplest form, for the perimeter of this shape.

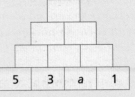

4 Simplify $4g + 3h + g + 5 + 2h$.

I can simplify expressions like $2x - 3y - x + y + 4$.

5 Simplify these.

(a) $10v - 2 - 8v + 7$

(b) $7j + 9k - j - 2k$

(c) $6 + 7w - 1 - 10w$

(d) $3y - 3z + 4y - 7 + 2z$

I can multiply out brackets from expressions like $7(4c - 9)$.

6 Multiply out the brackets from these.

(a) $5(6 - h)$　　　　(b) $3(2w + 5)$

(c) $4(3t - 1)$　　　　(d) $5(3 - 2b)$

(e) $6(m + n)$　　　　(f) $2(3b + c)$

⑲ No chance!

This is about probability.

The work will help you

◆ list outcomes systematically

◆ find probabilities in more complicated situations

A Probabilities

Thirty days hath September,
April, June and November,
All the rest have thirty-one
Except February all alone,
With twenty-eight days clear
And twenty-nine in each leap year.

Twelve cards with the names of the months are shuffled.

- What is the probability (as a fraction)
  of picking each of these?

A month with fewer than 31 days in it

A month starting with the letter J

A month with 31 days in it

A month with the letter R in it

A month ending with the letter Y

This wheel is used in a game at a school fête.
The wheel is fair.
Players pay 10p for a card and get a prize if it wins.

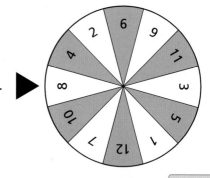

- What is the probability of each of these cards winning
  when the wheel is spun?

- What is each card's probability of not winning?

- Could more than one card win on a single spin of the wheel?

- Do any of the cards deserve a better prize than others?

- Make up some more cards.
  Give each card's probability of winning.

The number 1

The number 12

A red number

An odd number

An even number

A number less than 4

A number in the range 1–5

A number greater than 10

A1 (a) What is the probability of getting a 7 on the wheel?

(b) What is the probability of not getting a 7 on the wheel?

A2 What is the probability of each of these 'events' happening?

(a) a white number   (b) a number from 7, 8, 9, 10, 11, 12

(c) a prime number   (d) a non-prime number

(e) one of the numbers 1, 2, 3, 4   (f) a number not 1, 2, 3, 4

A3 (a) What do your answers to (c) and (d) add up to?

(b) Is this the same for (e) and (f)?
Explain your answer.

A4 (a) Write down all the square numbers on the wheel.

(b) What is the probability of getting a square number on the wheel?

(c) What is the probability of not getting a square number?

A5 (a) Write down all the triangle numbers on the wheel.

(b) What is the probability of getting a triangle number?

(c) What is the probability of not getting a triangle number?

A6 In the National Lottery, balls are numbered 1 to 49.

Find the probability of each of these events
(i) happening and (ii) not happening, for the first ball chosen

(a) It is an odd number.   (b) It is a square number.   (c) It is a prime number.

(d) It is a triangle number. (e) It is a multiple of 5.

A7 A bag contains 7 white, 5 red and 3 black beads.
If a bead is taken from the bag what is the probability of it being

(a) white   (b) red   (c) green

(d) white or red   (e) not white   (f) black

A8 The probability of getting a red from a bag of beads is $\frac{3}{5}$.

What is the probability of not getting red?

A9 A box contains black, blue and red pens.

The probability of randomly choosing a black pen is $\frac{12}{25}$.
The probability of choosing blue is $\frac{9}{25}$.

What is the probability of choosing red?

A10 There are 24 beads in a bag and the probability of getting an orange one is $\frac{2}{3}$.
How many of the beads are orange?

A11 There are 21 yellow beads in a bag and the probability of getting one of them is $\frac{3}{7}$.
How many beads are there altogether in the bag?

B All the outcomes

Coin game

I flip two coins.
If both land heads, you win.
If they are different, I win.
If they are both tails, we flip again!

Beat that!

I roll a dice. If I get a 6, it doesn't count,
and I roll again until I get 1, 2, 3, 4 or 5.

Now you roll. If your score is bigger than mine,
you win. If it's the same or less, then I win.

Dice difference

I roll two dice.
If the difference between the scores
is less than 2, you win.
If it's 2 or more, I win.

- Is the teacher playing fair in each of these games?
  How do you decide?

B1 A game is played with these two sets of cards.
One card is picked at random from each set.

(a) Copy and complete this list of all the
possible outcomes.

Heart	Spade
2	2
2	3

(b) What is the probability that

(i) both 2s are picked   (ii) both cards have the same number

(iii) the spade number is greater than the heart number

B2 A game is played with three coins.
The list of all the outcomes has been started here.

1st coin	2nd coin	3rd coin
H	H	H
H	H	T
H	T	H
H	T	T

(a) Copy and complete the list of outcomes.
(You should have eight altogether.)

(b) What is the probability that the coins land as

    (i) three tails   (ii) two heads and one tail (in any order)

    (iii) all three the same   (iv) more heads than tails

    (v) the same number of heads as tails

B3 In a game you spin these fair spinners together.

(a) List systematically all the pairs of numbers you could get.

(b) What is the probability of getting a 3 and a 5?

(c) What is the probability of getting two odd numbers?

B4 A card is selected at random from a set containing
the ace, king, queen and jack of clubs.
At the same time, a counter with black on one side
and red on the other is flipped.

(a) List all the outcomes for this.

(b) What is the probability that the card is a queen and
the counter lands red?

Card	Counter
A	B
A	R
K	B

(c) What is the probability that the counter lands black
and the card is either a king or a queen?

B5 A game is played with three fair spinners.
Each spinner has an apple, a lemon and a bell on it.

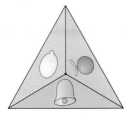 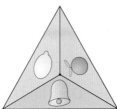 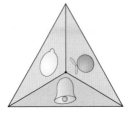

(a) Use the letters A, L and B to list all the possible outcomes
when the three spinners are spun together.

(b) Find the probabilities that the spinners land with

    (i) three bells   (ii) three the same

    (iii) exactly two the same   (iv) all three different

B6 Tom and Anabelle decide they want two children.
Assume each child is equally likely to be a boy or a girl.
What is the probability they have

(a) two girls   (b) two children of different sex

C Listing with grids

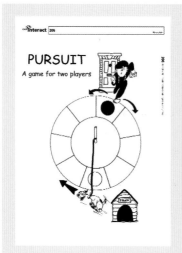

You need sheet 206, two four-sided dice and two counters of different colours.

- Postie is being chased by Fang.
  Fang can only go clockwise.
  Postie can go either way to escape.

- Fang catches Postie if either he lands on Postie or Postie lands on him.

- Postie goes first and rolls the two dice.
  He can move, in either direction, the total score on the dice.

- Fang throws the dice and moves clockwise that score.

- Continue until Postie is caught.

In each of these, it is Postie's go. (Postie is the red counter.)

Which way should he go, clockwise or anticlockwise?

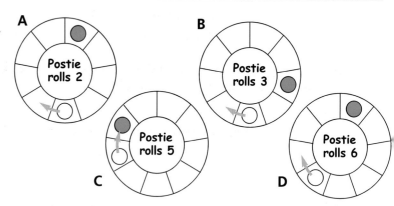

The outcomes of rolling two four-sided dice are   1, 1   1, 2   1, 3   1, 4
                                                  2, 1   2, 2   … and so on.

These outcomes can be shown as points on a coordinate grid.

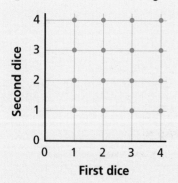

Or you can use a grid like this.

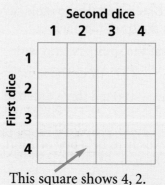

This square shows 4, 2.

The grid can be used to show, for example, total scores.

	Second dice			
	1	**2**	**3**	**4**
1	2	3	4	5
2	3	4	5	6
3	4	5	6	7
4	5	6	7	8

(First dice)

C1 Two four-sided dice are rolled.
From the last grid on page 130, find the probability that the total of the two scores is

(a) 0

(b) 3

(c) greater than 3

(d) less than 3

C2 Copy and complete this grid to show all the total scores with two ordinary six-sided dice.

Find the probability that the total score is

(a) 7   (b) 10

(c) 2   (d) an odd number

(e) a prime number   (f) greater than 10

Second dice

First dice	1	2	3
1	2	3	4
2	3	4	5
3	4		

C3 (a) What score are you most likely to get with two six-sided dice?

(b) What scores are you least likely to get?

(c) Make a list of all the total scores and their probabilities.

C4 In another game, two six-sided dice are used, but instead of the total, the **difference** between the numbers is used.

For example, 3, 5 gives a difference of 2.

(a) Make a grid showing the differences for all the possible outcomes.

(b) Find the probability that the difference is

(i) 2   (ii) 1   (iii) 0   (iv) 4 or more   (v) 6

C5 This set of cards is used in a game called 'Salty Dog'.

  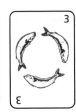  

A blue set and a green set of the five cards are used.
One card is taken from each set.

Make a grid of all the possible outcomes and use it to find the probability that the two cards chosen

(a) have the same number   (b) are both multiples of 5

(c) are both less than 5   (d) have a total of 8 or more

(e) are both mermaids   (f) have 3 or less on the blue card

D Which is more likely?

Two classes have each designed a Wheel of Fortune for a school fête.

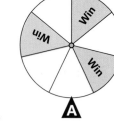

They each charge 10p a go and have the same prizes.

Which would you rather have a go on?

The probability of a win on A is $\frac{3}{7}$. On wheel B it is $\frac{5}{12}$.

Turning fractions into decimals, $\frac{3}{7} = 3 \div 7 = 0.428\ldots$ and $\frac{5}{12} = 0.416\ldots$

So you have a slightly higher chance of winning on wheel A.

D1 This is a scratch card.
You pick **one** box and scratch the surface.
You win if you find a star.

> **Be a Star!**
> Scratch
> just
> one   Find a star
> box   and win £1

Below are three possible card designs with all the stars showing.
If you couldn't see the stars, which gives the best chance of winning?

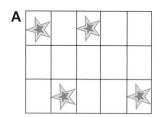

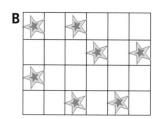

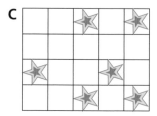

D2 Which of these is more likely? Explain why.

A Rolling a number greater than 4 on an ordinary dice

B Picking a weekend day when picking a day at random from the days of the week

D3 Which of these is more likely? Explain why.

A Getting more heads than tails when four coins are flipped

B Picking a heart from a pack of cards with no ace of clubs

D4 Find the probability of each of these events and say which is more likely.

A Getting a total score of 6 or more with two 6-sided dice

B Getting a total score of 12 or more with two 12-sided dice

What progress have you made?

Statement

Evidence

I can work out the probabilities of different outcomes in complex cases.

1 A Wheel of Fortune has the numbers 1 to 15 on it. In one spin, what is the probability of getting,

(a) a six

(b) an even number

(c) a number greater than 10

(d) a triangle number

I can list all the outcomes in a situation and use this to find probabilities.

2 A spinner is divided into three equal sections with pictures of a star, a moon and a sun.

(a) List all of the outcomes if three of these spinners are used.

(b) What is the probability the spinners show

(i)   three stars

(ii) all the same

(iii) three different symbols

(iv) two or more with the same symbol

I can use a grid to show all the equally likely outcomes in a situation.

3 Two fair spinners are used with the numbers 1 to 5 on them.

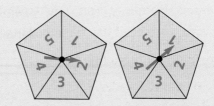

(a) Draw a grid to show all the equally likely outcomes.

(b) Find the probability that

(i) the spinners show the same number

(ii) the total of the numbers is 7

20 Recipes

This work will help you

◆ calculate quantities using the unitary method

A How much?

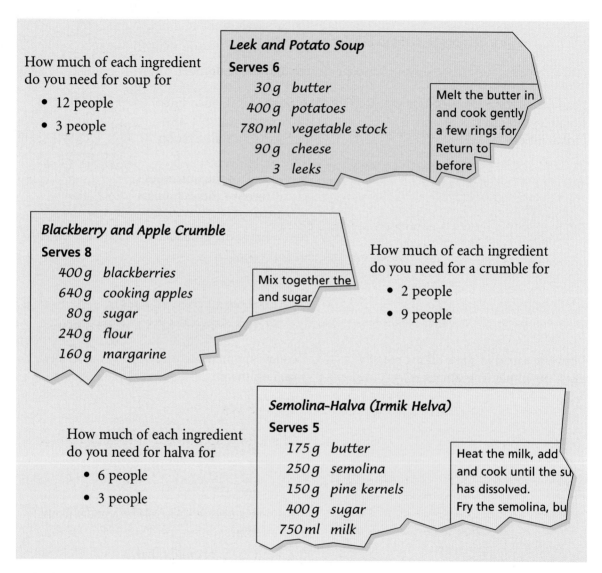

How much of each ingredient do you need for soup for

- 12 people
- 3 people

Leek and Potato Soup

Serves 6

30 g	butter
400 g	potatoes
780 ml	vegetable stock
90 g	cheese
3	leeks

Melt the butter in
and cook gently
a few rings for
Return to
before

Blackberry and Apple Crumble

Serves 8

400 g	blackberries
640 g	cooking apples
80 g	sugar
240 g	flour
160 g	margarine

Mix together the
and sugar

How much of each ingredient do you need for a crumble for

- 2 people
- 9 people

How much of each ingredient do you need for halva for

- 6 people
- 3 people

Semolina-Halva (Irmik Helva)

Serves 5

175 g	butter
250 g	semolina
150 g	pine kernels
400 g	sugar
750 ml	milk

Heat the milk, add
and cook until the su
has dissolved.
Fry the semolina, bu

Calculate the amount of ...

A1 ... sugar in a blackberry and apple crumble for 4 people.

A2 ... potatoes in a pot of leek and potato soup for 18 people.

A3 … pine kernels in semolina-halva made for 10 people.

A4 … butter needed for leek and potato soup for 9 people.

A5 … apples in a blackberry and apple crumble for 10 people.

A6 … leeks in leek and potato soup for 8 people.

A7 … sugar in a piece of semolina-halva for 1 person.

A8 … sugar in a blackberry and apple crumble for 10 people.

A9 … cheese in leek and potato soup for 10 people.

A10 … semolina needed for semolina-halva for 8 people.

A11 … apples in a blackberry and apple crumble for 11 people.

A12 … milk in semolina-halva for 2 people.

A13 … cheese in leek and potato soup for 5 people.

A14 … flour in a blackberry and apple crumble for 3 people.

A15 … butter in semolina-halva for 16 people.

A16 … vegetable stock in leek and potato soup for 47 people.

A17 … cheese in leek and potato soup for 125 people.

A18 … fruit in blackberry and apple crumble for 10 people.

A19 … butter in a meal for 33 people of leek and potato soup followed by semolina-halva.

In your school …

A20 … how much margarine would be in enough blackberry and apple crumble for everyone in your class?

A21 … how many leeks would be in enough leek and potato soup for everyone in your school?

A22 … how much semolina would be in enough semolina-halva for all the teachers in your school?

B The unitary method

> You need 400 g blackberries in a crumble for 8 people.

> So how much do you need in a crumble for 7 people?

8 people need **400** g

÷ 8 ↓   ↓ ÷ 8

1 person needs **50** g

× 7 ↓   ↓ × 7

7 people need **350** g

> This is called the **unitary method** because you first find out how much **one** person needs. One person is a **unit**.

B1 Here is part of a recipe for saffron-rice.

(a) How much rice would you need to make saffron-rice for one person?

(b) How much rice would you need to make enough saffron-rice for 9 people?

(c) How much water would you need when making saffron-rice for 3 people?

(d) What quantity of raisins would you need in saffron-rice for 19 people?

> **Saffron-rice (Zerde)**
> **Serves 4**
> 120 g   rice
> 1600 ml   water
> 400 g   sugar
> 80 g   raisins

B2 3 identical sacks of cabbages weigh 24 kg altogether.

(a) How much does one sack weigh?

(b) How much will 5 sacks weigh?

B3 The trays of strawberries in these piles are identical.

Pile Y is 90 cm high and weighs 12 kg.
Calculate the height and weight of piles X and Z.

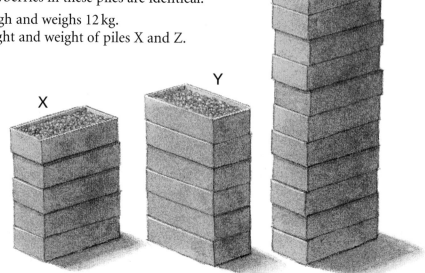

B4 Eight identical sticks of rock are laid end to end.
The total length is 320 cm.

What will be the length of five of the sticks of rock laid end to end?

B5 In an old recipe for liquid fertiliser, the following trace elements
should be added to 5 litres of water.

Boric acid	70 g
Zinc sulphate	2 g

How much of each should be added to

(a) 3 litres of water (b) 8 litres of water

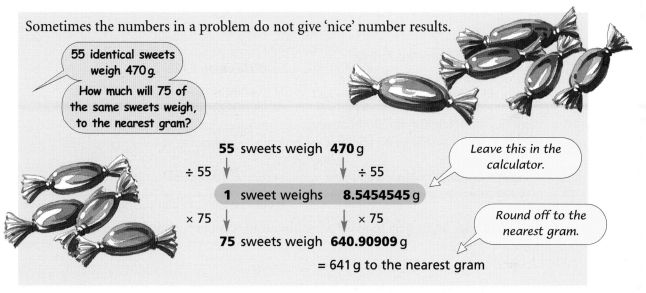

Sometimes the numbers in a problem do not give 'nice' number results.

55 identical sweets weigh 470 g.

How much will 75 of the same sweets weigh, to the nearest gram?

55 sweets weigh **470** g

÷ 55 ↓   ↓ ÷ 55

Leave this in the calculator.

1 sweet weighs **8.5454545** g

× 75 ↓   ↓ × 75

75 sweets weigh **640.90909** g

Round off to the nearest gram.

= 641 g to the nearest gram

B6 To make Ezogelin soup for 6 people you need 100 g rice.
How much rice, to the nearest gram, do you need to make Ezogelin soup for 19 people?

B7 To make cheese pastry for 3 people you need 70 g yoghurt.
How much yoghurt, to the nearest gram, do you need
to make cheese pastry for 35 people?

B8 70 sheets of filo pastry have a total thickness of 8.5 cm.
How thick will a pile of 250 sheets be?

B9 Here is part of a recipe for pumpkin pie.
Work out how much of each ingredient
you need in a pumpkin pie for 50 people.

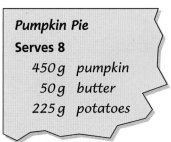

Pumpkin Pie
Serves 8
450 g *pumpkin*
50 g *butter*
225 g *potatoes*

The big biscuit

The largest biscuit ever made was a chocolate chip cookie with a diameter of 10.36 m.
It was made at the annual Riponfest, Wisconsin, USA on 11 July 1992.
This biscuit contained nearly 4 million chocolate chips.

Serves 8163

576 kg	flour
272 kg	sugar
345 kg	soya oil
11.4 kg	salt
6 kg	vanilla essence
9 kg	powdered eggs
4 kg	baking soda
123 litres	water
plus 3 839 207	chocolate chips

Mix all of the ingredients in a large bowl.
Add the chocolate chips and beat thoroughly.
Transfer dough mixture to biscuit tin via trailer lorry.
Bake on top of a rotating tin for 3 hours.
Allow to cool.
Slice using ten pizza cutters soldered together at 10 centimetre intervals.

Adapt this recipe accurately to make a big biscuit to serve every pupil in your school.

What progress have you made?

Statement	Evidence
I can calculate quantities using the unitary method.	1 A recipe for lemon ice-cream is for 6 people. The recipe uses 420 ml of double cream. How much double cream would be in lemon ice-cream for (a) 3 people (b) 5 people 2 I paid £1.65 for 3 identical pasties. How much would I pay for 7 pasties? 3 A pile of 16 identical cookery books is 38 cm high. How high will a pile of 35 of these books be, to the nearest cm?

138

㉑ Substituting into formulas

This work will help you

◆ work out the value of expressions

◆ form expressions and formulas

A Review

A1 Midchester Marquees hire out large tents.
They program their computer with rules for their orders.

For example, this is the rule for the hire charge for a tent.

$c = 6a + 50$

c is the hire charge in £,
a is the area the tent covers in square metres.

(a) How much will they charge for a tent that covers 40 square metres?

(b) (i) What is the area of a tent that measures 10 m by 10 m?

  (ii) How much is the hire charge for this tent?

(c) What is the hire charge for a tent that is 9 m by 21 m?

A2 Here are some other rules that Midchester Marquees use.
In each one, a stands for the area the tent covers in square metres.

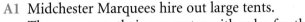

$s = 2(a - 5)$	s is the maximum number of seats.
$w = 3(a + 25)$	w is the cost in £ of a wooden floor.
$m = 2a + 50$	m is the cost in £ of floor matting.
$t = \frac{a}{10} - 10$	t is the maximum number of tables.
$d = \frac{a + 30}{2}$	d is the delivery charge in £.

(a) For an exhibition, a company hires a 200 m² tent.

  (i) How many seats can they get in?

  (ii) What is the delivery charge?

  (iii) How much more does a wood floor cost than a matting one?

(b) Work out the values of s, w, m, t and d for each of these tents.

  (i) A tent measuring 15 m by 20 m

  (ii) A tent that is 50 m by 50 m

A3 Work out the value of each of these expressions when $h = 12$.

(a) $4h + 1$ (b) $\frac{h}{2} + 8$ (c) $\frac{h + 20}{4}$ (d) $5(h - 3)$

(e) $\frac{h}{3} - 1$ (f) $3(h + 1)$ (g) $2h - 11$ (h) $\frac{h - 2}{5}$

A4 Work out the value of each of these expressions when $h = 8$.

(a) h^2 (b) $h^2 + 1$ (c) $h^2 - 4$ (d) $h^2 - 40$

B The right order

When there are no brackets, multiply or divide **before** you add or subtract.

Work out the value of
$10 - 2g$ when $g = 3$.

$$10 - 2g$$
$$= 10 - 2 \times 3$$
$$= 10 - 6$$
$$= 4$$

Do the multiplication first.

Work out the value of
$6 + \frac{h}{2}$ when $h = 8$.

$$6 + \frac{h}{2}$$
$$= 6 + \frac{8}{2}$$
$$= 6 + 4$$
$$= 10$$

Do the division first.

B1 Work out the value of each of these expression when $a = 2$.

(a) $10 + 3a$ (b) $10 - 3a$ (c) $3a + 10$ (d) $3a - 10$

B2 Use the rule $h = 4(12 - k)$ to work out h when

(a) $k = 5$ (b) $k = 3$ (c) $k = 0$ (d) $k = 12$

B3 Use the rule $t = 10 - 2s$ to work out t when

(a) $s = 2$ (b) $s = 5$ (c) $s = \frac{1}{2}$ (d) $s = 0$

B4 Here is part of Matt's homework. Both his answers are wrong!
Work out the correct answers for him.
Show your working.

Work these out.

(a) $4(10 - g)$ when $g = 6$

$$4(10 - g)$$
$$= 4 \times 10 - 6$$
$$= 40 - 6$$
$$= \underline{34} \quad \text{✗}$$

(b) $20 - 2h$ when $h = 5$

$$20 - 2h$$
$$= 20 - 2 \times 5$$
$$= 18 \times 5$$
$$= \underline{90} \quad \text{✗}$$

We need to talk about this, Matt.

B5 Use the rule $a = 6 - \frac{b}{3}$ to work out a when

(a) $b = 6$ (b) $b = 12$ (c) $b = 0$ (d) $b = 3$

B6 Work out m in each of these rules when $n = 6$.

(a) $m = \frac{12 + n}{9}$ (b) $m = 3 + \frac{n}{2}$ (c) $m = 3(8 - n)$ (d) $m = \frac{12 - n}{3}$

B7 The ground clearance of a lorry or car is the distance between the bottom of the lorry and the ground.

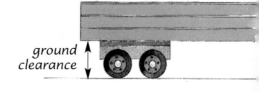

For this lorry the formula for the ground clearance is

$$d = 100 - 5w$$

d is the ground clearance in centimetres,
w is the weight the lorry is carrying in tonnes.

(a) Work out d when $w = 10$.

(b) What is the ground clearance when the lorry is carrying 8 tonnes of sand?

(c) What is the clearance when $w = 6.2$?

(d) What is the ground clearance of the lorry when it is empty?

(e) The lorry should not be driven if the ground clearance is less than 30 cm.
What is the maximum weight the lorry can carry?

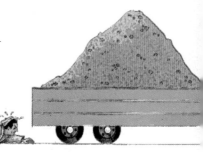

B8 At ground level, water boils at 100°C.
The temperature at which water boils is called its 'boiling point'.

As you go up a mountain, the boiling point changes.

The formula for the boiling point is

$$b = 100 - \frac{h}{1000}$$

b is the boiling point in degrees C,
h is the height in feet.

(a) Work out b when $h = 5000$.

(b) What is the boiling point when $h = 2000$?

(c) What is the boiling point at 3000 feet?

(d) Ben Nevis is about 4000 feet high.
What is the boiling point of water on top of Ben Nevis?

(e) Mount Everest is about 30 000 feet high.
What is the boiling point of water on top of Mount Everest?

C Including squares

When expressions involve squares, square **before** you multiply, divide, add or subtract.

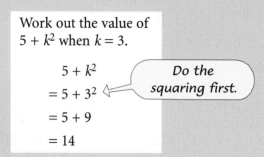

Work out the value of
$5 + k^2$ when $k = 3$.

$5 + k^2$

$= 5 + 3^2$ ← Do the squaring first.

$= 5 + 9$

$= 14$

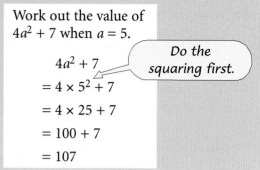

Work out the value of
$4a^2 + 7$ when $a = 5$.

$4a^2 + 7$

$= 4 \times 5^2 + 7$ ← Do the squaring first.

$= 4 \times 25 + 7$

$= 100 + 7$

$= 107$

C1 Work out the value of each of these expressions when $a = 5$.

(a) a^2 (b) $2 + a^2$ (c) $2a^2$ (d) $2a^2 + 10$

(e) $3a^2$ (f) $4 + 3a^2$ (g) $50 - a^2$ (h) $4a^2 - 20$

C2 Work out the value of y in each of these rules when $x = 10$.

(a) $y = \dfrac{x^2}{2}$ (b) $y = \dfrac{x^2}{5}$ (c) $y = \dfrac{x^2 - 30}{5}$ (d) $y = \dfrac{110 - x^2}{5}$

C3 Here is part of Joy's homework. Both her answers are wrong!
Work out the correct answers for her.
Show your working.

Work these out.

(a) $10 - h^2$ when $h = 3$

$10 - h^2$

$= 10 - 3^2$

$= 7^2$

$= \underline{49}$ ✗

(b) $4m^2 + 20$ when $m = 5$

$4m^2 + 20$

$= 4 \times 5^2 + 20$

$= 20^2 + 20$

$= 400 + 20$

$= \underline{420}$ ✗

Talk to me about this, Joy.

C4 In which of these rules does $z = 12$ when $y = 2$?

$z = 3y + 6$ $z = 3y^2$ $z = 18 - 3y$ $z = 6(4 - y)$ $z = 4 + y^2$

C5 Which of these rules give a negative value for a when $b = 10$?

$a = b^2 - 20$ $a = 10 - 2b$ $a = 100 - 2b^2$

$a = 2(b - 20)$ $a = \dfrac{b^2 - 10}{5}$

C6 Work out the value of $(k-3)^2$ when $k=7$.
Remember to work out what is in the brackets first.

C7 Work out the value of each of these expressions when $n=5$.

(a) $(n+5)^2$ (b) $(n-1)^2$ (c) $(2n+1)^2$ (d) $(2n-1)^2$

C8 Work out m in each of these rules when $n=4$.

(a) $m=10-2n$ (b) $m=5(7-n)$ (c) $m=1+n^2$ (d) $m=2n^2$

(e) $m=\dfrac{n^2}{8}$ (f) $m=9-\dfrac{n}{4}$ (g) $m=(n+1)^2$ (h) $m=1-n$

(i) $m=3n^2-10$ (j) $m=\dfrac{30-n^2}{7}$ (k) $m=50-3n^2$ (l) $m=\left(1+\dfrac{n}{2}\right)^2$

C9 When a car brakes it leaves skid marks on the road.

This rule tells you roughly how long a skid will be in metres.

$$L=\frac{s^2}{75}$$

L is the length of the skid in metres, s is the speed in miles per hour (m.p.h.).

(a) Work out L when $s=30$.

(b) A car is moving at 15 m.p.h. and then skids to a stop.
Roughly how long will the skid marks be?

(c) Roughly how long will the skid marks be for a car moving at 45 m.p.h?

(d) How long will the skid marks be for a car moving at 70 m.p.h?
Give your answer correct to the nearest metre.

(e) A car is travelling straight towards a wall at 90 m.p.h.
The wall is 80 metres away when the driver begins braking.

Will the car hit the wall?

(f) A car leaves skid marks 48 metres long.
About how fast was the car moving?

Grand Prix   a game for 2, 3 or 4 players

- You need sheet 215 and two dice – one marked 0, 0, 2, 2, 4, 4,
the other 3, 3, 5, 5, 7, 7.

On your turn
- Unless the square says otherwise, pick which dice to use.
- Roll the dice to see what value n will have.
- Work out the value of the expression on the square.
- Move forward that number of spaces.

- You have to go clockwise round the board twice.
- The first past FINISH the second time is the winner.

D Forming formulas

D1 The Rugged Walk outdoor centre organises walking trips.

They always take 3 sandwiches for each person and an extra 4 for emergencies.

(a) How many sandwiches would they take for 6 people?

(b) Copy and complete this table.

It shows p (the number of people) and s (the number of sandwiches).

p (number of people)	s (number of sandwiches)
1	
2	10
3	
4	
5	
6	

(c) Which of these is a formula for the number of sandwiches?

$s = p + 4$ $s = 3p + 4$ $s = p + 3$ $s = 4p + 3$

D2 Susie's Scramblers are a motorcycle team. When they go to competitions, they take their bikes and some new tyres.

They always take 2 new tyres for each bike and an extra 5 new tyres for emergencies.

(a) They take 7 bikes to the Cow Top meeting. How many new tyres do they take?

(b) For the Three Counties competition, they can only manage to take 2 bikes.

How many new tyres will they take?

(c) Copy and complete this table.
It shows b (the number of bikes they take) and t (the number of new tyres).

(They never take more than 7 bikes to a meeting, so stop at $b = 7$.)

b (number of bikes)	t (number of new tyres)
1	
2	

(d) Write down a formula connecting b (the number of bikes they take) and t (the number of new tyres).

Write it in the form $t = ...$

D3 H J Phillips sell building materials such as sand and gravel.
Sand costs £6 a tonne, plus a delivery charge of £30.

(a) How much would it cost to have 5 tonnes of sand delivered?

(b) How much would 7.5 tonnes cost?

(c) Write down a formula for the cost of having sand delivered.
(Choose your own letters to stand for the weight of
the sand in tonnes and the cost in £.)

(d) The largest lorry that H J Phillips have will carry 17 tonnes of sand.
Work out the cost of having this full lorry of sand delivered.

(e) Jim paid £102 for a load of sand.
How much did the load weigh?

D4 Each pattern in this sequence is a square grid of dots.

(a) How many dots will there be in pattern 5 of this design?

(b) How many dots will there be in pattern 10?

(c) What is the number of the largest pattern you can make from 80 dots?

(d) Which of these formulas tells you the number of dots in the nth pattern?
(d stands for the number of dots in the pattern.)

$$d = n \qquad d = 2n \qquad d = n^2 \qquad d = n + n$$

(e) Use the formula to work out the number of dots in the 15th pattern.

(f) Which pattern is made from 169 dots?

D5 This design is very similar to the one in question D4,
but each pattern has two more dots.

(a) How many dots will there be in pattern 5?

(b) What is the formula that tells you the number of dots in the nth pattern?
(Use d to stand for the number of dots in the pattern.)

(c) Use the formula to work out the number of dots in the 20th pattern.

(d) Which pattern is made from 326 dots?

E Words to symbols

Sue has some coins in a bag.

Let *n* stand for the number of coins that Sue has.

Jaz has twice as many coins as Sue.

Then Jaz has **2n** coins…

Sandy has 10 more coins than Jaz.

…and Sandy has **2n + 10** coins.

E1

Harry has made a column of cubes.

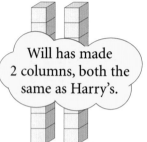

Will has made 2 columns, both the same as Harry's.

Chaz has made a column with 2 more cubes than Harry's.

Let *n* stand for the number of cubes in Harry's column.

(a) Which expression tells you the number of cubes Will made?

n^2 2 + 2n   2n

(b) Which expression tells you the number of cubes Chaz made?

n – 2   2n + 2   n + 2

E2

Liz has a pile of tiles.

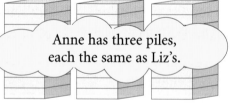

Anne has three piles, each the same as Liz's.

Let *n* stand for the number of tiles that Liz has.

(a) Which one of these expressions tells you the number of tiles Anne has?

n + 3 $\frac{n}{3}$ 3n   3 + n

(b) Mary has three fewer tiles than Liz.
Write an expression that tells you how many tiles Mary has.

Mary has three fewer than Liz.

(c) Sarah has five fewer tiles than **Anne**.
Write an expression that tells you how many tiles Sarah has.

E3 Jake has some pancakes.   Kevin has four times as many pancakes as Jake.

Let p stand for the number of pancakes that Jake has.

(a) Write an expression for the number of pancakes that Kevin has.

(b) Diane has twice as many as
Jake, and another 12.

Write an expression for the number of
pancakes that Diane has.

E4 Callum thinks of a number and multiplies it by 4.
He takes the answer away from 25.

Suppose c stands for the number he first thinks of.
Which of these expressions shows the
result that Callum ends up with?

$25 - 4c$ $4(25 - c)$

$4c - 25$ $4(c - 25)$

E5 Rebecca thinks of a number and takes it away from 10.
Then she multiplies the answer by 3.

$3r - 10$ $10 - 3r$ $3(r - 10)$

Suppose r stands for Rebecca's number.
Which of these expressions shows her result?

$3(10 - r)$

E6 Annie has some dog biscuits.
Bekky has 3 times as many as Annie.
Catch has 20 less than Annie.

Let n stand for the number of dog biscuits that Annie has.

(a) Write an expression for the number of biscuits Bekky has.

(b) Write an expression for the number of biscuits Catch has.

E7 This bag was full of 100 cubes.
Then Zafreen took some cubes out.

(a) Suppose Zafreen took out 10 cubes.
How many cubes would be left in the bag?

(b) Let z stand for the number of cubes Zafreen takes from the full bag.
Which of these expressions tells
you the number of cubes left?

$100 + z$ $100 - z$ $z + 100$

$z - 100$

(c) Yasin also starts with a bag of 100 cubes.
He takes twice as many cubes out as Zafreen.

Write an expression for the number of cubes left in Yasin's bag.

What progress have you made?

Statement	Evidence

I can work out the value of simple expressions, including those with brackets.

1 In the rule $s = 3t - 6$, work out s when

   (a) $t = 4$ (b) $t = 10$ (c) $t = 3$

2 In the rule $w = \dfrac{d}{2} + 3$, work out w when

   (a) $d = 4$ (b) $d = 0$ (c) $d = 10$

3 Find the value of each expression when $g = 6$.

   (a) $5(g - 4)$ (b) $5g - 4$ (c) $2(g + 10)$

I can work out the value of expressions where the order matters.

4 Work out each of these when $a = 4$.

   (a) $1 + a^2$ (b) $3a^2$ (c) $16 - \dfrac{a}{2}$

5 Sally begins a course of vitamin pills.
She uses the following rule to work out how many pills she has left.

$$P = 100 - 3d$$

P is the number of pills left and
d is the number of days she has been taking the pills.
Use the rule to calculate how many pills Sally has left after 10 days.

I can write an expression or formula for a situation in words.

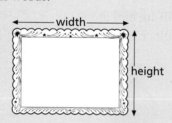

6 Nigel makes different types of picture frame. The width of a 'Fancy Frame' is always 15 cm more than its height.

   (a) One Fancy Frame is 60 cm high.
       How wide is this frame?

   (b) Write a formula connecting w (the width) and h (the height) of a Fancy Frame.

7 Sharon has some stamps. Henry has three times as many stamps as Sharon.
James has 50 fewer stamps than Sharon.

s is the number of stamps that Sharon has.

   (a) Write an expression for the number of stamps that Henry has.

   (b) Write an expression for the number of stamps that James has.

Review 3

1 Work out   (a) 7^2 (b) 5^3 (c) $(^-3)^2$ (d) $(^-2)^3$

2 For this spinner, what is the probability of
each of these events happening?

   (a) the number 18   (b) a square number

   (c) a prime number   (d) a multiple of 4

   (e) not a multiple of 4   (f) less than 10

3 (a) What is the square of 20?   (b) What is the cube of 100?

4 Simplify each of these.

   (a) $7a + 4 + 5a + a + 2$ (b) $4b + 2 + 3c + b + 4c$ (c) $8d - e - 2d + 3e$

   (d) $5f - 4 + 3g + 6 - 4g$ (e) $4(h + 3)$ (f) $5(2j - 3)$

5 Measure this parallelogram
and work out its area.

6 A coin is flipped and this 5-sided spinner is spun at the same time.

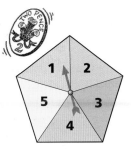

   (a) List systematically all the possible outcomes.

   (b) What is the probability that the coin lands heads up and the
spinner lands on 2?

   (c) What is the probability that the coin lands tails up and the
spinner lands on an odd number?

7 Find the area of
this triangle.

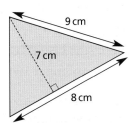

8 Find the value of each expression when $c = 3$.

   (a) $2c + 5$ (b) $5(c + 4)$ (c) $15 - 4c$ (d) $2c^2$

   (e) $4 + 5c$ (f) $(c + 2)^2$ (g) $40 - 2c^2$ (h) $\dfrac{c^2 + 7}{2}$

9 Six video tapes take up 15 cm of shelf space.
How much shelf space would 22 tapes need?

10 The area of this triangle is 60 cm². Work out the missing length.

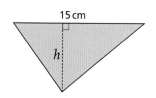
15 cm

11 Write down

(a) both the square roots of 81   (b) the cube root of 64   (c) the cube root of ⁻1

12 In the wall the value of each brick is found by adding the values in the two bricks below.

(a) Copy and complete this wall.

(b) If $t = 3$, what number will be on the top brick?

(c) What value for t gives 42 on the top brick?

| 4 | t | 3 | 5 |

13 Nibbly biscuits come in four different size packets.

The medium packet has 10 more biscuits than the small packet.
The large packet has twice as many biscuits as the small packet.
The extra-value packet has twice as many biscuits as the medium packet.

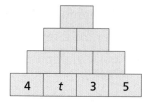
small
medium
large
extra-

If b is the number of biscuits in the small packet, write expressions for the number of biscuits in

(a) the medium packet   (b) the large packet   (c) the extra-value pack

14 (a) Write down an expression for the total length of wire needed to make this star. Lengths are in centimetres.

(b) If $x = 6$, how much wire would be needed to make one star?

(c) If 60 cm of wire is used for one star, what is the value of x?

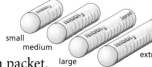

15 Sarah and Emma have made their own 4-sided dice from clay.

(a) Sarah thinks that hers is a fair dice.
If she rolls it 240 times, how many times would she expect it to score 1?

(b) Emma has already experimented with her dice, rolling it 100 times.
Here are her results.

(i) What is the relative frequency of getting 1 on Emma's dice?

(ii) Out of 240 rolls how many ones would Emma expect to get?

Score	Total	
1	ЖЖ ЖЖ ЖЖ	15
2	ЖЖ ЖЖ ЖЖ ЖЖ II	27
3	ЖЖ ЖЖ ЖЖ ЖЖ ЖЖ ЖЖ	30
4	ЖЖ ЖЖ ЖЖ ЖЖ ЖЖ ЖЖ III	28

16 Work out the area of this trapezium.

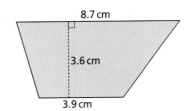

8.7 cm

3.6 cm

3.9 cm

17 This 5-sided spinner is spun twice and the scores added together.
Copy and complete this grid to show the possible totals.

Use your grid to help you work out the probability of scoring

(a) 7
(b) an odd number
(c) a square number
(d) less than 9
(e) the cube root of 27
(f) What percentage of the scores are greater than 28?

		Second spin				
		1	2	5	10	20
First spin	1	2	3	6	11	21
	2	3				
	5					
	10					
	20					

18 Here is part of a recipe for wild rice and bean salad.

(a) What weight of French beans would be needed for 4 people?

(b) How much wild rice would be needed to serve 15 people?

(c) How much white rice, to the nearest 10 grams, would be needed to serve 25?

(d) What is the ratio of wild rice to white rice in this recipe?
Give your answer in its simplest form.

Wild rice & bean salad

Serves 6
150 g French beans
150 g broad beans
50 g wild rice
175 g white rice
50 g mushrooms
30 ml chopped fresh thyme

19 When a stone is dropped this formula tells you roughly how far it will have fallen.

d is the distance fallen in metres.

$$d = 5t^2$$

t is the time taken in seconds.

Hayley drops a stone from a bridge into a river in a ravine below.
The stone hits the water after 3 seconds. Roughly how far is the river below the bridge?

20 The probability of getting a pen from a mixed bag of pens and pencils is $\frac{3}{8}$.

(a) What is the probability of getting a pencil?
(b) If there are 15 pens in the bag, how many pens and pencils in total will there be?

22 Scaling

This is about scaling shapes up and down.
The work will help you

- ◆ spot shapes that have been scaled
- ◆ use scale factors
- ◆ use and make scale drawings

A Spotting enlargements

Len is a photographer.
He has taken this photo
of his brother Bert.

Len makes some enlargements of the photo.
He also makes some fakes.

A

D

B

C

F

G

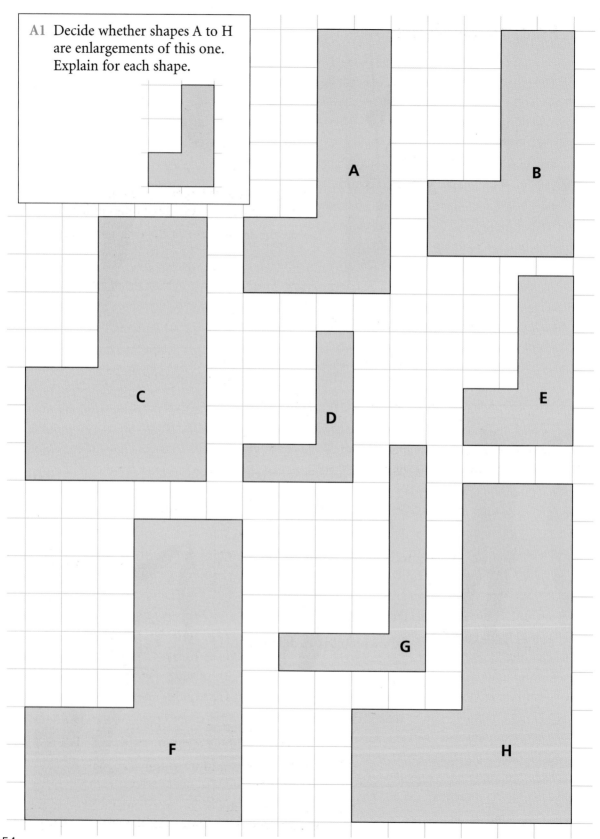

A1 Decide whether shapes A to H are enlargements of this one. Explain for each shape.

B Enlarging a shape

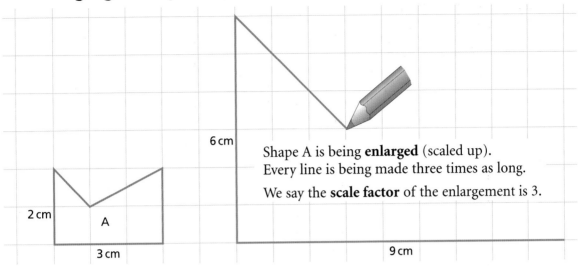

Shape A is being **enlarged** (scaled up).
Every line is being made three times as long.

We say the **scale factor** of the enlargement is 3.

B1 (a) Copy shape A on to centimetre squared paper and
complete the enlargement of it.

Check each side of the enlarged shape is three times as long as the
corresponding side in shape A. (Include the sloping sides in your check.)

(b) What can you say about the angles of the enlarged shape,
compared with the angles in shape A?

B2 Enlarge each of these shapes with the scale factor given.
Check the lengths of all the enlarged sides.

(a) scale factor 2

(b) scale factor 3

(c) scale factor 4

B3 Clubs and businesses often have a logo.

Design a small logo of your own on squared paper.

Now make an enlargement of it.
Choose your own scale factor.

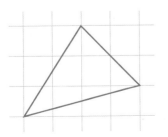

B4 (a) Copy this triangle on to centimetre squared paper.
Now draw an enlargement of it with scale factor 2.

(b) Find the perimeter of the original triangle by
measuring the sides to the nearest 0.1 cm.

(c) Find the perimeter of the enlargement. How does it
compare with the perimeter of the original triangle?

B5 These are sketches of a logo drawn to different scales.
Work out the missing measurements.

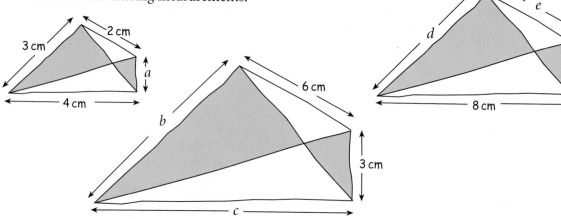

B6 Answer this on sheet 216.

B7 Answer this on sheet 197.

C Scaling down as well as up

C1 Copy this shape on to squared paper.
Scale it down using a scale factor of $\frac{1}{2}$.
This means dividing every length by 2.

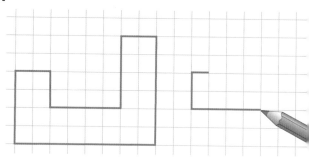

C2 Scale down each of these shapes using the scale factor given.

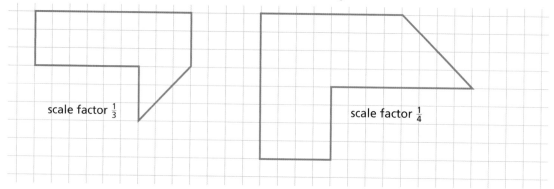

scale factor $\frac{1}{3}$

scale factor $\frac{1}{4}$

C3 Enlarge this shape on squared paper,
using a scale factor of $1\frac{1}{2}$.

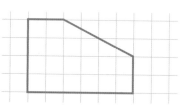

Enlarging to make smaller

Although scaling down with scale factor $\frac{1}{2}$ makes a shape smaller, this process is often called **enlargement** by scale factor $\frac{1}{2}$!

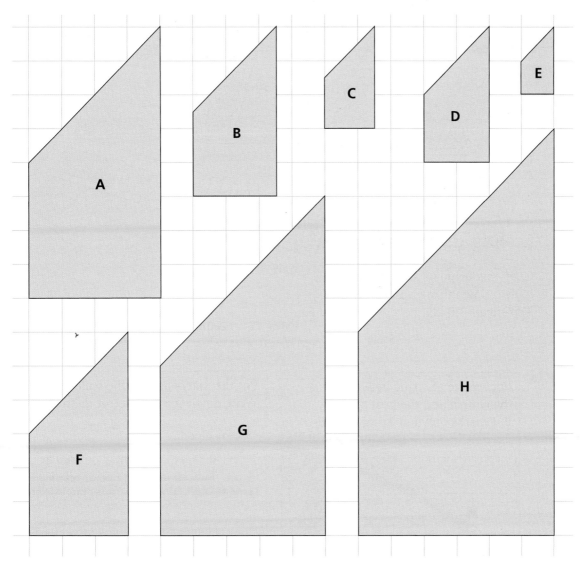

C4 Which shape above can be produced by scaling down H using a scale factor of $\frac{1}{3}$?

C5 Which shape is an 'enlargement' of shape H with scale factor $\frac{1}{2}$?

C6 What are the scale factors for these enlargements?

    (a) G to E   (b) A to D   (c) A to E   (d) F to E   (e) H to C

*C7 What are the scale factors for these enlargements?

    (a) D to F   (b) F to D   (c) A to F   (d) G to A   (e) D to G

D Scales for maps and drawings

This is a map of a village.
You can think of it as a scaled-down drawing.

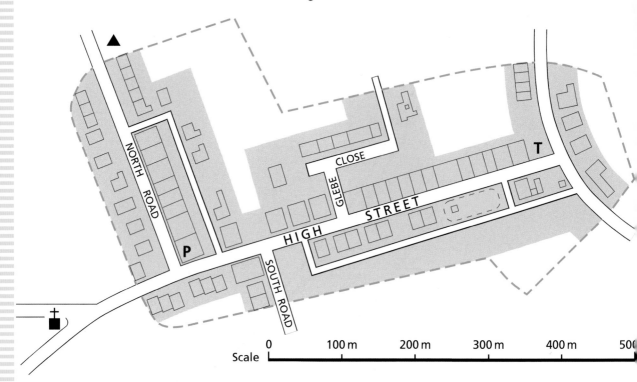

D1 (a)

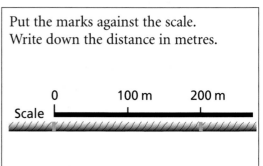

| Put a piece of string between the church and the post office. Put marks on your string like this. | Put the marks against the scale. Write down the distance in metres. |

(b) Find the distance from the post office to the youth hostel (▲) in the same way.

(c) How far is the public telephone (T) from the post office in metres?

(d) How far is the post office from the junction of South Road and High Street?

(e) How far is the public telephone from the junction of Glebe Close and High Street?

D2 The dotted line shows a nature walk round the village.

(a) How long is the walk in metres?   (b) How long is it in kilometres?

D3 What distance does 1 centimetre on the map represent?

This map shows the east end of the village, drawn to a larger scale.
Holmcroft and The Manor are two large houses.

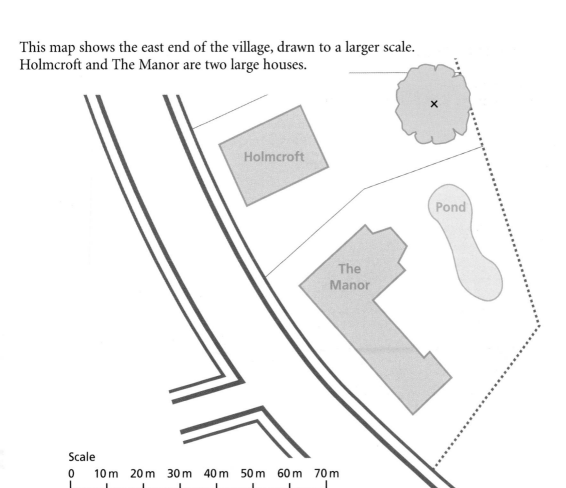

D4 What does 1 centimetre on this map represent?

D5 (a) Measure the length of the pond on the map with your ruler.
What is the length of the real pond?

(b) The front of The Manor faces the road.
How long is the front of The Manor in metres?

(c) There is a tree behind Holmcroft.
How far is its centre from the back of Holmcroft?

D6 (a) Measure the length and width of the table (or desk) you are working on.
Record the measurements to the nearest centimetre.

Make a scale drawing of the top of your table.
Use a scale where 1 cm represents 10 cm.

(b) If a computer keyboard 45 cm by 15 cm was put on your table,
how big would it be on your drawing?

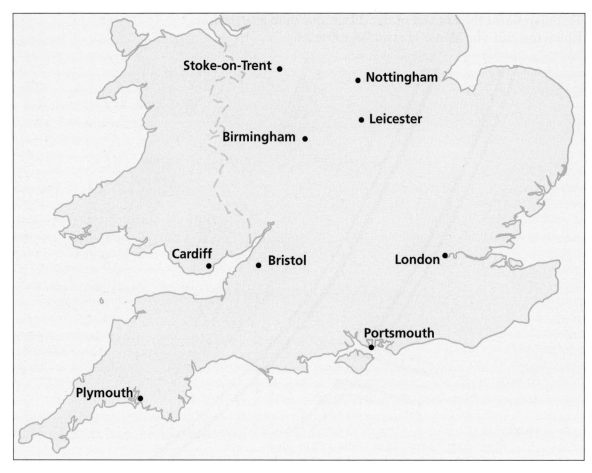

On this map 1 cm represents 20 miles.

D7 Find these distances in miles 'as the crow flies' (in a straight line).

    (a) Plymouth to Cardiff   (b) Plymouth to Portsmouth

    (c) Stoke-on-Trent to Nottingham (d) Birmingham to Leicester

    (e) Nottingham to Portsmouth   (f) Nottingham to London

    (g) Cardiff to London   (h) London to Stoke-on-Trent

D8 Use string to find roughly how far it is **by boat**

    (a) from Plymouth to Cardiff   (b) from Portsmouth to London

D9 A small plane takes off from Bristol with enough fuel to fly 90 miles. Which of these cities could it get to?

        Stoke on Trent   Nottingham   Birmingham

          Leicester   Portsmouth   Plymouth

D10 These buildings are drawn to a scale where 1 cm represents 50 metres.
Measure them and work out their actual height.
(Include the spires that are shown.)

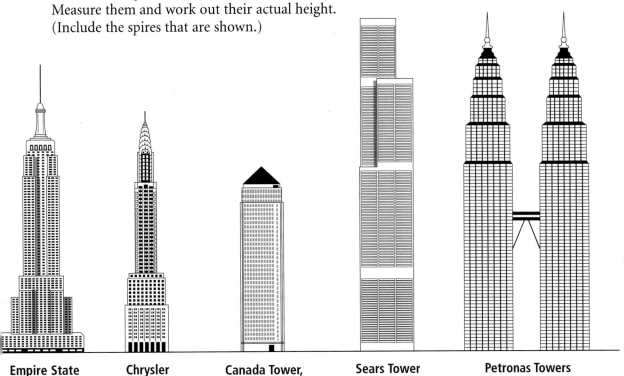

Empire State Building   **Chrysler Building**   **Canada Tower, Canary Wharf**   **Sears Tower**   **Petronas Towers**

D11 This is a sketch of a rectangular field.

(a) Make an accurate drawing using a scale where 2 cm represents 1 metre.

(b) On your drawing, measure the length of the dotted line to the neareast 0.1 cm.

(c) Work out the length of the footpath in real life.

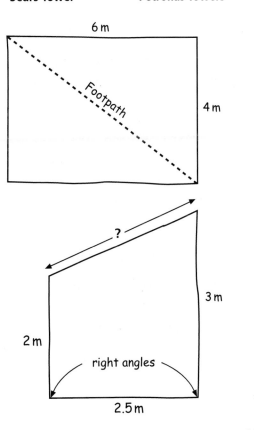

D12 This is a sketch of the end of a shed.

(a) Make an accurate drawing using a scale where 5 cm represents 1 metre.

(b) Measure the length of the sloping edge at the top, to the neareast 0.1 cm.

(c) Work out the length of the sloping edge in real life.

161

D13 How long would these be, drawn to a scale where 1 cm represents 20 metres?

    (a) A football pitch 80 m long   (b) A boating lake 130 m long

D14 How long would these be, drawn to a scale where 1 cm represents 50 metres?

    (a) A street 250 m long   (b) A footpath 380 m long

D15 This sketch shows the measurements of a bedroom.
Make an accurate drawing to a scale where 5 cm represents 1 metre.

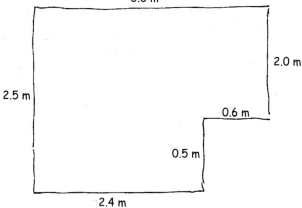

D16 What will these measurements of the Humber bridge be, drawn to a scale where 1 cm represents 100 metres?

    (a) The 1420 metre length of the central span

    (b) The 290 metre height of the towers

D17 What will these measurements of the Akashi Kaikyo bridge be, drawn to a scale where 1 cm represents 200 metres?

    (a) The 1990 metre length of the central span

    (b) The 300 metre height of the towers

D18 The real Chartres Cathedral is 110 metres high.

What scale is this drawing of it?

D19 The real Eiffel Tower is 300 metres high.

What scale is this drawing of it?

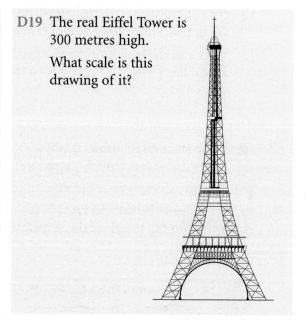

E Ratios

Another way to give the scale of a map or plan is to write the **ratio**

distance on map or plan : actual distance

To do this we must measure both distances in the **same units**.

For example, on this room plan, 1 cm stands for 2 m.

So the scale of the plan, as a ratio, is   **1 cm : 2 m**
Change the 2 m into centimetres: **1 cm : 200 cm**
Leave out the units and write it as   **1 : 200**

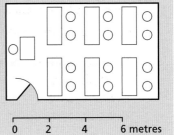

0   2   4   6 metres

E1 Write each of these map scales as a ratio.

    (a) 1 cm stands for 50 cm (for short we say 1 cm to 50 cm)

    (b) 1 cm to 1 m   (c) 1 cm to 5 m   (d) 1 cm to 20 m

E2 (a) Write the scale of the map on page 158 as a ratio.

    (b) Do the same for the map on page 159.

E3 Write each of these map scales as a ratio.

    (a) 1 cm to 100 m   (b) 1 cm to 500 m   (c) 1 cm to 200 m   (d) 1 cm to 1 km

E4 Write the scale of the drawings of the towers on page 161 as a ratio.

E5 For each of these scales, how many metres does 1 cm represent?

    (a) 1 : 200   (b) 1 : 4000   (c) 1 : 250

E6 This map of a lake is drawn to a scale of 1 : 2500.

    (a) How many metres does 1 cm represent?

    (b) Measure the map and find the actual length
        of the lake (the dotted line).

    (c) Find the distance between the two places
        marked A and B.

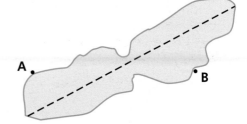

A scale written as a ratio usually begins 1 : ...

Suppose a plan has a scale where 2 cm stands for 1 m.

Write it as a ratio: 2 cm : 1 m
Change the 1 m into centimetres: 2 cm : 100 cm
Leave out the units: 2 : 100
Simplify: 1 : 50

E7 Write each of these scales as a ratio beginning 1 : ...

    (a) 2 cm to 50 cm   (b) 2 cm to 1 m   (c) 5 cm to 1 m   (d) 5 cm to 1 km

What progress have you made?

Statement

Evidence

I can identify enlargements and work out their scale factors.

1 (a) Which of the shapes A, B or C is an enlargement of shape S?

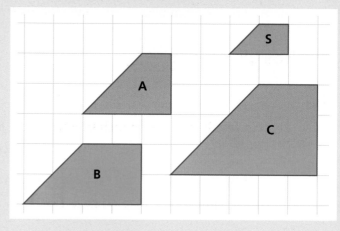

(b) What is the scale factor of the enlargement?

I can work out lengths when shapes have been scaled.

2 These are sketches of a design drawn to different scales. Work out the missing measurements.

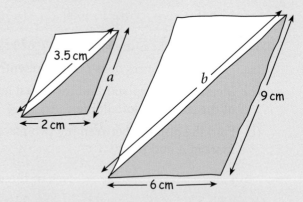

I can work with distances on a map.

3 A map is drawn to a scale of 1 cm to 5 km.

(a) An island is 2.4 cm long on the map. How long is the real island?

(b) The distance between two towns is 60 km. How far apart will they be on the map?

I can find the ratio of two quantities expressed in different units.

4 Write each of these map scales as a ratio.

(a) 1 cm to 10 m   (b) 1 cm to 50 m

(c) 1 cm to 2.5 m   (d) 2 cm to 1 km

㉓ Approximation and estimation

This work will help you
- ◆ round numbers to one significant figure
- ◆ estimate the result of a calculation by rounding

A Rough estimates

Seats

This activity is described in the teacher's guide.

The calculations 4×2, 40×20, 4×200 are all closely related.

Here is one way of finding the answer to 40×20 . You do it in stages:

$4 \times 2 = 8$

$4 \times 20 = 80$

$40 \times 20 = 800$

A1 Work these out.

(a) 30×2 (b) 30×20 (c) 40×5 (d) 40×50 (e) 400×50

(f) 6×20 (g) 6×200 (h) 60×200 (i) 60×20 (j) 40×30

(k) 20×50 (l) 300×30 (m) 50×30 (n) 40×40 (o) 80×200

A2 Work out a rough estimate for each of these.

(a) 18×31 (b) 48×39 (c) 22×57 (d) 41×62 (e) 78×31

A3 In a plantation there are 72 lines of trees, with 29 in each line.
Roughly how many trees are there altogether?

A4 A large car park has 38 rows of car spaces, with 21 spaces in each row.
Roughly how many spaces are there altogether?

A5 Work out a rough estimate for each of these.

(a) 204×39 (b) 197×29 (c) 301×68 (d) 41×502 (e) 796×48

B Rounding to one significant figure: whole numbers

News Breaker

3000 attend opening concert

In fact 3425 people attended this concert. In the newspaper headline 3425 has been rounded to the nearest thousand.

The Flame Throwers' first ever live concert was attended by 3425 people. The applause at the end lasted for nearly half an hour, and

The thousands figure is the **most significant figure** in the number 3425.

700 copies of new single sold in first minute

The latest single by The Wheelibins sold 682 copies in the first minute, it was claimed by their agent last

The most significant figure in 682 is the hundreds figure.

When 682 is rounded to the nearest hundred, it becomes 700.

In both headlines the numbers have been rounded to **one significant figure**.

B1 Round each of these numbers to one significant figure.

(a) 523   (b) 6974   (c) 486   (d) 1067   (e) 82

(f) 3684   (g) 677   (h) 2679   (i) 8731   (j) 608

B2 Write your own headline for each of these, rounding each number to one significant figure.

(a) 276 people take part in a sponsored cycle ride.

(b) 215 children pass their cycling proficiency test.

(c) A school raises £923.75 for the victims of a hurricane.

(d) 6848 school fair programmes are sold.

B3 Round each of these numbers to one significant figure.

(a) 53 123   (b) 78 227   (c) 61 063   (d) 48 372   (e) 13 404

B4 Write a headline for each of these, rounding each number to one significant figure.

(a) 24 376 people used the town's buses last week.

(b) A teacher won £58 621 in a lottery.

(c) 748 520 people used the underground last Sunday evening.

B5 Round each of these numbers to one significant figure.

(a) 98   (b) 956   (c) 6500   (d) 40 098   (e) 85 000

C Estimation: whole numbers

Worked example

Find a rough estimate for 324 × 78.

Round each number to one significant figure: 300 × 80 = **24 000**

3 × 8 = 24
30 × 8 = 240
300 × 8 = 2400
300 × 80 = 24 000

C1 Work out a rough estimate for each of these.

    (a) 51 × 38   (b) 631 × 18   (c) 48 × 316   (d) 77 × 92

    (e) 117 × 49   (f) 31 × 188   (g) 620 × 58   (h) 921 × 78

C2 A rectangular plot of land is 68 m by 223 m. Estimate its area roughly.

C3 Estimate the area of each of these rectangular plots.

    (a) 42 m by 218 m   (b) 178 m by 44 m   (c) 234 m by 57 m   (d) 405 m by 12 m

    (e) 98 m by 306 m   (f) 77 m by 822 m   (g) 621 m by 296 m   (h) 188 m by 215 m

C4 Kirsty buys a weekly magazine costing £3.95 each week.
Estimate how much she pays in a year.

D Rounding to one significant figure: decimals

The most significant figure in each of these numbers is shown in bold.

It is the first non-zero figure working from the left.

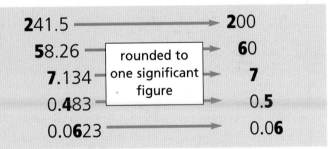

241.5 → **2**00
58.26 → **6**0
7.134 → **7**
0.**4**83 → 0.**5**
0.0**6**23 → 0.0**6**

(rounded to one significant figure)

D1 Round each of these numbers to one significant figure.

    (a) 52.3   (b) 4.827   (c) 6.89   (d) 23.047   (e) 82.56

    (f) 0.364   (g) 0.713   (h) 0.052   (i) 0.0755   (j) 0.0164

D2 Round each of these numbers to one significant figure.

    (a) 5478   (b) 386   (c) 6.044   (d) 0.027   (e) 831.8

    (f) 647   (g) 0.0072   (h) 1.058   (i) 327.55   (j) 0.0944

D3 Round each of these numbers to one significant figure.

    (a) 0.977   (b) 0.0928   (c) 0.0964   (d) 30.98   (e) 0.065

    (f) 33 512   (g) 0.3046   (h) 2.0077   (i) 0.0092   (j) 0.0098

E Multiplying decimals

Multiplying a number by 0.1 is the same as finding a tenth of it. Every digit moves **one place to the right**.

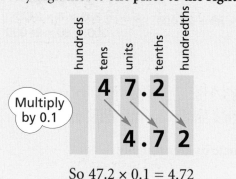

So 47.2 × 0.1 = 4.72

Multiplying a number by 0.01 is the same as finding a hundredth of it. Every digit moves **two places to the right**.

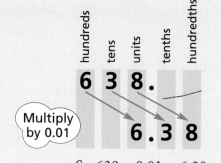

So 638 × 0.01 = 6.38

E1 Work these out.

(a) 42 × 0.1

(b) 122 × 0.01

(c) 5.8 × 0.1

(d) 302 × 0.1

(e) 3080 × 0.01

(f) 20.8 × 0.1

(g) 2.6 × 0.01

(h) 0.07 × 0.01

You can work out **0.3 × 0.2** like this. Start with **3 × 2** and do it in stages:

3 × 2 = 6

0.3 × 2 = 0.6

0.3 × 0.2 = 0.06

Similarly with **300 × 0.4** :

3 × 4 = 12

30 × 4 = 120

300 × 4 = 1200

300 × 0.4 = 120

E2 Copy and complete these.

(a) 3 × 4 = 12
0.3 × 4 = ...
0.3 × 0.4 = ...

(b) 4 × 5 = 20
4 × 0.5 = ...
0.4 × 0.5 = ...

(c) 3 × 5 = 15
30 × 5 = ...
30 × 0.5 = ...

(d) 2 × 7 = 14
0.2 × 7 = ...
0.02 × 7 = ...

(e) 5 × 0.5 = 2.5
50 × 0.5 = ...
500 × 0.5 = ...

(f) 40 × 2 = ...
400 × 2 = ...
400 × 0.2 = ...

(g) 0.6 × 3 = ...
0.06 × 3 = ...
0.06 × 30 = ...

(h) 0.5 × 9 = ...
0.5 × 0.9 = ...
0.5 × 0.09 = ...

E3 Work these out.

(a) 0.3 × 0.3

(b) 0.4 × 30

(c) 0.2 × 400

(d) 300 × 0.6

(e) 80 × 0.5

(f) 0.2 × 0.2

(g) 0.6 × 500

(h) 80 × 0.8

E4 Work these out.

(a) 0.8 × 0.02

(b) 30 × 0.04

(c) 0.01 × 700

(d) 60 × 0.02

(e) 200 × 0.7

(f) 0.08 × 20

(g) 0.1 × 2000

(h) 40 × 0.04

F Estimation

Worked example

Find a rough estimate for 42×0.568.

Round each number to one significant figure: $40 \times 0.6 = 24$ ⟵

$4 \times 6 = 24$
$40 \times 6 = 240$
$40 \times 0.6 = 24$

F1 Work out a rough estimate for each of these.

(a) 5.1×0.31 (b) 421×0.22 (c) 0.48×0.316 (d) 3.7×0.92

(e) 133×0.49 (f) 0.031×82 (g) 6.25×0.058 (h) 91.6×0.78

F2 Estimate the area of each of these rectangles.

(a) 48.2 m by 2.23 m   (b) 1.78 m by 0.44 m   (c) 223.4 m by 0.57 m

(d) 0.34 m by 0.78 m   (e) 0.19 m by 0.33 m   (f) 64.1 m by 0.029 m

F3 Gareth worked out 43.5×39.6 and got the answer 7122.6.
By finding a rough estimate, show that Gareth's answer must be wrong.

F4 Which of the numbers below is closest to the answer to 0.18×324 ?

     0.006   0.06   0.6   6   60   600   6000   60 000

F5 A roll of kitchen foil, when fully unrolled, is 20 m long and 0.3 m wide.
Calculate the area of the foil.

F6 Work out a rough estimate of the area of each of these rolls of foil.

(a) 27.5 m long and 0.52 m wide   (b) 24.3 m long and 0.57 m wide

What progress have you made?

Statement	Evidence
I can round whole numbers to one significant figure.	1 Round each of these numbers to one significant figure. (a) 438 (b) 7867 (c) 46 327
I can estimate when multiplying whole numbers.	2 Estimate the results of these multiplications. (a) 38×42 (b) 287×59 (c) 814×388
I can round decimals to one significant figure.	3 Round each of these numbers to one significant figure. (a) 36.73 (b) 0.512 (c) 0.0763
I can estimate when multiplying decimals.	4 Estimate each of these. (a) 43.21×0.592 (b) 0.315×0.234 (c) 0.0375×71.08

24 Bearings

This work will help you

◆ measure and record a direction as a three-figure bearing

◆ fix the position of a point by using its bearings from two other points

A Direction

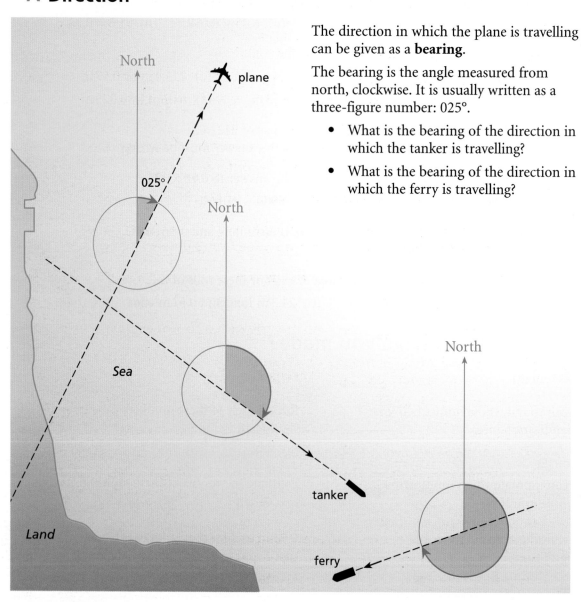

The direction in which the plane is travelling can be given as a **bearing**.

The bearing is the angle measured from north, clockwise. It is usually written as a three-figure number: 025°.

- What is the bearing of the direction in which the tanker is travelling?

- What is the bearing of the direction in which the ferry is travelling?

You need sheet 202.

A1 The dotted lines show the route of the ferry from Ballycastle to Church Quarter.
Measure the bearing of (a) the first part of the journey (b) the second part

A2 A boat leaves Ballycastle and travels on a bearing of 040°. Draw its path.

A3 A boat leaves Bull Point and travels on a bearing of 140°.
Draw its path and mark where it reaches the coast of the mainland.

A4 A boat sails from Cooraghy Bay on a bearing of 200°. Draw its path.

A5 A helicopter flies over Rue Point on a bearing of 310°.
Will the pilot see Bull Point on her left or her right?

A6 A speedboat leaves Kinbane and travels on a bearing of 075°.
Draw its path. (You will need to draw a line going north through Kinbane.)

A7 Draw the line from Colliery Bay on a bearing of 330°.
A company wants to build an oil platform 6 km from Colliery Bay along this line.
Mark the position where they want to build the platform.

A8 A buoy is 3.5 km from Bruce's Castle on a bearing of 175°. Mark its position.

A9 Measure the bearing of the line going from Killeany to the Coastguard Station.
We call this **the bearing of the Coastguard Station from Killeany.**

A10 Draw the line from Doon to Rue Point and measure the bearing of Rue Point from Doon.

A11 Find the bearing of
(a) Rue Point from Cooraghy Bay   (b) Ruecallan from Church Quarter

A12 A boat leaves Ballycastle. It first sails on a bearing of 030° for 5 km.
It then sails for 2 km on a bearing of 110°. Draw its path.

Measure how far it is now from Ballycastle and its bearing from Ballycastle.

A13 A yacht is in distress. Coastguards record its bearing from Doon (080°)
and its bearing from Cooraghy Bay (140°).

Draw the line from Doon on a bearing of 080° and the line from Cooraghy Bay
on a bearing of 140°. Mark the position of the yacht.

A14 A boat is drifting out of control.
Coastguards record its bearings from Bull Point and from Rue Point.

Time	Bearing from Bull Point	Bearing from Rue Point
2 p.m.	170°	235°
3 p.m.	140°	270°

Mark the two positions of the boat. Mark the point on the coast of Rathlin Island
that the boat is heading towards.

B On the moors

You need sheet 203.

B1 The scale of the map on sheet 203 is 4 cm to 1 km.
If you want to draw a line on the map to represent 3 km, how long will you draw it?

B2 What length in centimetres represents

(a) 4.5 km   (b) 2.8 km   (c) 1.6 km   (d) 4.9 km   (e) 0.8 km

B3 A line on the map is 16 cm long. How many kilometres does it represent?

B4 What is the real length of a line which on the map is of length

(a) 8 cm   (b) 15 cm   (c) 7.2 cm   (d) 10.4 cm   (e) 5.4 cm

To avoid calculations of distances, you could make a 'scale ruler' by copying the scale of the map along a straight edge (for example, a folded piece of paper).

B5 Janice goes for a walk on the moor. She starts at Ridgeway Cross.
She walks for 2.8 km on a bearing of 064°.
Then she walks for 2.2 km on a bearing of 335°.

(a) Draw her walk.   (b) How far is she from the nearest road?

B6 Grant starts at Portford Bridge. He walks for 1.6 km on a bearing of 208°.
Then he walks for 1.2 km on a bearing of 261°.

(a) Draw his walk.   (b) What is the bearing of Withypool Cross from his final position?

B7 Karina starts at Anstey Gate. She walks in a straight line to White Post.

(a) What bearing does she walk on?   (b) How far does she walk?

B8 Green Barrow is on a bearing of 130° from Landacre Gate and on a bearing of 010° from White Post. Mark its position on the map.

B9 There is a disused quarry on a bearing of 077° from Upper Willingford Bridge and 338° from Cloggs Farm. Mark it on the map.

B10 (a) Copy and complete this table of bearings.

RC to CF	CF to RC
CG to OB	OB to CG
PP to W	W to PP
WC to WP	WP to WC
RF to OB	OB to RF

CF = Cloggs Farm
CG = Coombe Gate
OB = Old Barrow
PP = Porchester's Post
RC = Ridgway Cross
RF = Red Ford
W = Willingford
WC = Withypool Cross
WP = White Post

(b) Can you see a connection between
'the bearing from X to Y' and
'the bearing from Y to X'?
Describe the connection.

C Bearings jigsaw puzzle

You need the jigsaw pieces from sheet 204, and sheet 205 to fit them on.

Each piece has the name of a tree on it.
Fit the pieces together following the information on them.

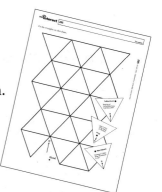

What progress have you made?

Statement

Evidence

I can measure and record a bearing.

1 On the map below, measure

   (a) the bearing of Kirk Farm from Alcote

   (b) the bearing of Sterndale from Kirk Farm

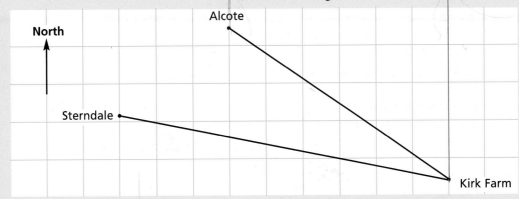

I can fix the position of a point given its bearings from two points.

2 Draw the square ABCD below to a scale of 1 cm to 5 km.

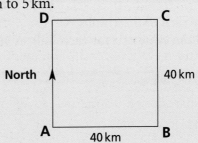

Find and label the point X whose bearing from A is 073° and from C is 202°.

I can plot a journey given the distance and bearing of each stage.

3 Draw the following journey on the same diagram as for question 2.

   D to P: 33 km on a bearing of 118°
   P to Q: 28 km on a bearing of 232°

25 Using equations

This will help you

◆ form equations from puzzles

◆ solve equations, including those that involve brackets and subtraction

A Walls

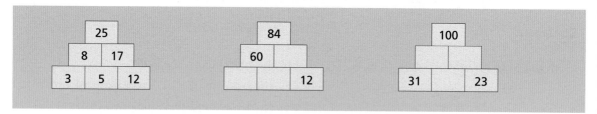

A1 Look at this wall.

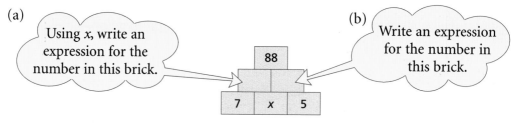

(a) Using x, write an expression for the number in this brick.

(b) Write an expression for the number in this brick.

(c) Add your answers to (a) and (b).

(d) Use your answer to (c) to write down an equation in x.

(e) Solve your equation. Copy and complete the wall to check.

A2 Copy each of these walls.
Find the value of x for each wall, as you did in question A1.

(a)
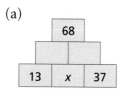

(b)
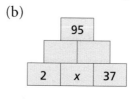

(c)
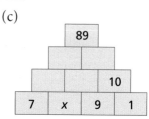

A3 Copy each of these walls.
Find the value of the letter in each wall.
Work out all the missing numbers in each wall.

(a)

70

| 17 | |

| 10 | | a | 6 |

(b)

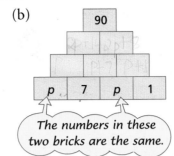

The numbers in these
two bricks are the same.

(c)

| 59 |

| 13 | 2m | m | 19 |

(d)

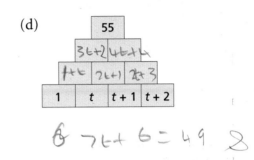

$7t + 6 = 49$

A4 In these walls, pick your own letter to stand for one of the missing numbers.
Work out the value of your letter.
Then find all the missing numbers in each wall.

(a)

| 71 |

| 3 | | 9 | 11 |

(b)

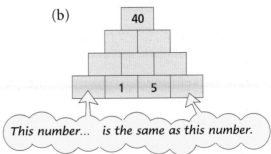

This number... is the same as this number.

*A5 Work out the missing numbers in these walls.

(a)

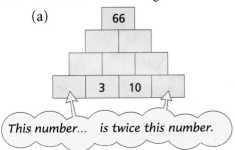

This number... is twice this number.

(b)

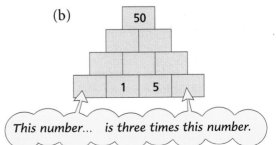

This number... is three times this number.

175

B Both sides

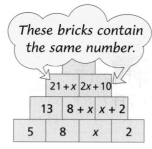

These bricks contain the same number.

21 + x 2x + 10

13 8 + x x + 2

5 8 x 2

$21 + x = 2x + 10$ *(take x off both sides)*
$21 = x + 10$ *(take 10 off both sides)*
$11 = x$

B1 Solve each of these equations.
Show all your working and check that each answer works.

(a) $3x + 23 = 4x + 12$

(b) $10 + 2x = 5x + 1$

(c) $7a + 1 = a + 43$

(d) $5g + 4 = 7g + 3$

(e) $1 + 11x = 61 + 5x$

(f) $2 + y = 2y + 1$

(g) $13p + 64 = 7p + 100$

(h) $25 + 4e = e + 100$

(i) $2x + 2\frac{1}{2} = x + 6$

(j) $t + 6 = 6 + 4t$

B2 (a) Copy and complete this working to solve $7(m + 3) = 3m + 65$.

(b) Check that your answer works in the original equation.

$7(m + 3) = 3m + 65$
$7m + 21 = 3m + 65$ *(multiply out brackets)*

B3 (a) Multiply out the brackets from $2(n + 3)$.

(b) Use your answer to help you solve the equation $2(n + 3) = n + 10$.

(c) Check that your answer works.

B4 Solve each of these equations. (Multiply out any brackets first.)
Show all your working and check that each answer works.

(a) $2(x + 12) = 7x + 4$

(b) $w + 44 = 3(w + 10)$

(c) $3(t + 11) = 4(t + 8)$

(d) $2(12 + d) = 7d + 9$

(e) $10(g + 1) = 6g + 54$

(f) $63 + 6k = 9(2 + k)$

(g) $2(8 + h) = 5(h + 2)$

(h) $3(r + 7) = 5(3 + r)$

*****B5** Work out the missing numbers in these walls.

(a)

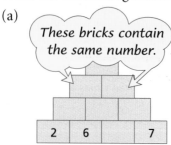

These bricks contain the same number.

2 6 7

(b)

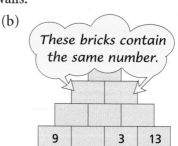

These bricks contain the same number.

9 3 13

C Think of a number

I think of a number.
I multiply it by 8.
I add on 6.
My answer is 110.
What was my number?

Jim

I think of a number.
I multiply it by 7.
I add on 9.
My answer is
13 times the number
I started with.
What was my number?

Ollie

C1 Turn Harry's number puzzle into an equation.
Solve the equation and check your solution works in the puzzle.

I think of a number.
I multiply it by 6.
I add on 20.
My answer is
10 times the number
I started with.
What was my number?

Harry

C2 Turn each of these number puzzles into equations and solve them.

(a) Jo thinks of a number.
She multiplies it by 9.
She adds on 18.
Her answer is 11 times
the number she started with.

(b) Iqbal thinks of a number.
He multiplies it by 4.
He adds on 100.
His answer is 8 times
the number he started with.

C3 Damian thinks of a number.
He adds on 10. ⟶
Then he multiplies by 3. ⟶
His answer is 42. ⟶

Let d stand for Damian's number.
He gets d + 10.
Now he gets 3(d + 10).
So 3(d + 10) = 42

Solve the equation to find the number
that Damian started with.

C4 Solve these puzzles.

(a) Jay thinks of a number.
She adds 4 to her number.
Then she multiplies by 5.
Her answer is 7 times as big
as her starting number.

(b) Hamish thinks of a number.
He adds on 12.
Now he multiplies by 6.
His answer is 8 times as big
as his starting number.

C5 Adie and Biff are both doing 'think of a number' puzzles.
They both start with the same number.
We will use n for the number they both start with.

Adie multiplies the number by 5 and then adds on 1.

$5n + 1$

Biff adds on 3 and then multiplies by 3.

$3(n + 3)$

They are surprised to find that they both end up with the same number.
So $5n + 1 = 3(n + 3)$

Solve the equation to find what number they both started with.
Check your answer works.

C6 Sofima and Will both think of the same number.
Sofima adds 2 and then multiplies by 5.
Will multiplies his number by 3 and adds 28.
They both get the same answer. What number were they thinking of?

C7 Cath and Janet start with the same number.
Cath adds 7 to her number and then multiplies by 3.
Janet multiplies her number by 7 and then adds 5.
Cath and Janet end up with the same answer.
What was their starting number?

D Subtracting

- How would you solve these equations?

$5a - 9 = 4a + 1$

$5b - 6 = 3b + 18$

$7b - 15 = 2b$

- What about these?

$7c - 5 = 5c - 1$

$d - 2 = 4d - 8$

D1 Solve $3t + 1 = 5t - 17$.
(Add 17 to both sides to start with.)
Check your solution works.

D2 Solve $9z - 7 = 4z + 3$.
(Add 7 to both sides to start with.)
Check your solution works.

D3 Here is part of Martin's homework.
It is not correct!
Explain what he has done wrong, and
write out a correct solution.

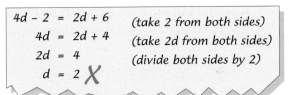

$$4d - 2 = 2d + 6 \quad \text{(take 2 from both sides)}$$
$$4d = 2d + 4 \quad \text{(take 2d from both sides)}$$
$$2d = 4 \quad \text{(divide both sides by 2)}$$
$$d = 2 \quad ✗$$

D4 Solve these equations.
Show your working clearly.

(a) $6b - 7 = 2b + 5$

(b) $4y + 2 = 7y - 10$

(c) $8h - 5 = 3h + 70$

(d) $2k + 13 = 5k - 2$

(e) $8m + 12 = 15m - 23$

(f) $45 + 3d = 8d - 55$

(g) $7f - 12 = 2f + 18$

(h) $2q - 0.8 = q + 1.2$

D5 (a) Multiply out the brackets from $3(x + 6)$.

(b) Use your answer to help you solve the equation $3(x + 6) = 5x - 2$.

(c) Check that your answer works.

D6 Solve each of these equations. (Multiply out any brackets first.)

(a) $5(t - 1) = 2t + 7$

(b) $10(h - 3) = 6h + 2$

(c) $13j - 55 = 3(j + 5)$

(d) $2a + 52 = 8(a - 7)$

(e) $q + 43 = 5(q - 1)$

(f) $2(3e - 1) = e + 23$

D7 Turn each of these number puzzles into equations and solve them.

(a) Harriet thinks of a number.
She takes away 3.
Then she multiplies by 4.
Her answer is twice
the number she started with.

(b) Kim thinks of a number.
He multiplies it by 7.
Then he subtracts 100.
His answer is 3 times
the number he started with.

D8 Solve $3z - 8 = z - 2$.
(Add 8 to both sides to start with.)
Check your solution works.

D9 Here is part of Maggie's homework.
It is not correct!
Explain what she has done wrong, and
write out a correct solution.

$$3s - 2 = 5s - 8 \quad \text{(take 3s from both sides)}$$
$$2 = 2s - 8 \quad \text{(add 8 to both sides)}$$
$$10 = 2s \quad \text{(divide both sides by 2)}$$
$$s = 5 \quad ✗$$

D10 Solve these equations.
Show your working clearly.

(a) $3n - 8 = 2n - 5$

(b) $4y - 1 = 7y - 10$

(c) $8t - 3 = 9t - 4$

(d) $3m - 10 = m - 2$

(e) $6x - 7 = 3x - 1$

(f) $2c - \frac{1}{2} = 6c - 12\frac{1}{2}$

D11 Solve each of these equations. (Multiply out any brackets first.)

(a) $2(y - 5) = 4y - 20$

(b) $5(g - 2) = 4g - 5$

(c) $8u - 50 = 6(u - 5)$

(d) $4(h - 1) = 7(h - 4)$

D12 Solve each of these equations.

(a) $7b - 6 = 3b + 2$

(b) $y + 6 = 3y - 4$

(c) $2h - 5 = h - 1$

(d) $5k - 2 = 3(k + 2)$

(e) $2m + 35 = 9m - 35$

(f) $3(d - 1) = 5(d - 3)$

D13 Shelagh and Rackpaal each think of the same number.

I take off 5 and then multiply by 6.

I multiply by 3 and then add 15.

They are surprised to find that they both end up with the same number. Work out what number they were both thinking of at first.

E Equations from pictures

Jim and Sarah have the same number of coins

Jim has 2 bags of coins and 25 extra coins.

Sarah has 3 bags of coins and 8 extra coins.

Each bag has the same number of coins in it. How many?

E1

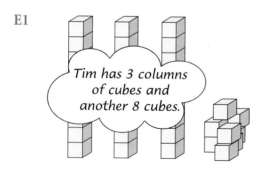

Tim has 3 columns of cubes and another 8 cubes.

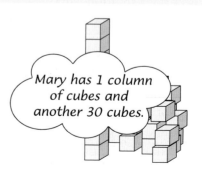

Mary has 1 column of cubes and another 30 cubes.

Each column has the same number of cubes in it, and Tim and Mary have the same number of cubes altogether.
How many cubes are there in each column?

E2 José has 3 suitcases of banknotes and another $1200.

Miguel has 1 suitcase of banknotes and another $4000.

Each suitcase has the same amount of money in it.
José and Miguel have the same amount of money each.

(a) How many dollars are in each suitcase?

(b) How much money do José and Miguel have each?

E3 There are 5 full coaches at a bus station, and another 26 passengers waiting for coaches.

At another bus station, there are 2 full coaches and another 131 passengers waiting.

Each coach holds the same number of people, and there are the same number of passengers at each bus station.

How many people does each coach hold?

E4 George has two packets of mints.
Suppose there are n mints in each packet.

(a) How many mints does George have left after eating 16?

(b) Hannah starts with 4 packets of mints. Then she eats 50!
How many mints does she have left?

(c) George and Hannah each have the same number of mints left.
Write an equation using n that tells you this.

Solve your equation to find the number of mints in each packet.

E5 There are 10 packets of woodscrews in a shop,
Sam steals 2 woodscrews from each packet.

Suppose there are w woodscrews in a full packet.

(a) Which of these expressions tells
you the total number of screws
after Sam stole some?

$10w - 2$ $\quad$ $10(w - 2)$ $\quad$ $w - 20$

(b) The number of woodscrews left is the same
as the number in 8 full packets.
Work out how many woodscrews there are in a full packet.

E6 Jenny and Bob are twins.
Jenny takes her age, multiplies it by 6 and takes off 15.
Bob takes his age, multiplies by 2 and adds 53.
The answer they both get is the age of their great-uncle Fred.

Work out the ages of great-uncle Fred and the twins.

What progress have you made?

Statement

I can solve simple wall problems.

Evidence

1 Find the value of the unknown letter in each wall.

(a)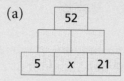

(b)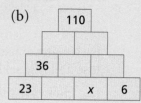

I can solve equations, including those with brackets.

2 Solve each of these equations. Show all your working.

(a) $3x + 5 = 2x + 8$

(b) $5y + 3 = 3(y + 7)$

(c) $2(h + 9) = 3(5 + h)$

I can solve equations involving subtraction.

3 Solve each of these equations. Show all your working.

(a) $5g - 12 = 3g + 8$

(b) $4(f - 3) = f + 9$

(c) $6d - 38 = 2d - 10$

I can form equations involving subtraction and solve them.

4 Turn each of these number puzzles into equations and solve them.

(a) Patrick thinks of a number.
He multiplies it by 6.
Then he takes off 52.
His answer is twice the number he first thought of.

(b) Rois and Maria each think of the same number.
Rois takes 6 off her number and then multiplies by 4.
Maria multiplies her number by 2 and then takes off 10.
They both get the same answer.
What number were they each thinking of?

26 Distributions

The work in this unit will help you

◆ revise frequency, mode, median, mean and range

◆ understand stem-and-leaf tables

A Median, range and mode

Here are the heights in centimetres of a group of 13 children.

130 123 141 150 139 134 126 137 156 142 147 135 145

We can see how these heights are spread out, or **distributed**, by drawing a **dot plot**.

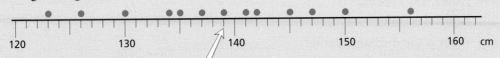

he dot plot shows that the heights re 'bunched' around the middle, ith fewer at each end.

*The **median** height is the middle height, 139 cm.*

Range = largest – smallest = 156 cm – 123 cm = 33 cm

A1 Find the median and range of the heights shown in this dot plot.

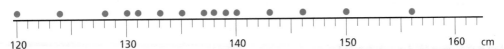

A2 Here are the weights in kg of a group of children.
  (a) Find the median weight.
  (b) Find the range of the weights.

37 51 41 45 52
57 39 42 56 46
46 50 48 38 41

With an even number of children, the median height is halfway between the middle pair.

123 127 130 132 132 134 **135** **138** 140 143 146 148 149 152

Median **136.5**

A3 Find the median and range of these heights in cm.

139 151 128 126 147 129
139 140 142 156 160 145

183

A4 Here are the heights, in cm, of some boys and some girls.

Boys	128	101	143	110	145	140	136	117
Girls	125	110	131	139	142	112	138	

(a) Find the range of the boys' heights.

(b) Find the range of the girls' heights.

(c) Which range is larger? What does this tell you about the boys' heights compared with the girls'?

A5 Charlie watched cars go by his house and noted down how many people were in each car. Here is his data, written out in order.

1, 1, 1, 1, 1, 1, 2, 2, 3, 3, 3, 3, 3, 3, 3, 4, 4, 4, 5

What is the median number of people in a car?

A6 Paula also noted the number of people in cars.
She made this tally table.

(a) How many cars did Paula observe?

(b) What is the median number of people in a car?

Number in car		Frequency
1	⊬⊬ ⊬⊬ ⊬⊬	15
2	⊬⊬ ////	9
3	⊬⊬ //	7
4	⊬⊬ /	5
5	///	3

A7 Zak summarised his car data in this frequency table.

Find the median number of people in a car.

Number in car	1	2	3	4	5
Frequency	7	10	11	6	4

A8 The most frequently occurring number of people is called the **mode**.
What is the mode for each of the data sets in A5, A6 and A7?

B Stem-and-leaf tables

An introductory activity is described in the teacher's guide.

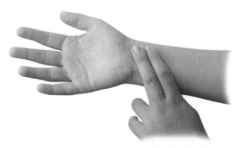

B1 This stem-and-leaf table shows the marks of some pupils in a test. Find

(a) the range of the marks

(b) the number of pupils who took the test

(c) the median mark

(d) the modal group

```
4 | 3 8
5 | 0 4 4 7
6 | 2 4 7 9 9
7 | 1 3 3 5 5 8 8 9
8 | 0 0 4 5 6
9 | 0 1 1
```

B2 Thirty pupils took a maths exam. There were two papers, each marked out of 100. Here are the results.

Paper 1	58	43	82	66	70	41	49	28	62	54
	80	44	72	70	45	49	55	61	54	63
	39	60	54	79	66	50	38	63	66	82

Paper 2	48	44	63	54	69	70	40	37	61	58
	56	35	42	51	28	34	39	41	44	38
	62	49	52	29	38	83	47	50	64	55

Make a stem-and-leaf table for each paper.
Which paper seems to have been harder? How can you tell?

B3 These are the weights in kg of 20 newborn babies.

3.0	3.2	4.1	3.8	3.7	2.5	1.7	2.3	3.3	2.8
1.9	3.1	2.6	3.3	2.5	4.0	2.7	3.4	2.8	1.9

(a) Make a stem-and-leaf table with the whole numbers as stems and the tenths as leaves. The table has been started here. ➤

1.	
2.	
3.	0
4.	

(b) What is the range of the weights?

(c) What is the median weight?

C Mean

Here are the players in a seven-a-side football team.   Their total weight is **519 kg**.

72 kg 75 kg 68 kg 81 kg 69 kg 84 kg 70 kg

519 kg

To find the **mean** weight, divide the total by the number of players: $\frac{519}{7}$ = **74.1 kg**
(to 1 d.p.)

C1 Here are the weights, in kg, of a group of babies.

Calculate the mean weight, to 1 d.p.

3.7	2.1	4.1	3.5	1.8	2.7	3.9
3.2	2.6	3.6	2.8	3.0	1.8	3.8	4.1

C2 These full-size drawings show some worms of two different species.

Species A

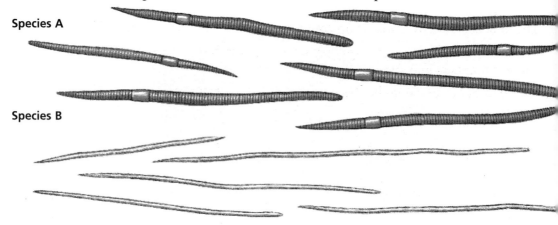

Species B

Find the mean length and the range of lengths of each species, in cm.
Write a couple of sentences comparing the two groups of worms.

C3 The fuel consumption of cars is measured in litres per 100 km.

Here are the fuel consumptions of some cars with two different types of engine.

Engine A	10.6	12.3	11.8	14.2	12.0	17.1	10.4	12.9
Engine B	13.5	16.1	12.9	15.8	16.7	15.5		

Use means and ranges to compare the two sets of data.

C4 The heights in cm of the players in
a seven-a-side football team are

163 169 165 165 168 171 161

All of these heights are over 160 cm.
The 'extra' heights above 160 cm are

3   9   5   5   8   11   1

(a) Work out the mean of these
extra heights.

(b) Write down the mean height of
the seven team members.

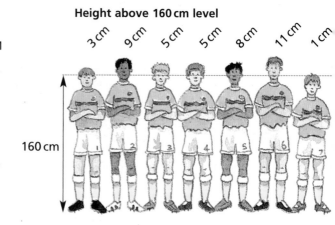

Height above 160 cm level

3 cm 9 cm 5 cm 5 cm 8 cm 11 cm 1 cm

160 cm

C5 Perry counted the matches in each of 12 boxes.

The numbers were   38, 35, 33, 37, 36, 35, 39, 40, 36, 32, 30, 38

Use a method similar to that in C4 to work out the mean number of matches.

D Discrete and continuous data

Discrete data usually comes from counting.

For example, the number of tomatoes on a plant can be 0, 1, 2, 3, …
but not numbers in between, like 1.7, 2.08, and so on.

This data about tomatoes has been **grouped**: 0–4, 5–9, 10–14, …

Number of tomatoes	0–4	5–9	10–14	15–19
Frequency	3	5	6	4

Because the data is discrete, there is a jump between
the end of each group and the start of the next.

The bars on the **frequency chart** can be labelled
as shown here.

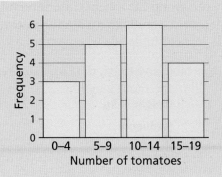

D1 Sam grows peas in her garden.
She grows two different varieties and wants to compare them.

She opens up 25 pods from each variety and counts
the peas in each pod.

Here are her results.

Variety A	12	7	10	9	16	14	8	18	13
	6	13	9	12	14	17	15	7	8
	20	12	11	21	3	4	11		
Variety B	10	5	9	12	11	7	12	9	17
	6	13	8	8	7	11	6	12	4
	7	9	11	6	8	14	8		

(a) Make a grouped frequency table for each variety.
Use groups 0–4, 5–9, and so on.

(b) Draw a frequency bar chart for each variety.

(c) Which is the modal group for variety A?

(d) Which is the modal group for variety B?

(e) Which variety has more peas in pods overall?

Continuous data usually comes from measuring.

If a baby weighs between 2 kg and 3 kg, its weight could be anything between 2 kg and 3 kg, for example 2.473 kg or 2.856 235 41 kg.

It depends on the accuracy of the weighing machine.

This dot plot shows the birth weights, in kg, of 16 babies.

We can group the weights into **intervals**, for example 1–2 kg, 2–3 kg, 3–4 kg, ...
There are no jumps between the intervals because the data is continuous.
But we have to decide where to put a weight of exactly 2 kg or 3 kg, and so on.

In this table and chart, the 2 kg baby has been included in the **upper** interval 2–3 kg.

Weight in kg	1–2	2–3	3–4	4–5
Frequency	1	5	6	4

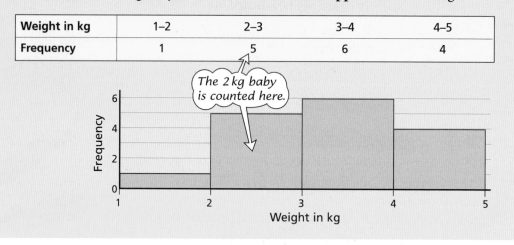

D2 (a) Use the dot plot to find the range of the babies' weights, as accurately as you can.

(b) Why is it not possible to find the range from the frequency chart?

D3 Jason measured the handspans of 20 girls and 20 boys.
Here are his results, in centimetres.

Girls	18.3	21.1	19.5	19.7	20.0	18.4	18.3	18.4	20.2	16.9
	20.4	17.6	19.5	18.0	18.3	17.2	16.0	17.8	18.9	19.1
Boys	17.6	22.5	19.7	21.9	22.4	21.0	22.5	21.8	21.1	20.3
	18.4	19.6	22.8	20.7	22.0	20.8	16.9	19.4	21.5	18.8

(a) Make a frequency table for each set of data, using intervals 16–17, 17–18, and so on.
When a value is on the boundary, put it into the interval above.

(b) Draw a frequency chart for each set of data.

(c) Write a sentence or two comparing the two sets of data.

D4 The teachers in a primary school asked all the children how long it took them to get home from school.

This chart shows the frequency distribution of the journey times.

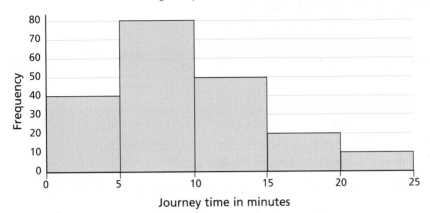

Journey time in minutes

(a) Karl says that the longest journey time is 25 minutes.
 Is he right? Explain your answer.

(b) Why is it not possible to find the range of the journey times from the chart?

(c) Which is the modal interval?

(d) What percentage of the children have journey times in the modal interval?

(e) If school ends at 3:45 p.m., what percentage of the children would get home at 4 p.m. or later?

D5 Draw a rough sketch of the kind of frequency chart of journey times you would expect to get for each of these schools.

(a) A school in a housing estate where all the pupils live very close to the school.

(b) A school which serves two villages some distance apart.
 The school is situated in one of the villages.
 About half the pupils come from this village and about half from the other.

(c) A school where most of the pupils live nearby, but a few live quite a long way away.

(d) A school where all the pupils live a long way from the school.

E Summarising and comparing data

It is often useful to summarise a set of data. This may make it easier
to compare it with other data.

To summarise data we need

some idea of the 'average' of the data	some idea of how spread out the data is

Measures of average

The word 'average' does not have a precise meaning. It is used to mean 'typical',
'representative', 'round about the middle, neither big nor small'.

In statistics, which is the science of handling data, there are several ways of getting a measure
of average. Three of these are the **mode, median** or **mean**.

Often one of these is a better measure of 'average' than the others.
It sometimes happens that none of them is a good 'average'.

E1 Here are the salaries of the people who work for a small company.
('k' means thousand.)

£8k, £9k, £9k, £9k, £11k, £11k, £13k, £30k, £53k

(a) Calculate the mean salary.
Does it give a good idea of a typical salary in the company?

(b) Write down the median salary and the modal salary.
Do either of these give a better idea of a typical salary?

E2 In another company the salaries are

£12k, £12k, £12k, £13k, £13k, £14k, £14k, £30k, £31k, £31k, £32k, £32k, £33k

(a) Find the mean, median and mode.

(b) Which gives the best idea of a typical salary in this company?

Measures of spread

Several different measures of spread are used in statistics.
The one we have met so far is the simplest: **range**.

E3 These are the salaries in two different companies.

Company A	£12k	£8k	£28k	£19k	£14k	£18k	£8k	£24k	£13k
Company B	£17k	£15k	£12k	£22k	£11k	£16k	£12k	£23k	

Calculate the mean and range of each company's salaries.
Write a couple of sentences comparing the two companies.

E4 These are the salaries in two more companies.

Company C	£15k	£10k	£12k	£30k	£24k	£28k	£12k	£26k	£23k
Company D	£14k	£15k	£10k	£21k	£14k	£16k	£20k	£30k	

Use the means and ranges to compare the two companies.

Relating two sorts of measurements

When studying a group of people or things, it can be useful to see how two different measurements (for example their height and their weight) are related.

A **scatter graph** is a good way to do this.

E5 A group of eight pupils were tested on their multiplication tables.
They then did some intensive practice.
After the practice they were tested again.

This is the data from the experiment.

Score before practice	5	3	6	4	8	6	2	8
Score after practice	7	7	8	6	5	7	6	9

(a) Draw and label axes like this.

Plot a point at (5, 7) to represent the first pupil.

Complete the scatter graph by plotting points the same way for the other seven pupils.

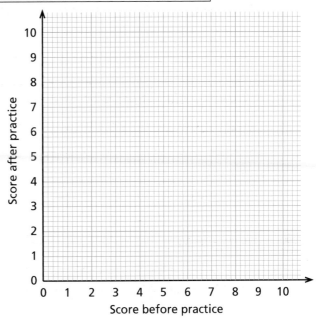

Answer these questions by looking at your scatter graph.

(b) Which are generally better, the before practice or the after practice scores?

(c) Which are more spread out, the before practice or the after practice scores?

(d) Is there anything unusual about any of the pupils' scores? Explain.

What progress have you made?

Statement

I can use a stem-and-leaf table.

Evidence

1 This stem-and-leaf table shows the ages of the people in a choir.

2	4 5 5 7
3	0 2 5 6 6 8 8
4	2 3 4 4 6 8 9 9
5	0 2 3 3
6	2 7

(a) How many people are there in the choir?

(b) What is the median age?

(c) What is the range of the ages?

I can make a frequency table and chart for continuous data.

2 Make a frequency table and chart for these children's weights in kg.

Use intervals 10–15, 15–20, and so on.

18.3	20.6	24.5	11.9	16.3
22.5	25.4	19.2	12.5	10.7
15.0	24.1	13.9	21.1	23.0

I can compare sets of data using measures of average and spread.

3 Colin weighed the apples from two different trees. Here are the results.

Tree A: mean 23 g, range 5 g

Tree B: mean 20 g, range 12 g

Write two sentences comparing the apples from the two trees.

I can draw a scatter graph.

4 Draw a scatter graph for a set of coins with these measurements.

Diameter (mm)	20	25	18	24	21	27	22	28
Thickness (mm)	2	2	1	2	2	2	3	3

A sense of proportion

This work will help you

◆ solve problems that involve quantities in direct proportion
◆ understand the link between graphs and direct proportion

A Double up

Which of these problems can be solved by doubling?

A A recipe for beef stew for four people uses 1 kg of beef.

How much beef would you need to make a stew for eight people?

B A man takes 1 hour to weed his garden.

How long would it take two men to weed this garden?

C £1 can be exchanged for 3 Altarian dollars.

How many Altarian dollars would you get for £2?

D An average two-year-old boy is 84 cm tall.

Find the average height of a four-year-old boy.

E It takes 3 minutes to boil an egg.

How long would it take to boil two eggs?

F Joy takes 2 hours to cycle 30 miles.

How long will it take her to cycle 60 miles?

G Joe needs $1\frac{1}{2}$ litres of paint for a floor with area 6 m².
How much paint is needed for a floor with area 12 m²?

A1 Which of these problems can be solved by halving?

A My recipe for chocolate mousse uses 100 grams of chocolate for four people.
How much chocolate will I need for chocolate mousse for two people?

B My dad weighed 80 kg when he was 40 years old.
How much did he weigh when he was 20 years old?

C It takes 3 hours for John and Margaret to paint their living room.
How long would it have taken John on his own?

D 6 kg is equivalent to about 13.2 pounds.
How many pounds are equivalent to 3 kg?

E It takes Carol about 2 hours to walk 5 miles on a level route.
How long will she take to walk $2\frac{1}{2}$ miles on a level route?

F Jo took 4 hours to climb about 1000 m to the top of the mountain Sgurr Choinnich.
How long would it take her to climb about 500 m to the top of Cracaval?

A2 Some of these problems involve direct proportion and some of them do not.

Solve only those problems that involve direct proportion.

A A recipe for leek soup for six people uses 30 grams of butter.
How much butter would I use to make a pot of leek soup for three people?

B It takes Jim two minutes to do the first question in his maths homework.
How long will it take him to do the next four questions?

C One inch is equivalent to about $2\frac{1}{2}$ cm. My middle finger is 3 inches long.
About how long is it in centimetres?

D A recipe for pink paint mixes 1 tin of red paint with 4 tins of white paint.
How many tins of white would you mix with 2 tins of red?

E It takes me about two hours to hoover and dust my house.
How long would it take three people to do the same job?

B Graphs

- Is the amount of double cream proportional to the number of people?

- Which graph could show the link between the amount of double cream and the number of people?

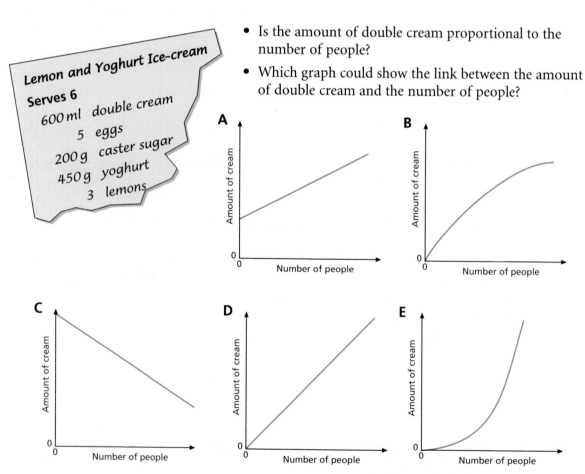

Lemon and Yoghurt Ice-cream

Serves 6

600 ml double cream

5 eggs

200 g caster sugar

450 g yoghurt

3 lemons

B1 One inch is equivalent to 2.54 cm.

(a) Which of the following four graphs shows the link between inches and cm?

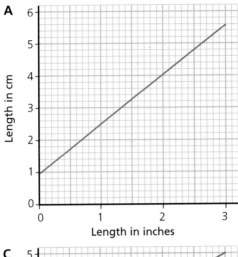

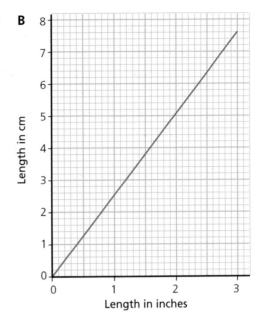

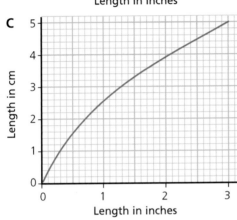

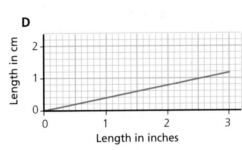

(b) Use the correct graph to estimate the number of centimetres in $1\frac{3}{4}$ inches.

B2 The recipe for lemon and yoghurt ice-cream for 6 people uses 200 grams of caster sugar.

(a) How much caster sugar would you need to make ice-cream for 12 people?

(b) Draw a graph of the amount of sugar against the number of people.

Use the scales on the right.

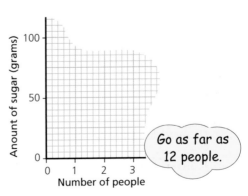

Go as far as 12 people.

(c) Use your graph to estimate the amount of sugar needed for ice-cream for

(i) 4 people   (ii) 10 people

C Conversion graphs

5 miles is approximately the same as 8 kilometres.

From this we can make a table of values …

Miles	0	5	10	15	20	25
Kilometres	0	8	16	24	32	40

… and draw a **conversion graph**.

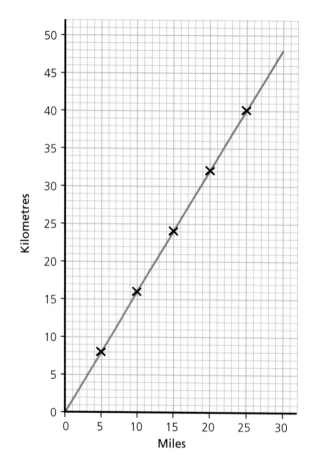

- Use the graph to convert 12 miles to kilometres.

- Use the graph to convert 43 kilometres to miles.

- Is the number of kilometres directly proportional to the number of miles?

- Which two rules below correctly link the number of kilometres (k) with the number of miles (m)?

$$k = \frac{m}{5} \times 8 \qquad k = \frac{m}{8} \times 5$$

$$k = m \times 0.625 \qquad k = m \times 1.6$$

C1 Use the graph to convert
   (a) 23 miles to kilometres
   (b) 45 kilometres to miles
   (c) 18 miles to kilometres
   (d) 22 kilometres to miles

C2 Convert 50 miles to kilometres. Show your method clearly.

C3 Convert 64 kilometres to miles. Show your method clearly.

This is a conversion graph (November 2001) for US dollars ($) and pounds sterling (£).

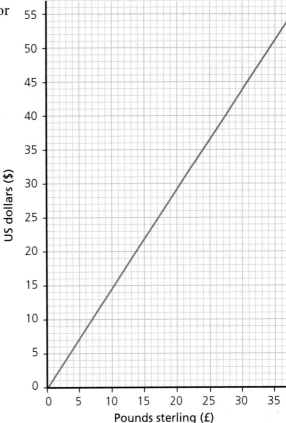

C4 Use the graph to convert
  (a) £15 to US dollars
  (b) $40 to pounds sterling

C5 An airport shop shows its prices in pounds sterling (£) and in US dollars ($).
  Use the graph to find the missing prices on these tickets.

  (a) Digital watch
       £35 / $......

  (b) Make-up bag
       £...... / $23

  (c) Perfume
       £11 / $......

C6 Find the current conversion rate for pounds sterling to US dollars.
  Draw a conversion graph for this rate.
  Make up some questions like those in C5 and ask someone else to try them.

C7 Large areas can be measured in square miles or square kilometres (km²).
  50 square miles is approximately equal to 130 km².

  (a) Draw a conversion graph for converting areas up to 50 square miles.
  (b) Use the graph to convert
    (i) 37 square miles to km²   (ii) 80 km² to square miles
  (c) Which rule below links the number of square miles (m) to the number of km² (k)?

  $$k = \frac{m}{50} \times 130 \qquad k = \frac{m}{130} \times 50$$

D The unitary method

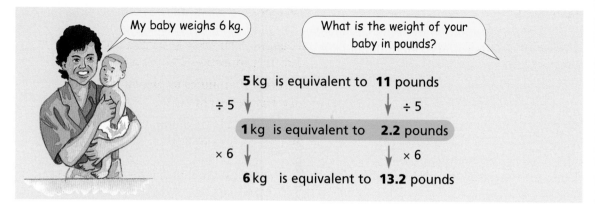

My baby weighs 6 kg.

What is the weight of your baby in pounds?

5 kg is equivalent to **11** pounds

÷ 5 ↓   ↓ ÷ 5

1 kg is equivalent to **2.2** pounds

× 6 ↓   ↓ × 6

6 kg is equivalent to **13.2** pounds

D1 A photocopier prints 220 copies in 4 minutes.
   (a) How many copies will it print in 1 minute?
   (b) How many copies will it print in 7 minutes?

D2 5 identical bricks weigh 14 kg.
   (a) What is the weight of 1 brick?
   (b) How much do 12 of these bricks weigh?

D3 8 pizzas cost £40.
   What will 5 pizzas cost?

D4 Jane changed £50 for 80 euros.
   Fiona changes £85 into euros. How many euros will she get?

D5 24 copies of a new book weigh 7.8 kg.
   How much will 55 of these books weigh, correct to one decimal place?

D6 Alice used 6.5 kg of grass seed to plant a lawn of area 150 m^2.
   How much grass seed would she need to plant a lawn of area 48 m^2?
   Give your answer correct to 1 d.p.

D7 These two pieces of metal are cut from the same sheet.
   The smaller piece weighs 8 kg.

   2.5 m

   4 m

   4 m

   6 m

   How much does the larger piece weigh?

D8 Josh painted a wall of area 35 m^2 and used 2.5 litres of paint.
   What area of wall could he paint with 9 litres of paint?

What progress have you made?

Statement

I can solve problems involving direct proportion.

I can use conversion graphs.

Evidence

1   The time Alan takes to paint a floor is directly proportional to the area.

  He takes 40 minutes to paint a floor that has an area of $16\,m^2$.

  How long will it take him to paint a floor that has an area of $8\,m^2$?

2   This is a conversion graph for litres and pints.

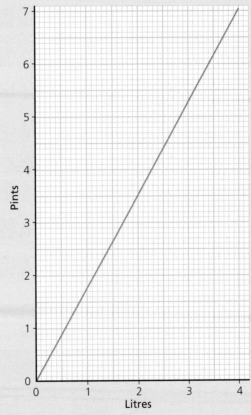

Use the graph to convert

(a) 3 litres to pints   (b) 1.7 litres to pints

(c) 6 pints to litres   (d) 2.5 pints to litres

I can solve problems involving direct proportion using the unitary method.

3   13 bottles of wine weigh 15.6 kg.
  What do 30 of these bottles weigh?

4   In March 2001, £10 was worth 24 Swiss francs
  How much was £26.50 worth in Swiss francs?

28 Fractions

This work will help you

- ◆ find equivalent fractions
- ◆ add, subtract and compare fractions
- ◆ multiply and divide using fractions

A Equivalent fractions

The fractions shown in green are **equivalent** to one another.

$$\frac{1}{3} = \frac{2}{6} = \frac{3}{9} = \frac{4}{12}$$

- Give some other fractions that are equivalent to $\frac{1}{3}$.

- Give some fractions that are equivalent to $\frac{2}{3}$.

$\frac{1}{3}$

$\frac{2}{6}$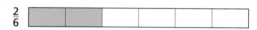

$\frac{3}{9}$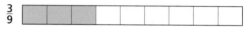

$\frac{4}{12}$

The fractions shown in red are equivalent to one another.

- Give some other fractions that are equivalent to $\frac{3}{5}$.

$\frac{3}{5}$

$\frac{6}{10}$

$\frac{9}{15}$

A1 Write some fractions equivalent to $\frac{1}{2}$.

A2 Which statement matches this diagram?

$$\frac{1}{3} = \frac{3}{9}$$

$$\frac{3}{4} = \frac{9}{12}$$

$$\frac{3}{6} = \frac{9}{18}$$

 =

A3 Draw a similar diagram to show that $\frac{3}{4} = \frac{6}{8}$.

A4 Use these diagrams to find the missing numbers here.

(a) $\frac{1}{6} = \frac{\square}{12}$

(b) $\frac{1}{\square} = \frac{3}{12}$

(c) $\frac{\square}{6} = \frac{10}{12}$

sixths

twelfths

quarters

This scale from 0 to to 1 is divided into fifths and twentieths.

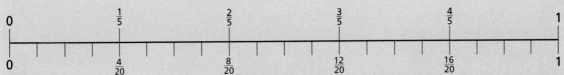

You can see that there are 4 twentieths in 1 fifth.

So you can change from fifths to twentieths by multiplying
the numerator (on top) and the denominator (on the bottom) by 4.

To change twentieths to fifths, divide numerator and denominator by 4.

Going from $\frac{12}{20}$ to the equivalent fraction $\frac{3}{5}$ is called **simplifying**.
A fraction which cannot be simplified any more is in its **simplest form**.

A5 Copy these and fill in the missing numbers.

(a) $\frac{1}{8} = \frac{?}{16}$ (b) $\frac{4}{5} = \frac{?}{15}$ (c) $\frac{2}{3} = \frac{12}{?}$ (d) $\frac{3}{8} = \frac{12}{?}$

(e) $\frac{25}{40} = \frac{?}{8}$ (f) $\frac{16}{24} = \frac{2}{?}$ (g) $\frac{18}{30} = \frac{?}{5}$ (h) $\frac{45}{75} = \frac{3}{?}$

(i) $\frac{1}{3} = \frac{4}{?}$ (j) $\frac{1}{5} = \frac{6}{?}$ (k) $\frac{1}{7} = \frac{?}{28}$ (l) $\frac{1}{10} = \frac{?}{50}$

(m) $\frac{3}{4} = \frac{?}{20}$ (n) $\frac{2}{9} = \frac{4}{?}$ (o) $\frac{5}{8} = \frac{?}{32}$ (p) $\frac{4}{11} = \frac{24}{?}$

A6 There are three sets of equivalent fractions muddled up here.
Can you sort them out?

$\frac{9}{24}$ $\frac{8}{10}$ $\frac{2}{3}$ $\frac{3}{8}$ $\frac{4}{5}$ $\frac{10}{15}$ $\frac{16}{20}$ $\frac{8}{12}$ $\frac{6}{16}$

A7 Simplify each of these fractions as far as possible.

(a) $\frac{4}{6}$ (b) $\frac{6}{12}$ (c) $\frac{15}{20}$ (d) $\frac{8}{16}$ (e) $\frac{18}{21}$

(f) $\frac{18}{45}$ (g) $\frac{10}{35}$ (h) $\frac{16}{20}$ (i) $\frac{16}{24}$ (j) $\frac{12}{60}$

A8 Simplify each of these fractions as far as possible.
One of them cannot be simplified – which one?

(a) $\frac{4}{12}$ (b) $\frac{20}{45}$ (c) $\frac{30}{50}$ (d) $\frac{28}{42}$ (e) $\frac{18}{54}$

(f) $\frac{9}{16}$ (g) $\frac{24}{30}$ (h) $\frac{24}{32}$ (i) $\frac{15}{35}$ (j) $\frac{25}{60}$

B Adding, subtracting and comparing

Adding and subtracting are straightforward when
the fractions have the same denominators (bottom numbers).

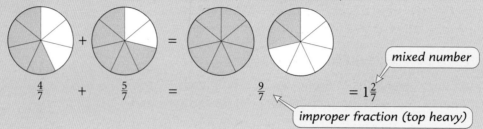

$$\frac{4}{7} + \frac{5}{7} = \frac{9}{7} = 1\frac{2}{7}$$

mixed number

improper fraction (top heavy)

B1 Work these out. Simplify your answers where possible
and write any improper fractions as mixed numbers.

(a) $\frac{1}{5} + \frac{3}{5}$ (b) $\frac{4}{7} - \frac{1}{7}$ (c) $\frac{7}{12} + \frac{1}{12}$ (d) $\frac{8}{9} + \frac{5}{9}$ (e) $\frac{7}{8} + \frac{3}{8}$

B2 Rebecca drinks $\frac{5}{8}$ of a can of lemonade. What fraction of the drink is left?

When one fraction's denominator is a multiple of the other,
you can use equivalent fractions to add or subtract.

For example, $\frac{1}{2} + \frac{3}{8} = \frac{4}{8} + \frac{3}{8} = \frac{7}{8}$

B3 Work these out.

(a) $\frac{2}{3} + \frac{1}{6}$ (b) $\frac{3}{4} - \frac{1}{8}$ (c) $\frac{3}{5} + \frac{1}{10}$ (d) $\frac{1}{4} + \frac{1}{16}$ (e) $\frac{5}{9} - \frac{1}{3}$

B4 Work these out. Simplify your answers where possible
and write any improper fractions as mixed numbers.

(a) $\frac{1}{2} + \frac{3}{16}$ (b) $\frac{4}{5} - \frac{3}{10}$ (c) $\frac{7}{12} + \frac{5}{6}$ (d) $\frac{5}{6} + \frac{2}{3}$ (e) $\frac{1}{4} + \frac{11}{12}$

Adding and subtracting fractions involve more work
when one denominator is not a multiple of the other.

B5 This strip has 12 equal parts.

Here $\frac{1}{3}$ of the strip is coloured.

Now an extra $\frac{1}{4}$ is coloured.

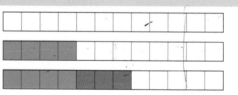

(a) What single fraction of the strip is $\frac{1}{3} + \frac{1}{4}$?

(b) What single fraction of the strip is $\frac{1}{3} - \frac{1}{4}$?

B6 Work these out, using the strip above if you like.

(a) $\frac{1}{4} + \frac{2}{3}$ (b) $\frac{2}{3} - \frac{1}{4}$ (c) $\frac{3}{4} - \frac{1}{3}$ (d) $\frac{3}{4} - \frac{2}{3}$

B7 Explain why it is helpful to think of a strip with 12 equal parts
when you want to add or subtract quarters and thirds.

B8 (a) Sketch a suitable strip for doing $\frac{1}{2} + \frac{1}{5}$.

(b) Write $\frac{1}{2} + \frac{1}{5}$ as a single fraction.

(c) Write $\frac{1}{2} - \frac{1}{5}$ as a single fraction.

(d) Write some other fraction additions and subtractions that can be done with this strip, and work out the answers.

B9 (a) Sketch a suitable strip for doing $\frac{2}{3} - \frac{1}{5}$.

(b) Write $\frac{2}{3} - \frac{1}{5}$ as a single fraction.

(c) Write $\frac{2}{3} + \frac{1}{5}$ as a single fraction.

(d) Write some other fraction additions and subtractions that can be done with this strip, and work out the answers.

B10 Work these out. Sketch or imagine suitable strips.

(a) $\frac{1}{5} + \frac{1}{4}$ (b) $\frac{1}{2} - \frac{1}{3}$ (c) $\frac{1}{8} + \frac{2}{3}$ (d) $\frac{2}{3} - \frac{1}{2}$ (e) $\frac{1}{3} + \frac{1}{10}$

(f) $\frac{1}{5} - \frac{1}{6}$ (g) $\frac{7}{10} - \frac{1}{3}$ (h) $\frac{3}{10} - \frac{1}{4}$ (i) $\frac{3}{8} - \frac{1}{3}$ (j) $\frac{2}{5} + \frac{1}{6}$

In the questions with the strips, you have been using equivalent fractions to make denominators the same before you add or subtract.

We call this 'finding a common denominator'.

You can set your work out like this.

$$\frac{3}{5} + \frac{1}{3} = \frac{9}{15} + \frac{5}{15} = \frac{14}{15}$$

B11 Work these out.

(a) $\frac{3}{8} + \frac{1}{5}$ (b) $\frac{2}{5} + \frac{1}{4}$ (c) $\frac{3}{4} - \frac{3}{5}$ (d) $\frac{5}{6} - \frac{3}{5}$ (e) $\frac{7}{8} - \frac{2}{3}$

B12 Work these out. Simplify your answers where possible and write any improper fractions as mixed numbers.

(a) $\frac{1}{12} + \frac{2}{3}$ (b) $\frac{1}{6} + \frac{3}{8}$ (c) $\frac{5}{6} + \frac{1}{4}$ (d) $\frac{7}{10} - \frac{4}{15}$ (e) $\frac{1}{2} + \frac{1}{3} + \frac{1}{4}$

B13 (a) What do the fractions in the top row add up to here?

(b) Copy the grid and complete it to make a magic square. Every row, every column and the two diagonals must have the same total.

$\frac{2}{5}$	$\frac{3}{20}$	$\frac{1}{5}$
	$\frac{1}{4}$	

*B14 A spider is at the bottom of a pit 2 metres deep.
One morning it starts to climb up the wall of the pit.
It climbs $\frac{2}{3}$ metre each day, then drops back $\frac{1}{5}$ metre at night.
When will it get to the top of the pit?

Comparing fractions

It is easy to see that $\frac{3}{5}$ is greater than $\frac{2}{5}$, because both fractions have the same denominator.

It is not so easy to see whether $\frac{3}{5}$ is greater or less than $\frac{2}{3}$.

One way to compare them is to change them to a pair of fractions with the same denominator (as you did when adding or subtracting).

$$\frac{3}{5} = \frac{9}{15}$$

$$\frac{2}{3} = \frac{10}{15}$$

So $\frac{3}{5}$ is less than $\frac{2}{3}$.

B15 Show which is the larger fraction in each of these pairs.

    (a) $\frac{1}{3}$ or $\frac{3}{8}$ (b) $\frac{2}{3}$ or $\frac{5}{8}$ (c) $\frac{3}{4}$ or $\frac{4}{5}$ (d) $\frac{3}{5}$ or $\frac{5}{8}$ (e) $\frac{3}{7}$ or $\frac{4}{9}$

    (f) $\frac{3}{8}$ or $\frac{4}{11}$ (g) $\frac{4}{7}$ or $\frac{3}{5}$ (h) $\frac{4}{9}$ or $\frac{9}{20}$ (i) $\frac{3}{4}$ or $\frac{7}{9}$ (j) $\frac{5}{7}$ or $\frac{7}{10}$

B16 In each of these, what fraction am I?

    (a) I am between $\frac{1}{2}$ and 1.
         My numerator is 5.
         My denominator is a square number.

    (b) I am greater than $\frac{1}{2}$ and less than $\frac{2}{3}$.
         My denominator is 2 more than my numerator.

    (c) I am between $\frac{1}{4}$ and $\frac{1}{2}$.
         My numerator and denominator add up to 7.

C Multiplying

$4 \times \frac{2}{3}$ means the same as $\frac{2}{3} + \frac{2}{3} + \frac{2}{3} + \frac{2}{3}$, which is $\frac{8}{3}$ or $2\frac{2}{3}$.

Similarly, $5 \times \frac{3}{4} = \frac{15}{4}$ or $3\frac{3}{4}$.

C1 Work these out.

    (a) $6 \times \frac{1}{13}$ (b) $2 \times \frac{2}{5}$ (c) $3 \times \frac{3}{11}$ (d) $5 \times \frac{3}{16}$ (e) $9 \times \frac{1}{9}$

C2 Work these out. Simplify your answers where possible and write any improper fractions as mixed numbers.

    (a) $6 \times \frac{2}{5}$ (b) $8 \times \frac{4}{5}$ (c) $10 \times \frac{3}{8}$ (d) $15 \times \frac{5}{6}$ (e) $12 \times \frac{5}{8}$

C3 (a) Work out $12 \times \frac{2}{3}$.

    (b) Work out $\frac{2}{3}$ of 12. What do you notice?

You can think of $\frac{1}{3}$ of 7 like this.

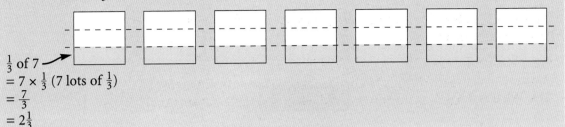

$\frac{1}{3}$ of 7
$= 7 \times \frac{1}{3}$ (7 lots of $\frac{1}{3}$)
$= \frac{7}{3}$
$= 2\frac{1}{3}$

C4 (a) Make a sketch of this diagram and shade it to show $\frac{1}{3}$ of 5.

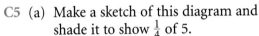

(b) Write $\frac{1}{3}$ of 5 as an improper fraction.

(c) Write $\frac{1}{3}$ of 5 as a mixed number.

C5 (a) Make a sketch of this diagram and shade it to show $\frac{1}{4}$ of 5.

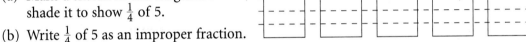

(b) Write $\frac{1}{4}$ of 5 as an improper fraction.

(c) Write $\frac{1}{4}$ of 5 as a mixed number.

C6 Work these out, giving each answer as a mixed number. Sketch a diagram if it helps.

(a) $\frac{1}{3}$ of 11 (b) $\frac{1}{4}$ of 9 (c) $\frac{1}{5}$ of 12 (d) $\frac{1}{8}$ of 15

You can think of $\frac{3}{4}$ of 5 like this.

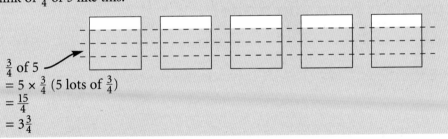

$\frac{3}{4}$ of 5
$= 5 \times \frac{3}{4}$ (5 lots of $\frac{3}{4}$)
$= \frac{15}{4}$
$= 3\frac{3}{4}$

C7 (a) Make a sketch of this diagram and shade it to show $\frac{2}{3}$ of 2.

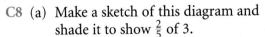

(b) Write $\frac{2}{3}$ of 2 as an improper fraction.

(c) Write $\frac{2}{3}$ of 2 as a mixed number.

C8 (a) Make a sketch of this diagram and shade it to show $\frac{2}{5}$ of 3.

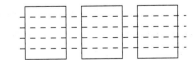

(b) Write $\frac{2}{5}$ of 3 as an improper fraction.

(c) Write $\frac{2}{5}$ of 3 as a mixed number.

C9 Work these out, giving each answer as a mixed number. Sketch a diagram if it helps.

(a) $\frac{2}{3}$ of 4 (b) $\frac{3}{4}$ of 7 (c) $\frac{2}{5}$ of 4 (d) $\frac{3}{8}$ of 11

D Dividing a whole number by a fraction

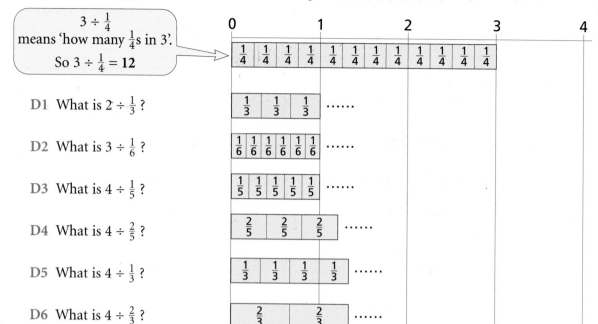

$3 \div \frac{1}{4}$
means 'how many $\frac{1}{4}$s in 3'.
So $3 \div \frac{1}{4} = 12$

D1 What is $2 \div \frac{1}{3}$?

D2 What is $3 \div \frac{1}{6}$?

D3 What is $4 \div \frac{1}{5}$?

D4 What is $4 \div \frac{2}{5}$?

D5 What is $4 \div \frac{1}{3}$?

D6 What is $4 \div \frac{2}{3}$?

D7 You can do these in a similar way, by imagining the diagrams.

(a) $6 \div \frac{1}{4}$ (b) $3 \div \frac{3}{4}$ (c) $6 \div \frac{3}{4}$ (d) $2 \div \frac{2}{3}$ (e) $6 \div \frac{1}{3}$

What progress have you made?

Statement	Evidence

Statement

I can simplify fractions.

Evidence

1 Simplify these as far as possible.

(a) $\frac{24}{30}$ (b) $\frac{27}{36}$

I can put fractions in order of size.

2 Which is larger, $\frac{5}{8}$ or $\frac{4}{7}$? Show your working.

I can add and subtract fractions.

3 Work these out.

(a) $\frac{1}{8} + \frac{1}{4}$ (b) $\frac{1}{3} + \frac{1}{10}$ (c) $\frac{2}{5} - \frac{1}{4}$

4 Give your answers to these as mixed numbers in their simplest form.

(a) $\frac{13}{15} + \frac{11}{15}$ (b) $\frac{7}{9} + \frac{3}{4}$ (c) $\frac{1}{3} + \frac{3}{4}$

I can multiply a whole number by a fraction.

5 Work these out.

(a) $15 \times \frac{3}{4}$ (b) $6 \times \frac{7}{8}$ (c) $7 \times \frac{2}{3}$

I can divide a whole number by a fraction.

6 Work these out.

(a) $12 \div \frac{1}{6}$ (b) $8 \div \frac{2}{3}$ (c) $8 \div \frac{4}{5}$

㉙ Constructions

This is about drawing accurately.
The work will help you

◆ draw triangles accurately

◆ use drawing methods involving ruler and compasses only

A Drawing triangles

The way to draw a triangle accurately depends on the information you are given.

Two angles and the side between them given

Draw the side accurately.
Mark the angles with an angle measurer.
Extend the arms of the angles to get the triangle.

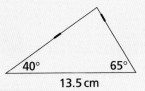

40° 65°
13.5 cm

Two sides and the angle between them given

Draw one side accurately.
Mark the angle with an angle measurer.
Draw the arm of the angle the right length.
Join up the third side.

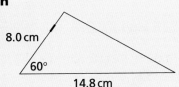

8.0 cm
60°
14.8 cm

Three sides given

Draw one side accurately.
Draw an arc with its centre at one end of this line
and your compasses set to another side's length.
Draw an arc for the third side centred at the other end of the line.
Join up the triangle.

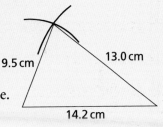

9.5 cm 13.0 cm
14.2 cm

A1 For each of these, draw the triangle accurately, label the vertices with their letters,
then measure and record the missing lengths and angles.

(a)

P
9.4 cm
38° Q
R 10.5 cm

(b)

A 11.2 cm
B
5.6 cm
9.8 cm
C

(c)

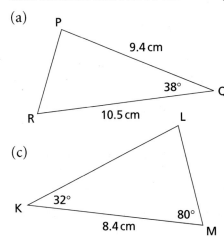

L
K 32°
80° M
8.4 cm

(d)

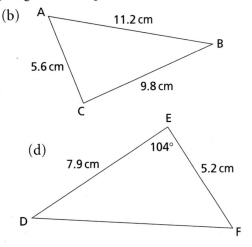

E 104°
7.9 cm 5.2 cm
D F

207

A2 For each of these triangles, draw a sketch showing the lengths and angles, then make an accurate drawing.

    (a) triangle ABC with AB = 6.3 cm, BC = 7.4 cm and AC = 10.5 cm

    (b) triangle PQR with PQ = 4.2 cm, PR = 8.0 cm and angle P = 90°

    (c) triangle LMN with LN = 7.5 cm, angle L = 65° and angle N = 50°

A3 Is it possible to draw triangles from this information? Try to do so.

    (a)

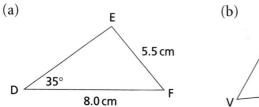

    (b)

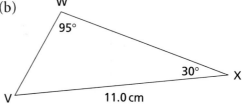

B Constructions with ruler and compasses

Construction 1

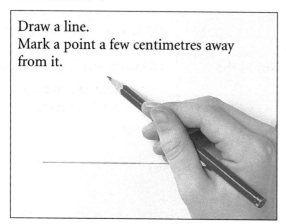

Draw a line.
Mark a point a few centimetres away from it.

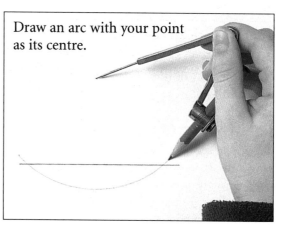

Draw an arc with your point as its centre.

Put the point of the compasses at one of the points where your arc crosses the line.

Draw an arc below the line.
You need not use the same radius as before.

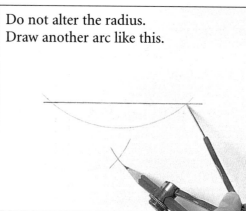

Do not alter the radius.
Draw another arc like this.

Draw a line from your original point to where the last pair of arcs cross.

• What can you say about this line?

Construction 2

Draw a line.
Draw an arc about this big with its centre at one end of the line.

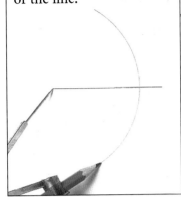

Keep your compasses the same radius.
Draw an arc with its centre at the other end of the line.

Draw a line through the points where the arcs cross.

• What can you say about this line?

Construction 3

Draw an angle about this size. Draw an arc with its centre at the vertex of the angle.

Draw two arcs with the same radius from the points where your first arc crosses the arms of the angle.

Draw a line from the vertex of the angle to the point where the last two arcs cross.

• What can you say about this line?

Construction 4

Draw a line and mark a point on it.
Draw arcs with the same radius and their centre at the point.

Draw two arcs with equal radius from the points where your first arcs cross the line.

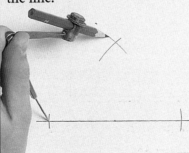

Draw a line from the marked point to the point where the last two arcs cross.

• What can you say about this line?

These are what the constructions on the last two pages give.

Construction 1: the perpendicular from a point to a line

Construction 2: the perpendicular bisector of a line

Construction 3: the bisector of an angle

Construction 4: the perpendicular to a line from a point on it

Select the constructions you need to answer these questions.

B1 Draw a right-angled triangle ABC, with the right angle at B.

Draw the perpendicular bisector of AB and of BC.

Where do the bisectors meet?

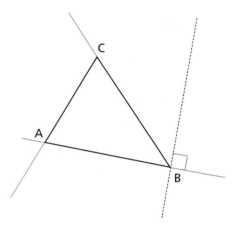

B2 Draw a triangle ABC and extend the sides AB, BC, CA as shown.

At B, construct a line perpendicular to AB.

At C, construct a line perpendicular to BC.

At A, construct a line perpendicular to CA.

Extend each of these lines (if necessary) to make a large triangle.

Measure the angles of this large triangle and the angles of the original triangle.
What do you find?

What progress have you made?

Statement	Evidence
I can draw a triangle accurately from given information.	1 Draw this triangle accurately. 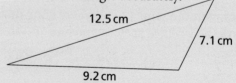

2 Draw triangle PQR, with QR = 8.5 cm, angle Q = 80° and angle R = 25°.

Statement	Evidence
I can do constructions using ruler and compasses only.	3 Draw an angle ABC. Construct the bisector of angle ABC.

30 Division

This work will help you

♦ divide without using a calculator

♦ estimate the answers to divisions

A Simplifying divisions

Another way to write $6 \div 2 = 3$ is like this. $\frac{6}{2} = 3$

You can often simplify a division by dividing 'top and bottom' by the same number.

$$\frac{120}{24} \xrightarrow[\div 4]{\div 4} = \frac{30}{6} = 5 \qquad \frac{900}{18} \xrightarrow[\div 3]{\div 3} = \frac{300}{6} \xrightarrow[\div 3]{\div 3} = \frac{100}{2} = 50$$

When dividing large numbers it often helps to divide top and bottom by 10 or 100.

$$\frac{6000}{20} \xrightarrow[\div 10]{\div 10} = \frac{600}{2} = 300 \qquad \frac{9000}{300} \xrightarrow[\div 100]{\div 100} = \frac{90}{3} = 30$$

Work these out.

A1 (a) $\frac{60}{15}$ (b) $\frac{90}{15}$ (c) $\frac{72}{18}$ (d) $\frac{54}{18}$ (e) $\frac{42}{14}$

(f) $\frac{125}{25}$ (g) $\frac{120}{15}$ (h) $\frac{96}{16}$ (i) $\frac{300}{75}$ (j) $\frac{150}{25}$

A2 (a) $\frac{800}{40}$ (b) $\frac{150}{30}$ (c) $\frac{2400}{60}$ (d) $\frac{18\,000}{60}$ (e) $\frac{2000}{40}$

(f) $\frac{3500}{500}$ (g) $\frac{32\,000}{400}$ (h) $\frac{1600}{40}$ (i) $\frac{3600}{900}$ (j) $\frac{27\,000}{30}$

A3 (a) $\frac{800}{16}$ (b) $\frac{800}{160}$ (c) $\frac{1500}{25}$ (d) $\frac{1800}{120}$ (e) $\frac{2000}{80}$

(f) $\frac{7500}{150}$ (g) $\frac{36\,000}{120}$ (h) $\frac{7200}{360}$ (i) $\frac{8000}{320}$ (j) $\frac{24\,000}{480}$

B Division with a decimal result

Examples

$\frac{6}{20}$ $\overset{\div 2}{\underset{\div 2}{=}}$ $\frac{3}{10}$ = 0.3 or $\frac{6}{20}$ $\overset{\div 10}{\underset{\div 10}{=}}$ $\frac{0.6}{2}$ = 0.3

$\frac{0.6}{20}$ $\overset{\div 2}{\underset{\div 2}{=}}$ $\frac{0.3}{10}$ = 0.03 or $\frac{0.6}{20}$ $\overset{\div 10}{\underset{\div 10}{=}}$ $\frac{0.06}{2}$ = 0.03

Work these out as decimals.

B1 (a) $\frac{4}{20}$ (b) $\frac{16}{80}$ (c) $\frac{15}{50}$ (d) $\frac{32}{40}$ (e) $\frac{24}{60}$

(f) $\frac{24}{30}$ (g) $\frac{14}{200}$ (h) $\frac{24}{400}$ (i) $\frac{120}{300}$ (j) $\frac{150}{500}$

B2 (a) $\frac{1.2}{20}$ (b) $\frac{1.5}{30}$ (c) $\frac{1.2}{60}$ (d) $\frac{0.8}{40}$ (e) $\frac{0.2}{50}$

With some divisions you cannot just 'see' the answer.
You can set out working like this.

$\frac{5}{8} = 5 \div 8$
$= 0.625$

$$\begin{array}{r} 0.6\ 2\ 5 \\ 8\overline{)5.0^2 0^4 0} \end{array}$$

B3 Work out   (a) $\frac{3}{8}$ (b) $\frac{7}{8}$

When you work out $\frac{1}{3}$ as a decimal, the calculation goes on for ever.
0.3333... is called a **recurring decimal**.

$$\begin{array}{r} 0.3\ 3\ 3\ 3\ 3\ ... \\ 3\overline{)1.0^1 0^1 0^1 0^1 0}\ ... \end{array}$$

B4 Change $\frac{2}{3}$ to a recurring decimal.

B5 (a) Work out $\frac{1}{9}$ as a recurring decimal.
(b) Repeat for $\frac{2}{9}$, $\frac{3}{9}$, ... and so on.

B6 When you work out $\frac{1}{7}$ as a recurring decimal, a group of figures recurs.

$$\begin{array}{r} 0.1\ 4\ 2\ 8\ 5\ 7\ 1\ 4\ 2\ 8\ 5\ 7\ 1\ ... \\ 7\overline{)1.0^3 0^2 0^6 0^4 0^5 0^1 0^3 0^2 0^6 0^4 0^5 0^1 0}\ ... \end{array}$$

Work out the recurring decimals for $\frac{2}{7}$, $\frac{3}{7}$, ... What do you notice?

C Dividing by a decimal

Sometimes you may need to divide by a decimal.

You can often change it to a whole number by multiplying 'top and bottom' by 10 or 100.

Examples

$$\frac{8}{0.2} \xrightarrow{\times 10} = \frac{80}{2} = 40 \qquad\qquad \frac{70}{0.1} \xrightarrow{\times 10} = \frac{700}{1} = 700$$

$$\frac{0.05}{0.01} \xrightarrow{\times 100} = \frac{5}{1} = 5 \qquad\qquad \frac{1.5}{0.03} \xrightarrow{\times 100} = \frac{150}{3} = 30$$

Work these out.

C1 (a) $\dfrac{6}{0.3}$ (b) $\dfrac{12}{0.2}$ (c) $\dfrac{18}{0.6}$ (d) $\dfrac{30}{0.1}$ (e) $\dfrac{2.4}{0.3}$

(f) $\dfrac{1.4}{0.2}$ (g) $\dfrac{3.2}{0.8}$ (h) $\dfrac{0.18}{0.3}$ (i) $\dfrac{0.06}{0.3}$ (j) $\dfrac{120}{0.4}$

C2 (a) $\dfrac{1.2}{0.03}$ (b) $\dfrac{2.8}{0.04}$ (c) $\dfrac{16}{0.08}$ (d) $\dfrac{0.8}{0.02}$ (e) $\dfrac{8}{0.04}$

(f) $\dfrac{0.6}{0.3}$ (g) $\dfrac{4}{0.05}$ (h) $\dfrac{0.15}{0.03}$ (i) $\dfrac{3}{0.01}$ (j) $\dfrac{28}{0.07}$

C3 For each of these problems,

- write the division that is needed
- work out the result
- check that your result gives a sensible answer to the original problem

(a) How many bottles of capacity 0.5 litre can be filled from a barrel containing 120 litres?

(b) A pizza weighing 0.2 kg is divided into 4 equal parts. What does each part weigh?

(c) How many lengths of copper pipe 0.25 m long can be cut from a pipe 3.0 m long?

(d) A certain stroboscope can flash every 0.03 second. How many times can it flash in 6 seconds?

(e) An ingot of gold weighing 0.4 kg is sold for £2400.00. Express this as a cost per kilogram.

D Rough estimates

You can get a rough estimate for a division by rounding the numbers to one significant figure.

Examples $\dfrac{785}{42}$ Rounding to one significant figure,

785 becomes 800

42 becomes 40

$\dfrac{800}{40} = \dfrac{80}{4} = 20$

$\dfrac{6.18}{0.17}$ Rounding to one significant figure,

6.18 becomes 6

0.17 becomes 0.2

$\dfrac{6}{0.2} = \dfrac{60}{2} = 30$

D1 Work out a rough estimate for each of these divisions.

(a) $\dfrac{621}{33}$ (b) $\dfrac{784}{39}$ (c) $\dfrac{5908}{28}$ (d) $\dfrac{32\,554}{614}$ (e) $\dfrac{8837}{32}$

(f) $\dfrac{2186}{479}$ (g) $\dfrac{81\,602}{378}$ (h) $\dfrac{77}{223}$ (i) $\dfrac{83}{1052}$ (j) $\dfrac{27\,660}{58}$

D2 Work out a rough estimate for each of these divisions.

(a) $\dfrac{42.1}{5.1}$ (b) $\dfrac{78.4}{3.9}$ (c) $\dfrac{392.8}{18.3}$ (d) $\dfrac{6.135}{19.7}$ (e) $\dfrac{5.88}{0.32}$

(f) $\dfrac{22.16}{0.48}$ (g) $\dfrac{58.32}{0.318}$ (h) $\dfrac{0.885}{2.89}$ (i) $\dfrac{1.893}{0.049}$ (j) $\dfrac{2.68}{0.058}$

D3 Estimate

(a) how many pieces of length 0.42 m can be cut from a strip of wood 7.85 m long

(b) how many glasses of capacity 0.32 litre can be filled from a jug holding 9.4 litres

(c) how many pieces of weight 0.575 kg can be cut from a cheese weighing 28.4 kg

What progress have you made?

Statement	Evidence
I can do divisions like $\dfrac{3600}{60}$, $\dfrac{36}{600}$, $\dfrac{36}{0.6}$ without a calculator.	1 Work out (a) $\dfrac{3600}{60}$ (b) $\dfrac{36}{600}$ (c) $\dfrac{36}{0.6}$ (d) $\dfrac{0.28}{0.4}$
I can estimate a division by rounding to one significant figure.	2 Work out a rough estimate for (a) $\dfrac{1895}{76}$ (b) $\dfrac{78}{396}$ (c) $\dfrac{58.4}{2.77}$ (d) $\dfrac{6.28}{0.31}$

31 Indices

This work will help you

♦ use a factor tree to write a number as a product of primes

♦ find the value of expressions such as 2^4 and 3^5

♦ find the value of expressions such as 5×10^4

♦ write, for example, $2^5 \times 2^3$ and $2^5 \div 2^3$ in the form $2^\blacksquare$

A Factor trees

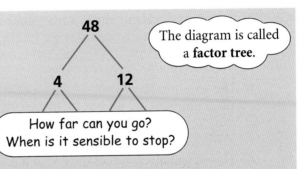

• Start with the number 48.

Think of a pair of factors that make 48, for example, 4 and 12.

Now do the same for 4 and 12.

The diagram is called a **factor tree**.

How far can you go?
When is it sensible to stop?

• Can you use your factor tree to write 48 as a **product of prime numbers**?

A1 (a) A factor tree for 40 can be started in different ways.
Here is one way.
Copy and finish the tree.

(b) Now start the tree in different ways and finish each one.
Do all the trees end with the same numbers?

A2 Make a factor tree for 24.

A3 Copy and complete these factor trees.

(a) 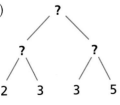 (b) 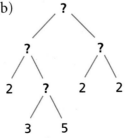 (c)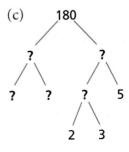

215

A4 (a) Make a factor tree for 36.

(b) Copy and complete the statement below to write 36 as a product of prime numbers.

36 = ☐ × ☐ × ☐ × ☐

A5 For each number below, make a factor tree and use it to write the number as a product of primes.

(a) 28   (b) 300   (c) 33   (d) 64

A6 Find the missing prime number in each of these products.

(a) $20 = 2 \times 2 \times$ ■

(b) $24 = 2 \times 2 \times$ ■ $\times 3$

(c) $30 = 2 \times$ ■ $\times 5$

(d) $54 =$ ■ $\times 3 \times 3 \times 3$

A7 Written as products of primes, some numbers use a mixture of 2s and 5s only. List all the numbers like this that are less than 100.

A8 (a) Write 70 as a product of primes.

(b) Use your product to decide which of these numbers are factors of 70.

*A9 (a) Write 198 as a product of primes.

(b) How does your product show that 6 is a factor of 198?

*A10 (a) Write 175 as a product of primes.

(b) How does your product show that 15 is **not** a factor of 175?

B Index notation

- Finish the factor tree for 243.

- Write 243 as a product of prime numbers.

- Can you think of a shorter way to write this product?

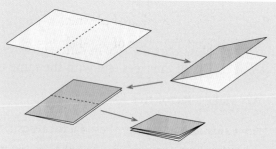

- Can you find a link between the number of times the paper is folded and the thickness?

Do not use a calculator for questions B1 to B6.

B1 Which of the expressions below is equivalent to 5^4?

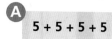
A   5 + 5 + 5 + 5

B   5 × 4

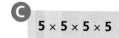
C   5 × 5 × 5 × 5

D   5 + 4

B2 We say 3^5 as 'three to the power five'.

Which expression is equivalent to 'four to the power three'?

 A 4×3 **B** $4 \times 4 \times 4$ **C** $3 \times 3 \times 3 \times 3$ **D** $4 + 4 + 4 + 4$

B3 The product $3 \times 3 \times 3 \times 3$ can be written as 3^4 using indices.

Write these products using indices.

(a) $5 \times 5 \times 5$ (b) $2 \times 2 \times 2 \times 2 \times 2$ (c) $7 \times 7 \times 7 \times 7$

B4 Match each expression on the left with its value on the right.

| 2^4 | 3^2 | 4^3 | 2^3 | | 8 | 16 | 9 | 64 |

B5 Find the value of each of these.

(a) 2^5 (b) 3^4 (c) 4^2 (d) 2^6

B6 What is the value of each of these?

(a) 2^2 (b) 3^3 (c) $2^2 + 3^3$ (d) $2^2 \times 3^3$

B7 Use a calculator to find the value of each of these.

(a) 3^5 (b) 6^4 (c) 2^{10} (d) 5^5

B8 (a) Do you think that 3^8 is greater or less than five thousand?

(b) Check your answer by working out the value of 3^8.

B9 Which is greater, 2^7 or 7^2?

B10 (a) Find the value of a^3 when $a = 6$.

(b) Find the value of x^5 when $x = 7$.

B11 Copy and complete the crossnumber puzzle.

Across	**Down**
1 $3^2 \times 7^2$	**1** $2^5 + 2^3$
4 $3^5 \times 2^2$	**2** 3^9
5 $8^3 + 2^4$	**3** $2^8 \div 2^3$
7 7^3	**5** $5^2 \times 2$
	6 $4^3 - 1^3$

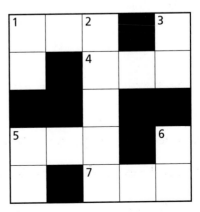

Here is a factor tree for 144.

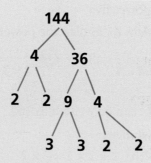

So we can write $144 = 2 \times 2 \times 2 \times 2 \times 3 \times 3$.

Using indices this is $144 = 2^4 \times 3^2$.

B12 (a) Make a factor tree for 360.

(b) Write 360 as a product of prime numbers using indices.

B13 Write the following numbers as products of primes using indices.

(a) 72   (b) 100   (c) 392

B14 What is the missing number in each statement?

(a) $150 = 2 \times 3 \times 5^{\blacksquare}$ (b) $504 = 2^{\blacksquare} \times 3^2 \times 7$

(c) $686 = 2 \times 7^{\blacksquare}$ (d) $375 = 3 \times \blacksquare^3$

C Powers of 10

C1 Copy and complete this table of powers of 10.

10^7	$10 \times 10 \times 10 \times 10 \times 10 \times 10 \times 10$	10 000 000	ten million
10^6	$10 \times 10 \times 10 \times 10 \times 10 \times 10$		
10^5			
10^4			
10^3			
10^2			
10^1			

C2 Match each expression on the left with its value on the right.

A 4×10^2 **B** 40×10^3 **C** 4×10^3 40 000   4000   400

C3 Work out the value of each of these.

(a) 5×10^4 (b) 23×10^3 (c) 20×10^7

C4 Which of these is equivalent to 5 million?

A 5×10^3 **B** 5×10^4 **C** 5×10^5 **D** 5×10^6

C5 Copy and complete this working to find the value of 2.5×10^3.

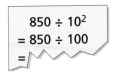

2.5×10^3
$= 2.5 \times 1000$
$=$

C6 Work out the value of each of these.

(a) 1.6×10^2 (b) 1.459×10^3 (c) 34.5×10^4

C7 Copy and complete this working to find the value of $850 \div 10^2$.

$850 \div 10^2$
$= 850 \div 100$
$=$

C8 Work out the value of each of these.

(a) $590 \div 10^2$ (b) $1917.4 \div 10^3$ (c) $3.8 \div 10^2$

Powers of 10 are very important as our number system is based on them.
Some prefixes stand for powers of 10.

For example:
- a **kilo**gram is 10^3 or **1000** or a **thousand** grams
- a **mega**death is 10^6 or **1 000 000** or a **million** deaths
- a **giga**tonne is 10^9 or **1 000 000 000** or a **billion** tonnes

---

C9 My electric fire gives out 2 kilowatts of power.
How many watts is this?

C10 In 1970 about 3 megatonnes of Atlantic cod were caught.
How many tonnes is this?

C11 Mercury is about 60 gigametres from the Sun.
How many metres is this?

C12 Which of these is not equivalent to 5 gigametres?

A 5 thousand million metres   **B** 5 million megametres

C 5000 megametres   **D** 5 million kilometres

D Combining powers

- Which of these can you write as a single power of 2?

A $2^4 \times 2$ **B** $2^4 + 2$ **C** $2^4 \times 2^2$ **D** $2^4 - 2^2$

E $2^3 \times 2^4$ **F** $2^3 \times 3^2$ **G** $2^5 \div 2^2$ **H** $2^4 \div 2$

D1 Write each of these as a single power of 5.

(a) $5^2 \times 5^3$ (b) $5^2 \times 5$ (c) 5×5^4 (d) $5^5 \times 5^2$

D2 What is the missing number in each statement?

(a) $4^\blacksquare \times 4^2 = 4^5$ (b) $7^3 \times 7^\blacksquare = 7^6$ (c) $9 \times 9^\blacksquare = 9^4$

D3 In each diagram, the expression in each square is found by multiplying the two expressions in the circles on either side of it.

Copy and complete each diagram.

(a) 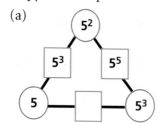 (b) 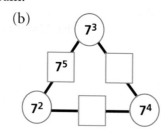 (c)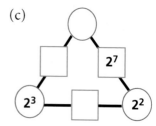

D4 Write each of these as a single power of 3.

(a) $3^3 \div 3$ (b) $3^3 \div 3^2$ (c) $3^4 \div 3$ (d) $3^4 \div 3^2$

D5 Write each of these as a single power of 2, where possible.

(a) $2^2 \times 2^6$ (b) $2^2 + 2^3$ (c) $2^4 \div 2$ (d) $2^4 - 2$

Some **algebraic expressions** involving indices can be simplified.

For example, $a^2 \times a^3 = (a \times a) \times (a \times a \times a)$

$= a \times a \times a \times a \times a$

$= a^5$

D6 Simplify these expressions.

(a) $b^3 \times b^2$ (b) $n^3 \times n^4$ (c) $y \times y^2$ (d) $x^3 \times x$

D7 In each diagram, the expression in each square is found by multiplying the two expressions in the circles on either side of it.

Copy and complete each diagram.

(a)

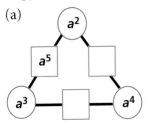

(b)

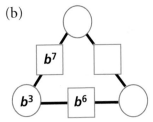

(c)

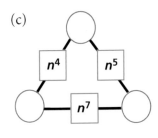

D8 Simplify these expressions.

(a) $a^2 \div a$ (b) $n^3 \div n$ (c) $m^3 \div m^2$ (d) $y^4 \div y^2$

What progress have you made?

Statement	Evidence
I can use a factor tree to write a number as a product of prime numbers.	1 (a) Make a factor tree for 80. (b) Use it to write 80 as a product of primes.
I can use index notation.	2 Write $5 \times 5 \times 5 \times 5 \times 5 \times 5$ using indices. 3 Use a calculator to find the value of these. (a) 2^8 (b) 3^7 (c) 5^4 4 (a) Make a factor tree for 200. (b) Write 200 as a product of primes using indices. 5 Copy and complete the statement below. $500 = 2^2 \times 5^{\blacksquare}$
I can work with powers of 10.	6 Work out the value of these. (a) 3×10^4 (b) 2.1×10^2 (c) $560 \div 10^2$ (d) $42.5 \div 10^3$
I can combine powers.	7 Write each of these as a single power of 2. (a) $2^5 \times 2^2$ (b) $2^3 \times 2$ (c) $2^3 \div 2$ 8 Simplify these expressions. (a) $n^4 \times n^2$ (b) $n \times n^3$ (c) $n^3 \div n^2$

Review 4

1 Copy this shape then enlarge it using

  (a) scale factor 2

  (b) scale factor $\frac{1}{2}$

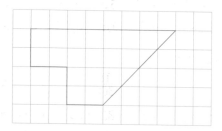

2 The Great Wall of China is 3460 km long.

  How long would this be on a map with scale 1 cm to 100 km?

3 Here are the heights of some plants, measured in centimetres.

15	38	35	21	41	30	18	21	31	28
32	22	12	34	22	40	36	34	24	25

  (a) Make a stem-and-leaf table for these heights.

  (b) What is the range of the heights?

  (c) What is the median height?

4 Write 280 as a product of primes using indices.

5 Round each of these numbers to one significant figure.

  (a) 280   (b) 4125   (c) 48.7   (d) 0.329   (e) 0.0299

6 Solve each of these equations. Show your working.

  (a) $7x + 4 = 3(x + 4)$ (b) $8p + 3 = 5p + 24$ (c) $3z + 16 = 5z$

  (d) $4(d - 2) = 3d + 1$ (e) $6r - 7 = 4r + 15$ (f) $3m - 1 = 7(m - 3)$

7 Here is a design for an earring, and an enlargement of it suitable for a necklace. They are not drawn accurately. Measurements are in centimetres.

  (a) What is the scale factor of the enlargement?

  (b) Work out the missing measurements.

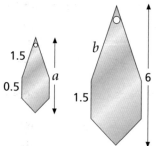

8 Without using a calculator work out the value of each of these.

  (a) 6×10^5 (b) 3.2×10^3 (c) $54.2 \div 10^2$

9 Without using a calculator work these out.

  (a) 0.2×0.4 (b) 40×0.3 (c) 500×0.07 (d) 0.03×0.5

10 A builder's site plan uses a scale of 1 : 400.

    (a) How many metres does 1 cm represent?

    (b) On the plan a wall is 5 cm long. How long will the actual wall be?

    (c) A driveway is to be 50 m long. How long will this be on the plan?

11 Work these out.

    (a) $\frac{7500}{250}$ (b) $\frac{18}{300}$ (c) $\frac{1.6}{40}$ (d) $\frac{0.27}{0.3}$

12 (a) A rectangular field is 82 m by 37 m. Estimate its area roughly.

    (b) A rectangular strip of land of area 38 m² and width 0.82 m is to be used for an experimental crop. Estimate the length of the strip of land roughly.

13 (a) Write down an expression for the perimeter of shape A.

    (b) Write down an expression for the perimeter of shape B.

    (c) The perimeters of the two shapes are the same.
Write down an equation and solve it
to find the value of p.

    (d) What is the perimeter of each shape?

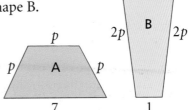

14 These are the weights of 8 clementines.

    (a) Find their mean weight.

    (b) What is the range of their weights?

    (c) The mean weight of 8 mandarin oranges is 181 g and the range is 53 g.
Write two sentences comparing the weights of the two types of orange.

15 Gemma and Kauseen both start with the same number.
Gemma multiplies her number by 6 then subtracts 14.
Kauseen adds 1 to her number then multiplies by 5.
They both end up with the same number.

What number did they start with?

16 Which of these two numbers is larger, and by how much? 2^{10} and 6^4

17 (a) Draw accurately triangle XYZ with XY = 6 cm, angle X = 30° and angle Y = 105°.

    (b) Measure YZ on your drawing.

    (c) Using ruler and compasses only, construct the line from Y that is perpendicular to XZ.

18 £20 was worth 3800 Japanese yen in January 2002.

    (a) How much was £27 worth in yen?

    (b) How much was 9000 yen worth in pounds?

19 Without using a calculator estimate the value of each of these.

(a) 53.2×0.381 (b) 781×21 (c) 319×0.742 (d) 0.039×28.9

20 Some pupils were asked to find the answer to a calculation on a computer.
The computer recorded the time (in seconds) each pupil took. Here are the results.

15.5	20.5	21.0	26.2	23.1	16.5	16.7	14.0
24.2	21.8	25.0	22.3	18.2	17.0	27.9	23.9
18.2	24.7	22.3	14.5	23.0	24.5	19.3	17.7

Make a frequency table and chart for these times. Use intervals of 10–15, 15–20 etc.
Which was the modal interval?

21 Simplify these expressions.

(a) $a^7 \times a^2$ (b) $a \times a^4$ (c) $a^6 \div a^4$

22 This sketch shows the position of three markers,
A, B and C on an orienteering course.

(a) Using a scale of 1 cm to 100 m draw
an accurate diagram showing
the position of the three markers.

(b) Use your diagram to find these bearings.
You may have to draw in some north lines.

  (i) The bearing of B from A

  (ii) The bearing of C from B

(c) Marker X is 430 m from C on a bearing of 250°.
Show the position of X accurately on your diagram.

(d) If Pam ran from A to B to C and straight back to A
how far would she have run?
Give your answer rounded to one significant figure.

23 Do each calculation.

Use the code to change the results into letters

Rearrange the letters to spell a food.

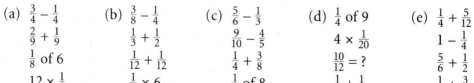

A	C	E	F	H	I	K	M	O	P	R	S	T	U
$1\frac{1}{3}$	$\frac{3}{4}$	$\frac{1}{2}$	$\frac{1}{6}$	$\frac{1}{8}$	$1\frac{1}{2}$	$\frac{2}{3}$	$\frac{5}{8}$	$\frac{7}{10}$	$2\frac{1}{4}$	$\frac{1}{3}$	$\frac{5}{6}$	$\frac{1}{10}$	$\frac{1}{5}$

(a) $\frac{3}{4} - \frac{1}{4}$ (b) $\frac{3}{8} - \frac{1}{4}$ (c) $\frac{5}{6} - \frac{1}{3}$ (d) $\frac{1}{4}$ of 9   (e) $\frac{1}{4} + \frac{5}{12}$

    $\frac{2}{9} + \frac{1}{9}$ $\frac{1}{3} + \frac{1}{2}$ $\frac{9}{10} - \frac{4}{5}$ $4 \times \frac{1}{20}$ $1 - \frac{1}{4}$

    $\frac{1}{8}$ of 6 $\frac{1}{12} + \frac{1}{12}$ $\frac{1}{4} + \frac{3}{8}$ $\frac{10}{12} = ?$ $\frac{5}{6} + \frac{1}{2}$

    $12 \times \frac{1}{8}$ $\frac{1}{4} \times 6$ $\frac{1}{6}$ of 8 $\frac{1}{2} + \frac{1}{5}$ $\frac{1}{5} + \frac{3}{10}$